ALL THAT I'VE SEEN

Failing Banks and Other Stories

Peter Nielsen

ALL THAT I'VE SEEN: Failing Banks and Other Stories

Copyright © 2017 by Peter Nielsen

All rights reserved. No part of this book may be reproduced in any form without permission in writing from the publisher, except by a reviewer who wishes to quote brief passages in connection with the review published in printed or electronic media. For permission requests, please address Publish Authority.

Published 2021, by Publish Authority
Newport Beach, CA & Roswell, GA USA
www.PublishAuthority.com

ISBN 978-1-954000-06-3 (Paperback)
ISBN 978-1-954000-07-0 (eBook)

Originally published 2017 by Dockside Sailing Press and is reprinted by permission of DSP and the author.

Printed in the United States of America

Praise for *All That I've Seen: Failing Banks and Other Stories*

5/5 Stars
Alden Lawrence
All that I've Seen is a book about faith, love and loyalty. The stories are both fascinating and emotionally honest. I got to read about the financial crash from the vantage point of an FDIC employee and about the civil rights movement from the point of view of a young child. Peter gives you a glimpse into the meaningful moments of his life. In a world full of cynicism and competition, it is refreshing to pick up a book that is honest and hopeful. A story of a life well lived.

Garrett Sanderson
All That I've Seen is a frank, poignant, insightful look at life through both a child's and an adult's eyes. Several chapters also illustrate Nielsen's wit. I was moved by how he confronted job loss and the difficulties of carrying out bank closings after joining the FDIC. Yet I was captivated most by Nielsen's childhood tales: his grandfather's ranch house, high school theater, and his tribute to UCLA's legendary coach, John Wooden. You'll re-live the awkwardness, humor and challenges of growing up from the parallels to what Nielsen shares about his own life journey.

5/5 Stars
Julie N.
I absolutely love *All that I've Seen*!!!! Peter's stories are simple, honest, tender, reflective. Some stories are really, really funny and some are tender and tug on my emotions. I highly recommend this book! Took me with him on his journey back in time. Reading this book made me realize we all have simple stories that make us who we are. Inspires me to find my

stories. Peter's memory and ability to pull out the simple things of life is remarkable and a gift.

5/5 Stars
D. Wells (retired banker)
I enjoyed reading *All That I've Seen*, with all the banking, Mormon and Utah references. His life coincided a lot with mine, growing up as a Mormon in California and spending summers in Utah with extended family in a farming community. Also attending college in Utah, although I was at the University of Utah where my mother had been a premed student. Our family left California every year the day after school was out to spend the summer in Delta, Utah where my parents were raised. Our father was a beekeeper who transported the bees to Delta for the alfalfa honey. As the author writes, I also spent my teenage years attending multiple church gatherings and going to dances. We attended Seminary from 6:30 to 7:30 a.m. on school days. There was an expectation of responsibility and performance from an early age. Expressions like "shorly" are very familiar. Most cannot recognize it but there is a Utah twang that is very distinct. It was fun to read about all the locations that I knew: Wasatch mountains, Ben Lomond Avenue in Ogden, Foothill Blvd. and East Bench in Salt Lake City. Peter Nielsen's book has encouraged me to reread the history of my pioneer ancestors who settled Utah, many walking across the plains and enduring the sadness of the handcart companies. As you know it is a Mormon thing to chronicle one's life. Peter Nielsen has written a remarkable history.

5/5 Stars
Kent Robertson
I am coincidentally reading Jordan Peterson's 12 Rules for Life as I read *All That I've seen*. Dr. Peterson observes that the human experience, though lived as facts and surrounded by material things is meaningless when described in those terms.

Humans experience chaos and order. What they know are emotions, relationships, pains, joys, fears, victories, love, meaning! Peter Nielsen has a gift. He is able to remember so many details of living and spin them into a beautiful tapestry of meaning, like a novel rather than the history he is creating for his posterity. We walk with him along the dividing line between order and chaos and fall in love with so many of the people in his life. It is an amazing work, created with skill and feeling. I look forward to his next installment.

5/5 Stars
K.S.
These stories have truly been heartwarming, touching and to the heart. The author has such a way with words, I truly love these stories.

5/5 *Stars*
Anonymous
All that I've Seen completely blew me away. This book is understated, humble, articulate, dripping with wisdom and experience. Peter's quiet dignity in a world of chaos and commotion is honestly refreshing. His writing style sort of sneaks up on you. You are reading along a nice story about Peter Nielsen and then all of the sudden kinda without realizing you get caught up in this web of tenderness and wisdom that leaves you contemplating the meaning of life. I highly recommend this book.

5/5 Stars
Kirsten Nilsson
Nielsen beautifully and deftly distills his own life experiences--some simple, some complex, many painful--into thoughtful observations of personal growth. His stories are gentle, warm and wise without being sickeningly sweet or sentimental. A lovely collection of short stories.

5/5 Stars
Ingrid Lola
Each of the stories in this collection are compelling and full of character, while spanning a huge range of experience and emotion. I laughed out loud and - I'll admit it - some of them made me tear up a little bit. I loved this collection and highly recommend it!

5/5 Stars
Julie Newcomb
In a very relatable narrative style, this book offers pearls of wisdom about living a truly good life. Thought provoking and uplifting lessons are offered in a collection of memories and stories that evoke real emotion. Highly recommend.

5/5 Stars
Jeff Peterson

All that I've Seen ... is understated, humble, articulate, dripping with wisdom and experience. Peter's quiet dignity in a world of chaos and commotion is honestly refreshing. His writing style leaves you contemplating the meaning of life. I highly recommend this book.

5/5 Stars
Steven Cantwell
What Nielsen gives us in *All That I've Seen*—his recent book of essays—are vivid encounters with both life's ordinary marvels and its harshest edges. Such intimate connections about what matters most—perhaps most immediate in the essay form—are the reason I read books. ... He is a born storyteller [and writes of his life's experiences] with searing honesty and humor. ... We can all hope another set of essays is in the works.

Dedication

This book is dedicated to my wife, Kathie, who has always helped me to see the big picture…in a story and in life. I met her on a picnic with my family when we were both only teenagers. We have 3 children now: Emily, who has a gentle soul and the most amazing blond curly hair. I mean Carol King type curls. She is a strong woman with a husband named Alden and three beautiful children. Sara, our second daughter is the most socially fearless person that I have ever known. She and her husband, Tom, also have three young children. We have a son too. His name is Jeff. He is the most hilarious person I know. He just graduated from business school in Irvine. He did his undergraduate work up in Salt Lake City (where his great grandfather studied). Now he's working in sales at a transportation company based out of Arkansas.

All of the stories I've written here are for them and anyone else who may be interested. They are true stories. All of them are about faith. These stories are about why I get up and stumble around each day, why I get up at five a.m. each morning and commute to the office. They are stories about why I continue to slug it out in this life even though I'm tired, or scared, or bored sometimes. They are, some of them, little fragments of memory about things that were almost inconsequential years ago. In some cases, though, they are vivid, almost radioactive pictures in my mind that are riveted there forever.

I am writing these stories down as they come to me. I'm writing them for Kathie, and for Emily, and Alden, Sara and Tom, and for Jeff. I am writing them for my grandchildren: Camille and Marilyn, Peter and Jeff, and for Harry and Owen. I am writing them for anyone else who wants to sit down and read.

Cover photo: Mountains in vicinity of Payson, Utah

Contents

Dedication   iii
Introduction   vii
Guatemala Map   190
   1. Staying True   1
   2. Failing Banks   4
   3. Anxiety   25
   4. The Piano Recital   34
   5. Paper Route   41
   6. Junior Varsity Football   50
   7. Getting Attention   59
   8. Bats In The Attic   65
   9. The Wizard of Westwood   74
  10. Crushing It   88
  11. Kathie   104
  12. The Pasture   120
  13. Jupiter Bowl   135
  14. Mission calls   148
  15. Driving Home   162
  16. Guatemala Arrival   177
  17. Volver, Volver   191
  18. I Didn't Think He'd Get Up Again   198
  19. Baby Blessing   204
  20. Bottle Caps   212
  21. Mission Ends   217
  22. Pheasant Hunting   223
  23. We Shall Overcome   233
  24. Final Thoughts   248

Photos   133-134
Acknowledgements   261
About the Author   263

Introduction

My name is Peter Nielsen. Every morning my alarm goes off at 5 a.m. I'm usually up before the alarm clock. I stare at it in the darkness until 5 a.m. comes and then I hear something from a selection of songs I've collected over the years. I rarely even have the time to recognize what song is playing before my hand, almost of its own will, pushes a button on the little plastic alarm clock and shuts it off.

Every morning, I lay there for a second as the fogginess in my brain gets pushed rudely and abruptly away. I am always amazed at how Kathie either never hears the alarm, or how she can lie so still and relaxed as I begin to move and fumble around for my glasses and the alarm button in the darkness. I get up and I put on a suit that I bought at one of those "buy one get three free" sales from Jos. A. Bank. I kiss Kathie goodbye and I stumble down the stairs into my little white Mini Cooper and drive down to the train station by my house.

Every weekday morning, I make my way onto the train and I find a seat and sit down. Most of the people are either sleeping or talking a little too loudly on their cell phones. The train ride takes an hour to get from Santa Ana, California to Union Station in downtown Los Angeles. It makes stops about every 5 or 10 minutes in places like Santa Ana, or Orange, or at Anaheim Stadium, where the Angels and Albert Pujols play. It makes a stop in Fullerton, where my dad grew up. It stops in Buena Park, Santa Fe Springs, Commerce, and Norwalk. Finally, the train lumbers to the end of the line at Union Station in Los Angeles.

Every morning it seems like more people than could fit in the train in the first place squirt out the doors and into the tunnels, stairs, and escalators. They scramble around like ants in all different directions. I am one of those working ants. I spend my days at a big Los Angeles-based bank on the 26th floor of a downtown skyscraper.

The other night we had some family over and we were watching a ballgame on TV. During one of the commercials, they showed a picture of the Los Angeles skyline. I could see on the screen the building I work in every day. So, I made my father, who had come over for some company and a bowl of soup, freeze the picture. I got up and pointed at what I thought had to be around the 26th floor of my building on the screen. I was impressed by it. The building looked established and solid. It looked like it had a real purpose. It was only a building, but for a second, as I looked at it there frozen on the screen, I felt a little like I'd made something of myself. I felt proud of where I'd come from and the work I do every day.

My family, however, wasn't as interested in my moment of reflection and they quickly told me that I was standing in the way of the TV. There were some comments about Los Angeles and how "the Lakers are sure falling apart this year," etc. and could we please unfreeze the screen so everyone could see the ballgame again.

Even though my family moved on, I kept thinking of seeing that building on TV and about what it meant to me. I've worked at one bank or another for most of my entire 35-year career. For a large part of that time, I've had to make the long commute from Orange County to Los Angeles every day. I've driven my car to Los Angeles. I've ridden the train to Los Angeles. I even took a taxi one day when I missed the train.

As I think about my time in Los Angeles, I realize that I spend a lot of my time on the train or up on the 26th floor of that downtown building. But that is not really where my true interests lie. I've always said, "I do this (banking) for them." I put on my suit and I commute to the 26th floor for my family. Because they've needed me to, and I have always done my best to keep the commitments I made to them. As I look back on my time working in Los Angeles at various banks, I think the best thing about my job (except that it helps us pay the bills every month) is that the commute gives me two hours each day to sit, and to think, and to remember, and sometimes to write about my life. When I write, I feel valuable and I feel important. I feel like I've amounted to something. I feel like I've amounted to more than just a worker ant on his daily commute. I feel like I have really lived. It's a part of this living that I want to share.

ONE

Staying True

Years before I'd ever held a job, when I was a teenager, I went to a youth activity at our church on a Tuesday or a Wednesday night down in Pacific Beach, California. Youth activities were on weeknights. My friends and I thought they were fun because there were a lot of pretty girls that came. We also liked them because, after an adult church leader talked to us a little about religion, we could usually finish off the night playing a game of pick-up basketball in a giant room they called the "Cultural Hall," which had a full basketball court in it with regulation baskets and a parquet wooden floor. It doubled as a performance hall with a big stage and a curtain. When we boys weren't playing ball in there, it was also used for concerts, recitals, and other big community presentations.

One night, they asked the 5 or 6 of us young men, before we played ball, to go in and sit down in a small classroom near the Cultural Hall for some kind of a lesson. I was sure they were going to teach us about church things, but when I went in the room, there was a man there that I hadn't met before. It turns out that he wasn't there to talk about religion, or basketball. They introduced him to us and told us that he was a cyclist.

I remember that he came all dressed in European-style cycling clothes and he brought with him a sleek racing bicycle. This was the 1970's, long before Lance Armstrong. It was even before Greg LeMond became the first American to win the Tour de France. The man's bicycle was new and it was shiny. It had lots of gears and stuff I'd never seen before on a bicycle. I noticed that the gear changer nobs were down on the very ends of the curved handlebars. This, I thought, must have been so he could shift gears without moving his hands or coming out of his aerodynamic racing position when he was going fast. The bike seemed very expensive. Calling it a "bike" instead of a "bicycle" still seems wrong somehow. He told us he was a professional cyclist and he explained that his bicycle was extremely lightweight. It was a lot lighter than the old Schwinn Varsity I used to ride around on.

He talked to us for a long time about cycling and about how much he loved it. He said if he could, he would ride or work on his bicycle every day, all day long. He showed us why his clothing worked better for racing than regular clothes. It was all so interesting that I don't remember thinking about basketball once.

He had brought in some extra bicycle wheels and he took one of them and set it sideways on a table in a weird looking metal stand. He kept talking to us as he slowly spun it around with his hand on the stand. He showed us how if you spin the wheel slowly in the metal stand you could easily tell if it was what he called "trued up" or if it wobbled as it spun around. He said if the wheels weren't true, and if they wobbled, you could still ride a bike. You might even be able to have some fun on it, he said, but it wouldn't ride as smoothly. It wouldn't work as well as it could. Then he pulled a little tool out of his bag and he showed us how to grab the wheel and put the tool at the base of one of the metal spokes and twist it so the spoke would get tighter. If you did this to enough of the spokes in the right places, you could "true up" the wheel and it would spin more like it was meant to, more like it was originally built to.

He finished up and we thanked him. We were ready to go to the Cultural Hall and play some ball. Just as we were getting ready to leave and he was putting his things away, almost as an afterthought, he told us that he thought we should think about "truing up" our lives so that we could spin like we ought to. He told us we should make whatever changes we needed to in order to live our lives more like we'd been born to live them. Then he said goodbye and asked us just to think about it.

I've been thinking about his little afterthought for over forty years and trying, and not always succeeding, to stay "trued up" like he said.

TWO

Failing Banks

About fifteen years ago, when my son Jeff was in middle school, he asked me what I do at work all day. Apparently, it was career week and he had an assignment to ask one of his parents what they did for a living. It made me feel good when he asked me about it. I tried to tell him about banking, and how I underwrite loans and get them approved by the bank's Credit Committee, but he rolled his eyes and said something about how I might as well have been speaking Chinese.

Banking is a respectable career but it can be complicated to explain. I tried again, from a different angle. This time, I told him about how bankers get to know a lot of people when times are good because we have access to a lot of money. He looked a little confused. I told him how I helped people get money and then use it to build things and start businesses. He looked at me like only a middle schooler can and he told me it sounded boring.

I knew I was failing with my description. I could see him wondering what his mom did and how maybe he could write about that instead. It was too bad, because I'd always kind of enjoyed work and I was making it sound awful. Each time I tried to explain, I got all caught up in banker-like technical talk that was not at all what he was looking for. I tried to explain about equity, and debt, and credit, and how it all worked, but I could see he wasn't getting it. Finally, I told him that I write long memos about complicated things and then I explain them to other people who ask me millions of questions about them. If I do it right, I said, I can lend some of the bank's money to people so they can buy things they need for their businesses. There is a lot more to it than that, but for middle-school career week, it was the best I could come up with.

That conversation happened around 2003 or 2004. I'd had a pretty good run as a banker by then. I had been at it for almost 20 years. I'd made a lot of loans and gotten a lot of people the money they needed so they could build a lot of things. Sometime back then, the Fed Chairman, Alan Greenspan, was interviewed about banking and the economy. He said he thought there was no need for any more government regulation. He said he was confident that "the markets would regulate themselves."

He was definitely right about that.

Over the years the markets, and particularly the banks, had been changing. They were becoming much more risky. In fact, things had changed *so* much that, by 2008, the markets were about to regulate themselves—in the form of a giant crash. Bankers, as a whole, had stopped being careful. Somewhere, the mindset had switched and banking became very aggressive.

There was more and more pressure on regular bankers like me to book all kinds of new loans. I had a boss back then who tried to motivate me by telling me that, as a banker, I was like a fighter pilot. I thought he was being ridiculous, but it was starting to dawn on me that the banking profession *definitely was* changing and getting much more aggressive. Other people besides bankers wanted in on this fighter pilot kind of mentality too. As a consequence, hugely risky loans were being made in an effort to drive up profits and qualify for giant pay increases.

In 2008, I was working for a large Ohio-based financial institution. Just before Christmas, everyone in our office crowded around a marble conference room table and listened to a voice coming from a tinny speakerphone in the middle of the table as a man in Cleveland told us we were all being laid off. He said that the market was crashing and they were closing down the office. All of us were losing our jobs. We hung up the phone, looked at each other for a second or two and then went home, just like that.

My son, Jeff, was now in college at the University of Utah. He heard that I'd lost my job and he sent me a little film clip that popped up one morning on my computer screen. It came with a message from him that said "Dad, you'll enjoy this." Apparently, in Salt Lake City there was a new development planned in the central downtown area. A high-rise building that had been the headquarters of my former employer had to be demolished to make room for the new project. The builder sent in one of those coordinated explosive demolition companies to blow up the old building. They filmed it as it came down in a giant cloud of dust and debris. You could see the name of my employer on the top of the building as it started to fall.

I watched Jeff's clip. At first, I felt like I shouldn't look at it. Part of me felt like I should turn it off. I was weirdly drawn to it, though. I knew the bank was still operating all over the U.S. and I told myself that if I had been one of the executives who made the decision to close down their offices in Southern California, I very well might have done the same thing. Still though, it hurt how they had swiped me aside like I was inconsequential. I couldn't tell if I felt like laughing or maybe crying. I did feel like watching the bank fall was a bit of poetic justice, though.

I'd been looking for a new job for months by then with no luck. Honestly, I was getting a bit discouraged. I leaned in closer to the video with an almost morbid curiosity and I watched the bank fall down and get covered up by the dust, over and over again. At one point, I chuckled from somewhere deep in my system. It was a weird awkward chuckle. It would have been embarrassing if anyone else had been around.

It turns out I had every right to be discouraged because right then, at that very same time, the entire financial world was, according to the news, in complete free-fall. One day we heard President Bush in an emergency news conference practically beg Congress to bail out the banks. The next day Congress said no and then, it seemed like minutes later, the stock market crashed. Congress huddled up again and this time they approved the biggest government bailout in banking history. At the same time, employers, and especially banks, were laying people off all over the place. Alan Greenspan was right. The markets were definitely regulating themselves. Times were getting very bad.

Banks all over the U.S. were beginning to show signs that our financial system was in real trouble. The Chairman of the FDIC, Sheila Bair, was getting to be a regular on financial TV shows explaining major government efforts to hold back the abyss. Wall Street firms that had been held up as pristine examples of financial strength were either failing or were about to fail. Unemployment was increasing. People I'd known my entire career were on the street. Some were having to switch to completely different industries in order to find work.

The Secretary of the Treasury and the President went on TV and announced that Congress had approved giving the banks a huge amount of money. They called it "TARP" money. They did it so the banking system in America, which was living only on fumes at that point, would have a chance to survive. I couldn't believe it—banking was supposed to be a stable profession. I would even learn later that there were people in Washington D.C. who spent their entire days back then trying to figure out how the government of the United States should respond if *every single bank* in the entire U.S. were to fail. It was not only possible; there were some very smart people who fully anticipatedcElhenny that it actually could happen.

I'd worked hard throughout my entire business life to carve out a successful career in banking. I'd spent good money studying finance and banking at some of the nation's best universities. On top of that, I'd worked at some excellent banks that had sterling reputations. I was on my way to a steady career on an even keel until that December day when I got laid off. Suddenly, being unemployed and not having an office to get up and go to each day was something I wasn't prepared for. It was hard to stay motivated, but I did. I looked for a job like the looking was my job. I must have called every single person in my contacts list. My motto was: If your name is in my phone and I remember what you look like, even if I haven't spoken to you in years, I am going to call you. But everyone I called told me the same thing. They said that they absolutely could not hire anyone until things cycled back around. That cycling, it turns out, would be painful and would take years, not just months.

In the end, I guess I got lucky. Just when it was almost completely impossible to find a job in my field, I came upon a government website and I applied for a job with the Federal Deposit Insurance Corporation in their new "West Coast Temporary Satellite Office." It was a Sunday when I learned that I got the job with the FDIC, and I was in church. It was morning and the bishop of our congregation had just spoken. I was opening a green standard-issue hymnal and getting ready to sing when my phone buzzed in my blazer pocket. Because I'd had a lot of free time, I'd figured out how to receive email on my phone, a new thing for me back then.

I really wasn't expecting to hear from anyone that day. It had been a few weeks since I'd gone in for my interview, and I remember wondering if they'd lost my application. But when I pulled my phone out of my pocket and peeked at it, I saw immediately that it was an offer of employment. I didn't sing the hymn with the rest of the congregation; instead, I read the message on my phone and I felt a great wave of relief. I also knew my job search was over, and that instead of being a banker, I was going to work for the FDIC. I was going to try and help fix what the banking system had broken.

I knew instantly that I would take the job but, to be honest, I wasn't really sure what I was getting myself into. On one of my first days at the FDIC I remember, before I left for work, stopping and telling my wife that I wasn't sure if working at the FDIC would be like working for a real professional organization, or more like working for the Department of Motor Vehicles, who I had always thought of as the perfect example of large-scale government bureaucracy.

A few weeks later, when I arrived at my new office early one morning, I was told that I needed to go back home and pack. I'd been "deployed," they said. The next thing I knew I was on my way to Georgia, sitting in the very last row of a large commercial airliner, directly in front of one of the two miniature bathrooms. I don't know what it is about airplanes and narrow aisles and bathrooms, but that day it seemed like an endless line of large strangers stood in the aisle during the whole flight. They bumped me, leaned over me, and rested themselves on the top of my seat. They had loud conversations as they waited in line, like I didn't even exist. I tried to shift around in my seat to get clear of them but they just kept coming and bumping and leaning and talking. I don't think the aisle was clear once all the way from California to Atlanta.

As we all bumped along above the deserts of Southern Nevada and the rain clouds over the Midwest, I sat and wondered, with every bit of turbulence, what it was I was getting myself into. They had actually used the word "deployed," when they told me I was going to that little town in Georgia. They said that The Georgia Department of Financial Institutions had decided to close the bank and that we at the FDIC had to be there to make sure its depositors got back everything they rightly deserved. *Really*—I thought— *was it necessary to use the word "deployed?"* Deployment is what the military does to young soldiers before they send them off into battle in places like Iraq or Afghanistan. I wasn't a soldier or even a young man anymore and I really hoped I wasn't heading into battle.

I picked up my suitcase when it rolled out of a chute down at baggage claim and dragged it behind me. One of the little black wheels on the bottom of the case had somehow worn down during the flight. When I rolled it behind me it limped and bumped along, with an odd sort of rhythm, almost like it had a handicap.

It was a humid and ridiculously hot day in Georgia. I don't think I'd ever been in the south before and I knew I'd never been at a bank closing. Before they "deployed" me, the people back home had told me not to worry. They said when I got to the hotel where we were meeting, I should find a short, red-haired woman named Tracy. They told me I would be on her team and she would show me what to do. I followed a map I'd printed out on MapQuest, parked my rental car, and checked into a Hampton Hotel somewhere on the outskirts of town. I'd been told to check in using an alias company name, something like "ABC Construction." They also informed me that I couldn't tell the hotel that I worked for the FDIC. When they asked, I told them I worked for The Department of Agriculture, which is actually true. I still don't have any idea why the FDIC is a part of the Department of Agriculture and not part of some financial department, but it is.

After I got to my room, I unpacked the suitcase with the bent wheel and got dressed in my navy-blue suit. Then I sat down on the corner of the bed and turned on the TV. I had still been in banking during the first several months of 2008 and I'd watched on the news as IndyMac Bank had failed and people stood in line in Pasadena in the heat of the summer. It seemed like everyone everywhere was watching on TV while all those people stood there to try to get their money back.

I'm pretty sure it was IndyMac Bank where a United States Congressman had gone on TV and told everyone to run and take their money out of the bank because it was in trouble. If there ever was a chance to save IndyMac Bank, it was long gone the second he said what he did. It was a horrible misuse of information that any responsible person, especially a U.S. Congressman, should have just kept to himself. It is hard to describe how this flippant comment by a man in such a responsible position made me feel. I wasn't working for the FDIC when he said it—I joined them later. But there is a reason that some information is privileged. Not only was it bad form, but it set off a real panic. I would learn over the next few months that real people got hurt.

When the TV show I was watching in my hotel room ended, it was about 3:00 p.m. I took a deep breath and stood up and I made my way downstairs to a big conference room near the lobby of the hotel. There was already a crowd of people standing in line to check in by two big wooden conference room doors. So, I stood and I waited in line. A tall, dark-haired woman I had never met found my name on a list she had and then looked up at me and smiled and said, "You're new. You're from the West Coast Temporary Satellite office." Then she told me to go in and find a seat somewhere. I wondered why they would name our office something so strange and transitory as the "West Coast Temporary Satellite office." On the one hand, they treated us almost like soldiers going into battle and on the other hand it seemed like they wanted us to remember that we were on the "B" team, and part of the "temporary" office.

She gave me a name tag and then I walked in through the doors into a very large conference room full of people. They were greeting each other and laughing like they all knew each other and like they'd been through this a million times. I sat down near the front just as a tall skinny man with a Texas accent stood up and introduced himself as the "Receiver-in-Charge." He was uncomfortable and awkward speaking to us all and he squirmed around like he was unsure of his footing. The way he stretched and moved and grimaced reminded me of the unsettled movements of Marty McFly's Dad in *Back to the Future*.

He cleared his throat, and coughed, and then ran his fingers through his dark black hair. Next he got our attention and said, at first softly, "Is anyone from the press here?" Then he cleared his throat again and, louder this time, asked, "Is anyone from the news media in the room?" He held his hand up over his eyes like he was shading them from the sun or something. He scanned out across the room as if he was on a watchtower looking out into the distance for the enemy. I wasn't sure what he would do if anybody from the media was there, but he sure looked like *he* knew. Then he summoned up some courage. He frowned and looked at us all uncomfortably and said, "Well, this closing is the worst-case scenario. Really, we do everything we can to avoid what is going to happen this weekend."

"I'm telling y'all, when we learn that a bank is going to have to close, we do everything to sell it to another bank. If that fails, we announce that it's closed and open it for a few weeks during normal business hours so people can come in and withdraw their insured deposits." He shifted his weight and leaned his elbow on his other wrist at his waist and he said, "This time folks, there's really nothing left. Nobody wants to buy this bank and it doesn't make sense to open it up for depositors. There's just not enough there." He stretched out and stood on his tippy toes like he was waking up or something. Then he said, "So, we're just going to close it down. We're going to have to dip into the government insurance fund, which we don't like to do unless there really is nothing left, and we're going to have to just mail checks to people who have money coming."

The insurance fund, I had learned, is completely separate and apart from bank funds. The bank funds, in this case, were gone. They had been squandered by the bank. The insurance fund is part of the government's pledge to guarantee bank deposits. It's a whole different pot of money that only got dipped into when a bank failed and people's deposits were at risk. The Receiver-in-Charge stopped and looked over us, into a distant corner of the room like he was disgusted. Then he went on and laid out what he called the staging of the night and how we were supposed to arrive at the failing bank.

He asked if it was anyone's first closing and I raised my hand along with a few other people in the room. He told us to be careful and not linger around outside the bank at night until after the first few days. "You never can tell how people will react," he said. "After the first couple of days, things should probably be calmed down." He told us how the bank had originally opened for business just after the Civil War and how it had helped with the rebuilding of the South. He said it was nothing short of a "tragedy" that it had failed like it did. He went on and talked all about the bank. He told us where the branches were and how it had been in the news, and that there had been a story alleging fraud in a part of the bank's mortgage portfolio.

I was positive that the bank had just made too many bad loans that people never had a chance to repay. The people who made the loans probably got huge bonuses based on how many new loans they could put on the books, so they ran as hard as they could at that goal. There was also a new thing called mortgage-backed securities that made more people even more money. These instruments required that even more mortgages get booked. Everyone was racing so hard to book new loans that they couldn't, or wouldn't, stop and ask themselves how, or if, all the new loans would get repaid. I was convinced that they did it for one reason and that was to make as much money as they possibly could for themselves.

There was never a question asked about whether this was a good idea. In the end, it wasn't. Reality caught up with them, and when the loans they had made couldn't be repaid, the banks they worked for ran out of money and failed.

I hadn't known it before that day in the hotel, but there is a very carefully choreographed procedure that the FDIC has used for years at bank closings. I listened and I tried to remember everything, but there were so many details. I was hoping the woman I was supposed to meet was somewhere in the crowd of people I didn't know, and that she was listening.

The awkward Receiver-in-Charge stopped talking and looked down. His voiced drifted like he was done. He walked back to his chair and he put his hands on the table in front of the room. He glared back up at the audience like he was a little angry at us. Then he sat down dismissively. I looked around and could see that everyone in the room was staring at him. I don't know about anyone else, but I know that I was dreading this night. I stood up to look for Tracy. She was there in front of me in a second, sticking her hand out and saying, "You're Peter, right?" I smiled and then I shook her hand. I liked her immediately. She was short and stocky and strong. She was as straightforward as a person can be. She shook my hand with a firm grip like she was not messing around and said, "I'm Tracy. You better get ready because we're gonna work hard this weekend. Are you up for it?" I assured her that I was up for it. She told me that the best way to learn how to close a bank was to jump in and do it. "We are the Asset Managers," she said. "We're going to do a lot of things. I'll show you how. Meet me in the lobby at 5:45 tonight. Okay?"

Then she turned like she had a million other things to do and started marching off to the door. Before she left, though, she stopped and thought for a second and then she turned around and came back to where I was standing in the giant conference room. She looked me over like she might beat me up or something and then she pointed at me as though she was drawing a line in the sand and daring me to cross it. She said in a very bossy tone, "Peter, this is going to be a stressful night." I was already sure it would be. The meeting with the Receiver-in-Charge had left me completely out of sorts. She said, "It might be stressful for you but you have to remember that it's much more stressful for the bank employees who are losing their jobs tonight." She went on, "When they bring in pizza tonight, those employees eat first. If there's an empty chair and there's a bank employee standing up anywhere, I better not see you sitting down. Remember, tonight our biggest job is to respect what they are going through. We are not here to punish anyone. We are the *good guys*." She almost spit when she talked. She was like a drill sergeant. "And we're gonna act that way too. You got it?" She pointed at me again and stared me down. I assured her that I got it and that I could do this. At that moment, I knew that I could believe in this process. I was completely on board.

Later that night, we followed the nervous Receiver-in-Charge's instructions. Tracy and I arrived at the bank and set to work. She set me up reviewing hundreds of borrower's loan files and completing an excruciatingly detailed Excel spreadsheet with all kinds of information about each one. The spreadsheet had so many names on it that it seemed like it would go on forever, like I could scroll down for hours and never get to the bottom of the document.

I set to work in a room that had, until that night, been the bank's basement. It was a stuffy little room with sterile block walls and no windows. My job, as Tracy had explained it, was to work with an older woman named Peach who had been an employee at the bank since she'd graduated from college. She had a smooth southern accent. She was proper and soft-spoken. She had been in charge of loan administration, and that very night, when the bank failed, she had lost the only job she'd had for over 40 years.

The small file room had a desk and a very modern computerized file retrieval system that must have taken Peach months to learn how to operate. I would read one of the names from my Excel file and she would punch some buttons and this automated file retrieval system would come to life. We watched through a fireproof window as these giant canisters of files would rumble around until a large metal opening under the window would open up to us. Then, by some almost scary marvel of modern technology, the file we had asked for would appear.

Our job was to find each file on the list, have the big machine retrieve it, and then look through it and make a record of its contents. We would look through a file and fill out our spreadsheet and then heft it back up into the big metal drawer. Then I would read the next name on my list and Peach would push some more buttons. The file cabinet would maneuver around again, like one of those conveyer systems that a dry cleaner uses to retrieve all of their newly cleaned clothes. Soon, when the exact file we needed would again "land" right in front of us, Peach would reach in and pull it out and then we'd do it again—and again, and again. Peach and I worked like this for hours until our legs and feet ached from standing.

Through it all, Peach was gentle and nice. She asked me about the FDIC. After a few polite questions, she asked if she really was going to get paid for the days she was working with us. I promised her that she would, and she smiled and said she was grateful. She said although it wasn't much "it was something." She said she knew she wouldn't sleep well that night. She'd never looked for a job before. She told me that, earlier in the night, when she heard the news that the bank had been closed, it had "stunned" her and she didn't feel like herself.

It was late in the night by then. I handed her one of the files so she could put it back in the drawer. Then I read aloud the next name on our list. "Jedediah Beauregard," I read quietly, almost reverently. It sounded to me like a classic southern name, like the name of a decorated Civil War soldier, and it demanded to be spoken with a proper southern accent. I knew I was tired and I took off my glasses, rubbed my eyes and said under my breath, "Jedediah Beauregard, now that's an unusual name." I wasn't really speaking to anyone; I wasn't even sure if I had said it or if I had just thought it.

Peach stood by the file drawer frowning, and I could see her body sag from the weight of my statement and from everything happening that night. She looked at me and said, "Poor Jedediah." She looked at the ground for a second and then back up at me and she told me how Jedediah's wife had been sick and he'd had to go into debt to pay for her medical care. Peach told me how Jedediah had driven his wife to the hospital in his truck nearly every day for months. She got slowly worse anyway, though, and then she died. Peach's voice was full of emotion when she said that Jedediah was devastated. To pay all of the debt he'd rung up for his wife's medical expenses, he'd had to sell his truck and their home. It was the home he'd grown up in when he was a boy.

I remember not being able to look away from Peach as she told me about Jedediah and his wife. When she finished, I looked down through the thick glass window at the file room and the endless stacks of files. I said, "Peach, do you know every one of the people in all of these files like you know Jedediah Beauregard?" She hesitated for a second. Then she nodded and quietly said, "Yes sir, I do."

Years before that night when I sorted files with Peach, I was in business school, in Claremont, California when the dean called me in to his office with a group of other students and asked us about our experience and our goals. I sat in a small circle with my friends and the dean, and I waited for my turn to talk. I was planning to tell him how I thought the management program could help prepare me to contribute to the world somehow, help me make it a better place, in a small way, for my two daughters when they grew up. I would tell him that my first semester had not been that hard but that I wanted the program to be more rigorous. I wanted to learn the business skills I would need to be ready for the world when I got out of school.

The dean started things off by asking a young man sitting to his left what he thought. The young man sat up straight and said that he was sure he could speak for us all when he said we were all there studying so that we could go out afterwards and make a lot of money. I remember looking at him as he answered, wondering if that was all he had to say. But he was as sure as he could be, and he seemed to be absolutely positive that money was the only motivation for everyone in the room. It surprised me when all the other students there nodded in agreement. I didn't disagree completely—I felt like it would be nice to make a good living if I could at the same time contribute to the world—but suddenly I felt like I'd missed something about why people really do study business. And maybe that something that I had missed was now wreaking havoc on the lives of regular people like Jedediah Beauregard, and on small towns like the one he lived in back in Georgia.

For months after I worked with Peach in Georgia, I went to many bank closings. Every time, I was sure the banks were failing because someone was reaching for too much money too fast, and the unsuspecting regular people in small towns and big cities across the country, like Peach and Jedediah, were the ones who were paying the price. They were losing the money that they had entrusted to the banks. I almost always thought of Peach and how she personally knew Jedediah Beauregard and every other person in the hundreds of files in that stuffy block-wall room. She not only knew their names, she knew them personally; they were her friends. To her, they were real people with real lives and real problems.

Later, after I'd been Asset Manager on several other closings, the FDIC asked me to be what they called "Branch Manager." One of the more difficult assignments that the Branch Managers had was to stand up in front of all the bank employees while someone from the state we were in announced to the bank employees that their bank had failed. Everyone would gasp and then he'd say that the FDIC was going to be the bank's receiver and deal with any of its remaining assets. In the worst cases, the State Regulator would make his announcement and then immediately turn the floor over to me. It seemed like every time, just before I started talking, the Regulator would hurry out the door of the bank. I would stand there for a minute and wait while he quickly left, and after he did, it was just me in the lobby with all of the employees. Most of them just stood there waiting and staring at me in disbelief.

Those moments were always deathly quiet, and horribly awkward. I hated the few seconds in between, and the big pause after the guy from the state made his announcement and walked out. Eventually, I would have to break the silence in the room and explain again that the bank had failed. I would tell them we were going to do everything we could to make whatever form of transition was needed a smooth one. I would always reach into my pocket and pull out a paper that had detailed instructions written on it. I usually told the employees that I needed to read it to them because there was a lot in it and I didn't want to forget anything. I wanted to be sure they heard it all. Then I read about what kind of closing we were doing. I said we would pay them for their help over the weekend. Sometimes, I had to tell them they were losing their jobs. I always thought about Tracy in Atlanta and how she told me it was about them, and I tried to give them some time to call their families and let them know what was going on. I tried to make sure I read the instructions slowly so they would be clear, but I always found myself hurried and nervous because the whole situation everywhere I went was just so sad and depressing.

One cold, late afternoon in Northern Utah I parked my rental car at a Shell gas station on the main boulevard near a small branch of a local bank. It was cold and windy when I got out of my car to meet a man wearing a dark suit from the Utah Department of Financial Institutions. I had never met him before that night. He was waiting for me with two Highway Patrol officers at a gas station that was across the street from the bank branch. The officers had been asked by another department of the FDIC to be there to help if anything got out of hand. It was almost dark and it started snowing while we were talking.

The man from the State of Utah was uncomfortable. He was a tall, mild-mannered person. He fiddled with his car keys and told me he'd never done this before. I remembered how I felt back in Georgia with Tracy and Peach. I told him that I knew it was stressful, but for us, it was about the bank employees. He seemed to take some comfort in that. We stood by our cars in the snow and briefly talked about how we would go in and wait in the lobby until the bank was closing for the day. We agreed that I would approach someone at the bank and let him or her know who we were, but that he would make the announcement that the bank had failed. He knew that all of the bank employees would lose their jobs that night, and he told me that it was nights like this when he hated his job. I told him he could leave right after he made his announcement if he wanted to. He just nodded and said, "Thanks."

At five minutes to five, we walked in and sat down in the lobby and waited. Right at 5:00 p.m., I got up out of my chair like we had planned and I walked across the tile floor and went to the window and spoke to one of the tellers. I think she was probably nineteen or twenty years old. I showed her the official FDIC badge I kept in my shirt pocket and I asked her if we could talk to the Bank's Manager. The young woman stepped back and straightened up when she saw my badge, like I had a disease or something. She didn't say anything. She just looked at my badge, looked up at me, and then pointed to another woman who was very busy, walking very fast across the lobby. I took a step toward her but, I swear without even looking at me, she held her hand up in the air and she shouted, "I know why you are here and I don't want to talk to you!" Then, she ducked her head down and went into her office and shut the big wooden door behind her. I looked at the man from the State of Utah. He looked like he might fall apart, like he was in pain, horrified by what was happening. I wasn't sure how to respond to either one of them, but I knew we had to talk to the Bank Manager. So, I started walking deliberately, but as calmly as I could, across the lobby toward her office. My friend from the State of Utah followed behind me.

We arrived outside her office door and I reached down and opened it slowly until I could peek through. I said, through the little slit in the door, "I know you don't want to talk to us but I have to tell you some things." Then I pushed the door open a little further. I could see that she was crying. Her name, she said, was Effie. I could tell by the questions she asked that she was in charge and she knew what she was doing. She was sharp and very well qualified.

I closed the door and we sat down on the other side of her big desk. Nobody said anything for a few minutes. I tried to come up with some words I could say that would be helpful. My new friend sitting next to me was clearly at a loss for words. There is a protocol that we were supposed to follow and I knew that I had jumped the gun. We were supposed to wait and not talk to anyone until I got a message on my Blackberry from the FDIC in Washington D.C. that the bank had officially failed. I had been caught up in the moment and done things out of order, and now I might be making the announcement before it was official. I didn't think I should do that, so we all just sat there in her office in awkward silence.

She was crying, and I was flustered, so I started talking. I told her that the bank had failed, or was about to officially fail, and how, for the next days or weeks, we were going to allow customers to come in and withdraw the amount of their "insured deposits." I told her we'd have a lot of people coming to work with us who were experts in insured deposits and very good at what they did. I said we would pay her employees on an hourly basis for every hour they agreed to work for us. I said I wasn't sure how long we would be able to pay them, probably a couple of weeks or so. I told her everything I knew, everything I could think of to fill the silence with what I hoped was practical information.

Her mascara dripped down from under her eyes. She wiped at it, smudging a little across her cheek. She didn't say anything at first, but just looked at me sadly, like she was giving up on a huge struggle that had started a long time before I got there. She looked at me like she was having a hard time deciding if she was sorry or if she was mad. It was very awkward. Finally, I felt like I had said it all. She wiped her eyes and then looked across her desk at me and with pain in her voice she almost yelled, "Didn't any bank out there want to buy us?" No, I had to tell her. The bank was being dissolved and in a few more weeks it would all be over. Just when I finished talking, my Blackberry buzzed in my pocket with the official bank closure announcement from Washington.

We all went back out into the lobby and she gathered up her team. I felt like they were all expecting me to be authoritative and imposing, like the FBI or the IRS would be. They expected me to be the government, to impose the law. They anticipated that I would start barking out orders and be detached and cold. Then the Utah Bank Regulator who had sat there silently up until this point, read a prepared statement and left, clearly glad to be out of such a sad, uncomfortable situation. I smiled halfway and then I read my prepared paper to a lobby full of sad employees. Some cried. I felt like I was telling them a dear friend had died. I had thought maybe they would be mad or scared, but for some reason I did not expect them to be just plain sad.

I read to them about how as Receiver, we'd be inviting depositors in to withdraw their funds. I told them what would occur the very next morning and that it would last for the next few days. I read everything on my list and then I stopped and I took a breath and looked at them. I told them I was hopeful that things could move ahead smoothly and I would do whatever I could to make that happen. They couldn't believe that no other bank wanted to buy them and they wanted to know why. I had to tell them that I didn't know why, that I wasn't in that part of the FDIC.

Over the next few days all of the bank customers in that small town came in to talk to a "Claims Administrator" from the FDIC to find out how much of their deposits was insured and how much they would be able to withdraw. One time, a family helped support an old man as he shuffled back across the lobby to the room I shared with the claims adjustor to find out if the bank had lost his money. I couldn't help but think of my grandfather. This particular bank closing was in an old building by a field, and when that family helped support the old man as he walked across the lobby, it reminded me of the little bank in the small Utah town that my grandfather lived in.

When my grandpa was middle-aged and I was a young boy, he called me "Pierre." He'd drive me down to his little office in that small Utah town at the foothills of the Wasatch Mountains and we would check his mail. Then I'd climb into the bed of his pickup truck and he'd climb into the cab and he'd take me down to a piece of flat land with a deserted-looking old barn that he called "the pasture." He'd roll up slowly to an old gate made of barbed wire and grey gnarled wood and he would whistle out of the window and shout to me, "Pierre, get up and jump over there and open up the gate! The animals aren't going to feed themselves!" I'd open the gate and his sheep would already be bouncing toward us. We'd feed them and I'd climb back in the back of the truck and we'd head home. I loved working with him like this.

Sometimes, on the way back to his house, after our chores were done and the animals were all fed, he'd stop by the local bank. Every time we did, he'd introduce me to all the people who worked in the bank. There was a loan officer named Reed who always stopped what he was doing and came over and shook my grandpa's hand and showed us around. Grandpa loved being a big shot there. I have no idea if he had a lot of money or only a little, but he liked to walk around the bank and act like he had a lot.

The thing is, the whole time I was working at the FDIC, I couldn't stop thinking of him. Every time an old man would hobble up to ask me as a representative of the FDIC if his money was still his, I would think of my grandfather and how he showed me off to the man named Reed in the lobby of the bank in his little town.

The night I read the instructions to the bank employees, after I went back to my hotel room, I sat on my bed in the dark and stared out the window at random gusty snowflakes that were fighting their way to the ground. I wondered before I fell asleep how I got here. Why was I the one talking to bank managers and breaking bad news to employees? When I met the bank employees that night, they didn't know if they should treat me like the enemy or like someone who was there to help them. I was asking myself the same question—was I the enemy or was I really there to try to help?

I worked at a lot of bank closings, always thinking of people like my grandpa, or like Peach in that Civil War town in Georgia, or like Effie when she told me to go away and cried in her office. It was hard. I felt like I shouldn't let it get to me like it did. I wondered almost every time why it all mattered so much to me. Other FDIC guys went out for drinks the night they closed down their branches and they laughed about it all. It seemed like it was all in a day's work for them. The personal stories behind each bank closure didn't seem to creep into their consciousness like they did mine. I couldn't laugh about it. To me, it was all too much. To me, it was all so sad.

I'd had too many experiences in my life that made it so that, even if I had wanted to, I couldn't separate my feelings from the things I was asked to do at work. I've always related to the little guy—the "common man." In this whole experience, it was uncomfortable for me to be a part of the big machine. I knew that the things I did had to be done. But that didn't make them easy to do and it certainly didn't make them any better for the employees of the banks I helped close. Since this experience, I've realized that when people talk to me about how much money they make, I'm never impressed by it. I don't spend time pondering the CEO's struggle. However, I have spent lots of time thinking about Peach and wondering if she ever landed on her feet.

THREE

Anxiety

Y ou know that moment when it's about to storm? It's almost electric. I mean, there's some kind of power in the air. The air feels heavy and musty, like it's coming to life. You can smell the dirt from fields and areas that aren't even nearby. It feels important, even crucial, like something big is about to happen.

I've never been in a big storm like a hurricane or one of those awful tornadoes that churn through farmlands and towns and leave rubble in their wake. But I can imagine how it would feel just before one hit. It would feel pregnant, like something life-alteringly giant is in the offing. But it must also at the same time feel pretty normal, like another day. I've heard that they often come by surprise and that's why people get hurt. They don't suspect anything is going to happen until long past when the air begins to feel heavy, when the news starts to broadcast warnings and/or the storm sirens start to wail and people run in a panic to find shelter.

One night, when I was much younger, I lived in a very small village that was located at the foothills of a giant ancient volcano in Guatemala. I slept on an old army cot in the hot, sticky night. I used to sleep with just a sheet over me each night and I had a way that I curled it around me to cover my body and up around and over my head so the wicked, humming, unfeeling mosquitos couldn't sneak in and get to my flesh while I was asleep, gouging out a hunk of it while injecting their poison.

    I was asleep under the curled-up sheet on the canvas cot. It was dark in the room. I don't know if it was the darkness in the room or the fogginess of a worn-out, dog-tired sleep, but I started hearing loud percussive sounds, like thunder, or howling like wind through a canyon. For a very brief time, before I was all the way awake, I felt like I was home. I felt like the air was cool again and I didn't know I should worry about things. I was unburdened and all the way asleep.

    The sounds got louder outside my dream and on the muddy roads outside my room. I hadn't moved yet in my sheets from my curled-up insect repellant position but I opened my eyes and looked at the white cotton shroud over my face. In the night, it looked almost purple or a deep midnight blue. What I was hearing were dogs and maybe wolves or whatever other carnivorous animals roam the jungles in Guatemala. They were loud, as if every scared or lonely animal was suddenly on hyper alert. They cried out in one giant collective moan in the deep black of midnight, as if they knew there was going to be a big storm, or perhaps some ancient folkloric spirit animal had risen to tell them that the end of days was at hand. And it wasn't just a few sleepless dogs howling at the moon in the darkness. I would dare to say that every single dog and cat and raccoon and monkey and any other animal anywhere near the house I was sleeping in was agitated and stirred up, feeling the electricity.

    I couldn't. I just laid there and listened to the weird, mythical cacophony. It was loud and it lasted only a minute or two and then it stopped. *What was that about?* I wondered from under my tangle of blue and purple sheets. I was glad it was over. I was glad whatever had roused them in the night had let them alone again. I never moved but I closed my eyes again and hoped I would drift off away from the scariness of animals howling, to a rest that I knew I badly needed.

It only took a minute until I again began to feel the fuzziness of sleep. Just as the whole weird episode of howling and screaming and anxiousness was fading from my conscious mind, and I was again surrendering, there was a loud bang like a thunderous snapping noise. If I'm being honest, this all happened in the same second. I remember it slowly, though. First, there was this sound of percussion again but this time it sounded like a big crack. Next, there was pitching and yawing. The foundation under me was moving and I could hear the old adobe walls moan under the strain of the heavy tile roof they were holding up. This time I did move. I sat straight up, the covers flying off me as I bolted to attention. I felt I should run or hide or do something. The ground was shaking and my old cot was rattling and squeaking. It was too late, though, to do anything except just hold on while the earth grumbled beneath me for a couple of very long minutes.

I sat there on my cot and just waited it out, hoping the thick adobe walls and roof would hold up and this would pass. I could hear the man who lived in the room next to mine shouting that night about *un tembloron*. I was afraid for a minute, and lucky, I guess, that this earthquake hadn't been worse.

I've wondered since that night—how it was that the dogs knew before there was any sign? What was it they sensed? How did they pick up on something that was about to happen? Could they feel it in the air like a rainstorm or a tornado? I guess I'll never know. I do know that it happened, though, just the way I've described it. The animals had some ability to sense what was going to happen and they were right about it. They could feel it in the heavy, pregnant air while I was asleep.

My friend Dan, a psychotherapist in Chicago, told me once that fear is driven somewhere deep in a primitive part of your brain called the amygdala. People who have anxiety aren't weak minded, he told me. In fact, he said, they are usually very smart. They just have a more active amygdala that fires when it doesn't need to. The dogs in their minds sometimes bark and howl and moan in the darkness, but then often times there's no earthquake, nothing to fear. When that happens, it's embarrassing to us and it's just very uncomfortable.

Many, many years after I came home from Guatemala, when I was no longer young, Dan and I were hiking with Marty, a very good friend I'd met my freshman year in college, and Kent, who lived near me in Orange County. We were out in the extreme wilderness in Southern Utah, a windswept orange-colored sandy landscape that is full of majestic, incredible cliffs and narrow slot canyons that hadn't budged for centuries. Places down there have abandoned, scary sounding names like "Coyote Gulch" or "Death Hollow" or "Devil's Garden." We weren't far from the place where a guy became famous for hiking alone when a boulder fell and crushed his arm. He spent 3 or 4 days figuring out that he'd have to cut his arm off with his dull pocket knife to free himself and survive.

We'd driven in a rental car out into the desert somewhere in Southern Utah and slept there, or tried to sleep there, in the sand until morning broke. When morning finally came, we began to walk. We walked and talked and walked and hiked in what has got to be one of the most beautiful wilderness areas in the Western United States. We hiked along down the sandy trails across what seemed like an empty endless desert. We went in and around the deep slot canyons and down long narrow troughs where millions of years of dripping rain and wind had carved out perfect pathways.

After a few hours, right where the trail took a turn and sloped steeply downward into a deep canyon, we all stopped one by one and just stared ahead at the towering pre-historic cliffs that were indescribably beautiful. Each one of us came to the point in the trail where this view of the deep canyon and soaring cliffs was most inescapable, and we stopped without even saying a word and just stared at it. You could only hear the wind and the sand shifting and sliding as we each stood there on it. I don't know how long we stayed there without speaking, I only really remember that moment, feeling dwarfed by the power and eons of time.

In all, our hike was about 12 or 13 miles long. It took all morning and most of a warm sunny afternoon. I could understand how the guy who cut his own arm off could get so lost and so alone. There were four of us together out there and the labyrinth of canyons and trails was so vast and spread out that I'm sure if we hadn't paid close attention, we could have gotten lost.

After a full day, we were all very tired. We came to a place where the trail doubled back around a huge mountain made of blunt sandstone. Now, after walking all day, we were only a few hundred yards away from where we had left our car the night before. The problem was that between us and the car (and the end of the trail), there was a short but steeply sloping rock wall. If we could climb up it we'd be back up out of the canyon.

I was exhausted. I only had a swallow or two of water left in my water bottle. I had my doubts about somehow scaling this slick rock wall. Marty stood at its base and thought about it for a second and then he pressed tight against the wall and shimmied up the steep, worn stone, slowly at first and then, after hesitating for just a few seconds, he caught his center of gravity near the top where the rock face for a few feet seemed almost vertical. Then he skipped up and over to the top where it leveled off again. He was way up there now, telling us we could do it, urging us to "go for it." Looking back at us, he said he was sure we could make it and it seemed easy to him now. Kent followed Marty. He slithered up the wall too, almost an instant replay of Marty.

Dan went next and I followed him. We were both up about 25 or 30 feet. Okay, it may very well have only been about 10 feet, but it felt scary high to me. As I lay there spread eagle against the hard, slippery stone I tried to push my weight into the wall and I pushed my tiptoes onto a tiny sliver of rock. My hands searched above me for something, anything to grab ahold of and to steady myself and my nerves. I was okay though. I felt pretty good. I'd just seen two of my friends lie on their bellies and then almost will themselves to stand and skip up through the difficult part. I felt like Dan and I would for sure be next.

Dan was above me to the right. We were both leaning into the dense orange stone face as much as we could and trying desperately not to slip. My legs were shaking from the long hike mostly but, honestly, I did not like where I was and my legs shook from the fear that I might slide off and fall onto the rocks below. There were only a few feet of true hairiness ahead, I told myself.

Dan's amygdala had to be firing. He was right there all stretched out just above me and to my right, barely holding on like I was. I was clinging on, searching the rock wall for a hand hold when I heard Dan start to shout or whine in a panicky, terrified voice. He squealed out the words "I'm slipping…I'm slipping!" and he moved his hands around above him reaching for a hold or a cleft or anything except smooth rock. Falling would hurt and, worse, I knew that if Dan fell and got hurt he would be at the bottom of the canyon and we'd have to somehow get back down there and figure out a way to get his injured body up and out and across the bumpy desert above us and into our rental car to a small-town clinic or hospital where they probably only spoke some ancient American Indian dialect.

I could see Dan's boot slipping down in front of me. He was definitely starting to fall. That fulcrum of balance or center of gravity that Marty and Kent had somehow managed successfully was going the other way for Dan. This all happened in nanoseconds. I could feel his moment of panic in my gut and, without even having time to think, I slapped my hand out onto the slick rock just below where Dan's boot was sliding down and, I am sure without thinking, he stepped on it…hard. It felt like a sledgehammer or a giant boulder would have felt if it smashed down on my hand. It only hurt for a second, though, because when he stomped on my hand, Dan caught himself and regained his footing and balance. In another second, he was off his belly and pushing with his legs upward and then running for a few steps to the top with the others.

I, on the other hand, was still there clinging to the side of the wall. I knew my next step would take me to where Dan almost slipped off onto the canyon floor. I could hear Marty and Dan encouraging me, but I suddenly found myself curled up on my cot in Guatemala with all the dogs barking and howling, warning me about something horrible that was about to happen.

It seemed like I should be able to do this. I'd just watched three of my friends do it. It certainly was not impossible. But there was a very stubborn part of me deep in my primitive brain that insisted that it was a stupid risk for me to take. I wasn't slipping like Dan had, but if I did there wasn't anyone there to let me mash their hand into the hard rock with my hiking boots and catch myself. This was the time where I absolutely had to decide if I should try this or if my system was really warning me that there was a horrible disaster looming.

I didn't move for a while. I just leaned in and pushed down with my tired legs so I wouldn't slip. I wasn't serenely weighing the pros and cons. My heart was racing and my mind was starting to get confused and panicky. I felt like the answer should be clear somehow, like it should just present itself and then I would willingly take the risk. I didn't trust my instincts. My instincts told me to edge back over and slide on down and not try to decide while I was trying to deal with a hurricane or a tornado I couldn't see but was right there at my doorstep with the potential to cause unspeakable, unforgivable damage.

Was this a random, overzealous firing of my amygdala or was I hearing the animals warn me in advance of a *tembloron*? I don't think it's ever easy to know. In fact, most of the time it's impossible. Most of the time, it's not clear to me at all, and I just have to decide. If I could just catch my balance, I thought, just do like the others and lean the right way, I'd be skipping up to the top and out onto the desert to the car, where we had water and snacks and we would sit there and laugh and forget about "that one scary moment" and talk about how awesome the hike was. But if I slipped or at that critical point my balance tilted the wrong way, it would be over in a second and I would fall and for sure get hurt and maybe worse.

So, I didn't move for a minute or two and I tried to clear my head and listen. I could hear the others up above me urging and encouraging me upward. Things slowed down. I could feel the afternoon sun on my back and the warmth radiating back at it from the sandstone wall I was clinging to. I could hear my heart beat in my ears as I rested my forehead on the smooth rock. For a second, I felt hyper-focused, noticing the smallest imperfections and dimples in the rock wall. I could smell the dust and feel the heat of the sun. I couldn't hear, or better said, I wasn't listening to anything outside of my own body. I just felt myself breathing and stretching and holding on.

I thought again about how I felt the answer should be clear, but it wouldn't come. I remembered when I was young and I had a friend named Christian whose little brother had fallen into a crevasse and died while trying to climb a mountain. I imagined that it happened at a moment just like this one. There was a risky point in the trail where he just had to pay attention and shift his weight at the right time and it would be nothing to even remember. Maybe he hadn't been paying attention or maybe he was leaning the wrong way in the wrong split second and then it was over. Just like that. I thought about my family and I asked myself if I should be taking risks like this one, like my friend's brother had.

If I went one way and was successful, I'd be up on top with my friends, done hiking for the day, and joking about the brief episode where Dan almost slipped off but then stepped on my hand and got his balance. If I went the other way and shimmied back down to the base of the cliff, I would have to hike back 12 or 13 miles over the trail we'd come in on, with dwindling water in my bottle and weary leg muscles. So, this was it, face my fear and risk a big fall and possible serious injuries or turn around and face defeat and exhaustion.

For a second, as I gripped onto the wall, I remembered a tennis match I had watched on TV a long time before. Two players had fought each other until they were both exhausted. One of them, at the end of the match, had volleyed the ball sharply back to the other side of the net with what looked like a clear winner. His opponent's momentum had taken him all the way off the court, to the other side, where he could only turn and watch. The ball smacked off the man's racquet and was moving forcefully down, a sure winner, when unexpectedly it slapped into the top of the net and then flopped straight up into the air a foot or two above the net. Both players could only watch as it hung there in the air. The one who hit it, who had felt so confident that he'd won the point, was now in this split second unsure, while the other player, standing helplessly on the other side of the court watching, was now hopeful that maybe he still had a chance.

I felt like I was right there in that moment like the tennis players or like my friend's brother before he fell. I knew I had thought about it long enough. It was time to move, to do something, to not be paralyzed any longer.

FOUR

The Piano Recital

It was the late 1960s. My Dad worked in the Pentagon, for the United States Air Force and my family lived in a small suburb of Washington, D.C. named Carderock Springs. It was a pretty exciting time to be growing up. Every year or so it seemed like another set of astronauts was flying into space trying to get to the moon before the end of the decade. We were all captivated. I spent a lot of time with my friend Sandy thinking and learning about the planets and playing at the pool with my friends and my authentic looking plastic GI Joe space capsule, throwing it into the air and watching it splash down into the deep end of the pool.

We used to all gather around our black and white television sets every time one of the real space ships appeared from nowhere in the sky with its parachutes popping open and then later plopping down in the ocean. When the Navy frogmen found them and pulled them out of their little tin can flying machines, we were all thrilled.

Mom woke me and my brother John up late one night and told us we needed to watch the TV with her because Neil Armstrong was about to walk on the moon. I remember watching with sleep in my head and my eyes as he climbed down the metal ladder from the lunar module. He was careful and then he sort of bounced on the last step up and out and onto the surface of the moon. We all stared at the TV and held our breath wondering what he would say. We listened as he said in an electronic sounding voice, "That's one small step for man, one giant leap for mankind." I wanted badly for it to be a giant leap for mankind. But, by the time Neil Armstrong walked on the moon, I wasn't so sure. I was starting to worry. A couple of things happened that made me feel like something was about to snap in the world around me, like it wasn't as fun as I had first thought.

A year or so before the moon landing, I have a hazy memory of swimming at the community pool one summer day. We were playing a game where one boy would tread water above the tiled lines at the bottom of the pool. The rest of us would jump in and try to touch the line before the boy could touch us. It was fun and a great way to deal with the sticky hot summer days in Maryland. We jumped in and out of the cool water at least a hundred times that day.

One time, when I came up from under the water to the edge of the pool and was about to climb out, I saw another boy I knew sitting alone with his mom on the wooden deck by an old vending machine near the pool clubhouse. I was about to call out to the boy but Sandy told me that I shouldn't bother them. He said they'd just learned that the boy's older brother had been killed in Vietnam. I held myself up against the side of the pool, water running down my face, my head just high enough above the deck so I could see them, and I watched as he and his mom sat there looking empty. I felt sad, like their world had ended. I felt a little hollow myself, and I lowered myself quietly and slowly back down into the water and swam away.

I'd had very limited experiences with death before that day at the pool. I'm sure I'd never seen the sorrow that goes with it. I didn't know that it could reach out and sting many more people than just close relatives or friends. I couldn't, no matter how hard I tried, make any sense of it.

I would have to face it again though, in the spring of 1968 when I was sitting in the back seat of my mother's car. It was night and we'd been shopping. It was warm outside. I know that because I was sitting there with the window rolled down waiting for Mom to put the groceries in the car. She was reaching in the driver's door, getting ready to sit down, when a woman she knew, a family friend, saw her and shouted from across the parking lot, "Marilyn!" Mom stopped and looked up. The woman was now running across the parking lot. Mom didn't sit down. She stood up by the car and waited.

I know that I had the window rolled down because I could hear everything this woman said. She stood there by my mom looking angry and scared. She sounded alarmed, almost panicky. She neatened up her hair-sprayed bouffant in the reflection in the car window and she said in a voice that was half horrified and half excited to be the one telling the news, "Marilyn, did you hear what happened in Georgia tonight?" Mom shrugged her shoulders and said, "No." "Martin Luther King was shot. He's dead! They killed him!" The woman was nearly yelling now. "You know what this means don't you, Marilyn? It means they'll come and they'll burn down Washington!"

I could feel the emotion in her voice, and now in my head, and I felt for a second like maybe the world really was ending. I squirmed in the back seat. I wanted to run somewhere and hide but I had to sit there while mom got in the car and drove away. She told us something about how she couldn't believe that her friend would talk like that in front of us. She told us not to worry. She told us "no one was going to come and burn Washington" and she drove us home.

I was still ten years old then when I started to notice feelings of unease about things. I began to feel a little unsure of my step. I watched pictures on the news about the war in Viet Nam and protests everywhere. I wondered who else was going to die. I worried about people in my family and others that I knew.

I don't remember if there were riots in the streets of Washington that summer. I've read since then that there were some. I've read that President Johnson signed the Civil Rights Act in 1964 and that he feared he was sitting on a powder keg, and that cities, especially southern cities, were hunkering down and getting ready to quash any civil rights protests with force. I remember war protests too, and hippies, and Bob Dylan singing "Blowin' in the Wind" and the Beatles singing a song called "Revolution."

People were starting to talk about drugs and flower power. Universities were getting shut down by student protesters. The Black Panthers were beginning to fight and in the 1968 Olympics two black U.S. athletes had had their medals taken away for holding their fists in the air and looking down during the national anthem. I felt like the whole world was a powder keg and no one really knew how things could be resolved.

In the beginning of the summer, after a few months had passed, I woke up one morning and went into the kitchen to grab something to eat. Mom and Dad had gone on a trip for my dad's job at the Pentagon and the Air Force had provided a sitter to stay with us while they were gone. I walked into our small kitchen half asleep, to get a bowl of cereal.

The woman who was staying with us was from somewhere in the South. She was short and pudgy and she had an accent when she talked. She was supposed to make our meals, but she didn't. She was a chain smoker and as soon as my parents left she had no trouble smoking everywhere in the house. She would smoke and cough and leave cigarette butts lying around all over the house in thin metal ashtrays she had brought with her. She was always coughing and making big gasping noises that sounded like she was about to die right there. I came around the corner into the kitchen that morning and she was standing there with the remaining half of a lit cigarette dangling from her lips. I almost gasped when I saw her. Her eyes narrowed when she saw me and she leaned against the kitchen counter. "They killed your boy last night," she drawled. I had no idea what she was talking about when she said, "Robert F. Kennedy," and then she sucked down hard on her cigarette.

I couldn't believe it. I just stared at her. I didn't know anything about politics and I was barely aware that there was a civil rights movement, but I knew this was wrong. I knew this was evil. Robert F. Kennedy and Martin Luther King Jr. spoke about things like love, equality, and fairness, and here in the space of just a few months both of them had been killed. There was no end in sight for the Vietnam War. We were ducking and covering in school emergency drills. Protestors were everywhere in Washington. I'd heard that a U.S. ship had been captured in Korea, and political ads with atomic mushroom clouds were being used to try to win votes in the presidential election. For me, back then, it felt pretty grim.

But, in the middle of all this, there was a moment when my dad brought a little sense of calm to things, a sense that maybe everything wasn't spinning completely out of control. It didn't seem that way at the time, but looking back now, he helped me hope that maybe cooler heads would prevail.

I was, at the time, going to Carderock Springs Elementary School, trying to learn to play the trumpet, and playing team ball at recess. One afternoon, my mom told me to get dressed in my church clothes because we had to go to my older brother's piano recital at a theatre in Washington, D.C. somewhere. I was, as almost every boy my age would be, against the idea. A piano recital, at that point in my life, seemed like nothing short of a boredom chamber. Mom and Dad weren't asking, though, so I got dressed and we drove down into the city.

After we got out of our car and walked up the sidewalk to the front of the theatre I could see a big crowd standing and arguing. We stood back with Mom, while Dad went up and listened. Apparently, the venue had been double booked. Our group of young, white, suburban piano students and their families had been scheduled to use the auditorium at the same exact time as a large group of African Americans. They were also dressed up. Some of them were wearing tuxedos.

After what I thought was a long negotiation, the two groups decided that our group should go first as we had young children and it was a school night. We filed into the theatre and filled up the seats and one by one young piano students got up and stumbled through their pieces. As seems to be the case at almost every piano recital I've ever been to, it went long. Our time was up and there were still three or four of the most accomplished students who had not yet played. Everyone inside and outside the theatre was getting tense with every missed note. We all knew we were going overtime and that the people outside had been very patient already. It looked bad. It was bad—the privileged white people sitting inside and listening, as the crowd of black people waited outside and simmered.

Eventually, a few of the men outside could take it no longer. During one of the last performances they burst through the doors and started marching down the aisles. They were angry, and rightfully so. They started silently walking in protest through the rows of families bumping them and causing people to twist in their chairs and turn their knees to get out of their way.

We were sitting near the front and I kept turning and watching the men behind me as they continued their protest. The piano music kept playing. I was sitting by my dad when the man came to our row. He was tall, and he had a black suit on. He was shaking he was so angry. He stomped down the row bumping people's knees. He looked fierce and ready for a brawl. When he came to us, I flinched and closed my eyes and curled up in my chair next to my dad to get out of the way. I wanted him to just go by, but to my horror, my dad reached up and grabbed the man's arm.

I could see the man bristle at my dad's touch and look down on us with disdain. I was sure there was going to be a fight or a struggle. I couldn't really imagine it, though, because I'd never seen my dad lose his cool. I was leaning as hard as I could into the corner of my seat. My dad held onto the man's arm. It was very tense and I braced myself. The man looked at dad and dad said something like, "If you'll sit down here by me we will be done very soon … please." The man looked at my dad without emotion. It wasn't an angry look. It was more like he was just feeling so frustrated and tired of being in the group that got taken advantage of. Maybe I'm reading into things here, but it seemed like there was zero feeling as he looked at my dad and at my dad's hand on his wrist. Then he sat down in the seat next to me and he watched the one last piano student nervously perform.

When the show ended, the crowd sprang to their feet and exited the building. I jumped up relieved that this ordeal was finally over. I was ready to run to the nearest exit. My dad leaned over, though, and told me that he thought these people had been very patient to wait for our group. He said that the least we could do would be to stay and listen to their music.

I'm a little ashamed to say that I had already been at the very fringe edges of my own ten-year-old patience limits, coming to my brother's recital in the first place, and the thought of enduring more classical music was much more than I thought I could bear. But Dad was insistent and so we found some new seats in the back and sat down. It was opera or some kind of very formal singing. Sometimes they sang in foreign languages. There was a piano player who was absolutely phenomenal. Finally, when their show ended, I jumped up ready to go again. But Dad grabbed my arm again and told me that he'd like to go up and meet the performers and tell them how much he appreciated their performances.

So, we did. We went up and stood in a long line and shook hands with each one of the people who had performed. I listened as Dad told each one of them how much he appreciated their patience and, more than that, their talent. Finally, well after midnight, we left the theatre and went home. I fell asleep immediately when I sat down in the car. It seemed to me, later when I thought about it, that what we did wasn't really a huge gesture. It was just a bit of courtesy and the result was good. It could have, in a second, before anyone had a chance to think of the right way to respond, gone out of control and moved from bad to much, much worse. But it didn't because, when it came right down to the moment that could have gone bad, both my dad and the man walking through the aisles decided to try for a better way.

FIVE

Paper Route

I had a paper route when I was a kid. My high school friend Chris Sadler got me the job. I used to wake up super early, when it was still dark, and find my way out to a small enclosure area by the garage where we kept our trash cans and where I kept my bicycle. It was always dark and I would feel around for my bike laying somewhere, wherever I'd let it fall the last time I jumped off it.

It had a light on the handlebars that was powered by a small generator attached to the front forks. The generator was grey metal and a little bigger than a walnut. When I pushed it into the "on" position, a part of it rubbed up against the front wheel and spun around however fast the wheel was turning. The light on the handlebars barely glowed if I was going slow or shined way ahead on the road in front of me if I was going fast down a hill.

I would get up and throw on a pair of old Levis and a T-shirt and put my big set of canvas paperboy bags over my shoulders. I'd grab a piece of bread or something from the kitchen and get on my bike, flip the generator on, and ride down the hill from my house to downtown La Jolla, CA. It was cold in the winter months and usually foggy. No one used bicycle helmets back then and I learned to ride sitting back on my seat with my hands off the handlebars and coast. That way I could hold my arms closer to me up under the oversized newspaper delivery bags so I wouldn't be as cold.

It was a mile or two ride from my house to the front steps of a bank building across the street from the old Post Office in downtown La Jolla, where the man we all called "The Manager" from the *San Diego Union* dropped a couple of bundles of newspapers for me very early every morning. I don't think I could have made it there earlier than the manager dropped the bundles even if I'd tried (which I never did by the way). I rode my bike there in the dark every morning and when I arrived, I stopped and laid it down next to me.

I knelt in front of each bundle and flipped them over and removed the little plastic strap holding all the papers together. There's a trick to undoing the plastic strap—a paperboy trick that my friend Chris taught me. It involved twisting the plastic and pealing it away on the underside. If you didn't know how to do that you would have to carry a knife or scissors or something with you in your bags. One of my rules as a newspaper carrier was to always travel as light as possible, especially on Sundays and on Thursdays when the papers had extra sections and more ads and they were thicker, fuller, and heavier. Carrying extra things, especially knives or scissors was just not a good idea.

I'd kneel in front of the bundle of papers and with a rapid fire technique born of months and months of daily practice I folded each paper, wrapped a rubber band around it, and then made a couple of organized piles of folded newspapers there on the sidewalk out in front of the closed and dark bank. I'd lay out my canvas bags and fill them up neatly on both sides. The bags were big and heavy and made of rugged white canvas. They had the *San Diego Union* logo on the front and back. I'd slide my head into the big hole in the middle of the bags and all of the papers would rest on my shoulders. On easy days, like Mondays or Tuesdays, this was no problem because there was less news or ads. They had fewer pages and they fit more easily into the bags.

On Thursday or a Sunday, the bags were always really heavy. In fact, sometimes I had to set up the bags on the stairs of the bank with the papers in them and the neck hole suspended in the air between the two different compartments that were now jammed with papers, and I'd lay down on the sidewalk and wiggle my way to get my head through the hole and then I'd shove the bags around and squirm myself under and around so the bags would rest on my shoulders. I'd have to push and strain until I was standing up and ready to get on my bike.

I always wanted to get all the papers the manager had dropped for me into the bag on the first try and not have to make two trips. This was impossible on Sundays and unadvisable on Thursdays. On those days, the bags were, in the beginning, swollen and heavy. With each house I'd stop at, as I pulled papers out of the bags to deliver them, the load got lighter and lighter. After dropping a few papers at people's houses, the whole delivery process became more manageable. Riding my bike then, and throwing, and managing things like curbs, and bumps, and sharp turns in alleys when it was still dark became doable.

My buddy Chris trained me in the finer arts of newspaper delivery. He was the one who showed me how to fold and rubber band a paper quickly. He told me how to maneuver the big canvas bags and still be able to ride a bicycle. While riding, he taught me to reach in and take a paper out and, if necessary, chuck it a long way onto someone's porch or down on the ground right by their door. One of Chris Sadler's great pearls of paperboy wisdom came when he told me that no matter what time it was, if I ever saw a customer who was awake, I should get off my bike and hand them their paper and say, "Good morning, I'm sorry I'm late this morning." He said people would be amazed at how early we were out and this would invariably lead to bigger tips at the end of the month when I went out to collect people's monthly payments.

Each day after our routes were over, Chris and I used to meet up at a local Jack in the Box restaurant on Pearl Street near the high school. Chris had worked out a deal with the people there that if he gave them a free paper, they would give him a "Breakfast Jack." When I showed up, he went back and talked to someone he knew and they decided that one free paper was now worth two free Breakfast Jacks. Every day for years, with no days off, we went to Jack in the Box and ate our Breakfast Jacks. We told each other all kinds of paperboy stories. He had been a paperboy long before I showed up on the scene and he had some great stories. The breakfast was like the reward for the hard work each day.

Delivering papers was not an easy task. First off, I would struggle to stand under the weight of a busy news day's papers. Then I would get on my bike and start to ride it to the first home. I'd reach in and pull a paper out of the bags and drop it or throw it to the customer's porch. After only a few deliveries like this the papers in the back of the bag would gradually start to weigh more than the ones in the front of the bag and the neck hole would get pulled up tight against my throat and it would start to choke me. This would cause increasingly difficult bicycling skills to be employed with less and less ability to balance and breath properly.

Eventually I would have to get off my bike and stand away from things and spin the bags around on me so the heavy back part would now be in the front and I could again ride my bike without fear of losing control. This maneuver was easy for a seasoned paperboy. The really advanced super-skilled guys who had years of experience could even sometimes do it while they were still riding their bikes. But it was an advanced paperboy skill that could only be developed by repeated effort and many bike crashes. I saw Chris do it once. When it was done correctly, it was a thing of beauty, like some kind of a ballet move. When my friend Chris did it, it looked completely effortless.

I tried it a couple of times when I was so sleepy that I should not even have been out riding a bike in the first place. I had not yet awakened to a level where I was able to evaluate things like the risk of crashing my bicycle in the road and the potential for pain or road rash on my arms and legs. A couple of times I tried it when I was so alert and daring that I thought I actually could swing the bags around and keep control of my bike. But each time, the weight of the lopsided bags would shift my center of gravity when I tried the big circular shoulder and upper body motion that I'd seen Chris do. The looping, spinning, off-balance movements required always made the bags swoosh outward. They always started going around but eventually somewhere in the spinning, when the bags pulled out and around, the neck hole would yank backwards and choke me and rub a big ridiculous looking red scraping rash / burn mark on my neck. It hurt; and by that time the bags would be in full swing and I would invariably be pulled to one side or another and lose my grip on the handlebars and end up in a crumpled heap of newspapers, twisted canvas bag, and spinning bicycle wheels, on the road or sidewalk.

There was one house on a street called Bluebird Lane that was a particularly difficult delivery. It was near the beginning of the route so my bags were always full when I approached. The customer had asked that the paper be delivered to their back sliding glass door which sounds fine except that I had to throw the paper from an alley that was about 30 or 35 feet away from the slider and up a large embankment covered with a weird succulent plant called "ice plant" that was all over the general La Jolla area. I would get off my bike and open their back gate, but only long enough to not alarm their large German Shepard dog. I don't know if the dog lived outside or if he was just out roaming around the yard. I usually had a paper out and ready to throw by the time I had pedaled up the alley to their back gate.

The throw had to be precise too because it was a long arcing downhill toss and they had a large rectangular swimming pool between me at the top of the hill and the door they wanted the paper to land at. Every day I prepared my paper in advance by double or even triple rubber banding it. That way, corners of the folded newspaper would not poke up and cause some aerodynamic disturbance that would end up with the paper either plunking into the pool or thunking resoundingly on their wood shingled roof. The customer told me they would never complain if I got a paper in the pool or up on the roof but they said they would if there wasn't one there by the door when they woke up.

Between the bags weighing me down, and the dog running toward me whenever I opened the gate, and the paper throwing precision required, I was never sure how many papers it would take to make a clean delivery and avoid a complaint to "The Manager." I think my record for a single day's folded and double and triple rubber-banded newspapers being launched from the top of the hill through the gate with the dog barreling toward me and then arcing gracefully but landing on the roof or in the swimming pool before I finally landed one where they wanted it was seven. I always imagined that an old man lived down there and he loved just sliding open his door and reaching down and picking up his morning paper, He probably had a gardener or a pool man who didn't mind fishing soggy papers out of the pool or getting them off of his roof. I always made sure there was a paper right there by the door even if there were several others all over his back yard.

One foggy cold winter morning I was riding along in old town La Jolla. It was early and still dark. I wasn't riding my usual bike that day. Something was wrong with it, and I was riding on a non-Sting-Ray, a non-paperboy type bike that had hand brakes and gears. It didn't have a light either. This bike didn't fit me as well. It was taller and more awkward than my regular bicycle. I was teetering along with a full set of bags on a downhill part of my route. I remember my legs were tired from having pedaled a big load of papers and myself up a big hill and I was relieved to have come to a small part of the road where I could coast for a minute.

I let go of the handlebars and I let the bike take me down the hill. It was a dangerous maneuver. I knew it, but I was getting pretty good at it by now so I leaned back and tried to close my eyes for a second and just coast down the hill. The same thing always happens though when you are coasting with no hands on a hill and you close your eyes. Invariably, the bike starts to wiggle and shimmy. I opened my eyes immediately and grabbed hold of the handlebars again and squeezed the hand brake lever a little and steadied the bike and felt relief that I'd corrected in time and was back in control.

I turned into a little driveway where I usually stopped and placed a paper on a little metal railing by the front door of the home of an older man. I'd see him there early some mornings because he used to wake up early. His light was on almost every day and sometimes he would see me coasting into the driveway of his little craftsman style home and he'd open the door and wait for me in his bathrobe. He was never smiling and he never said anything to me. He took the paper and nodded. I would smile and turn my bike around and continue on down the road.

This one morning, I didn't see him there at the porch. I placed the paper on his railing the way he liked it and I turned my bike around and headed back out his driveway. Usually, if I didn't think he was looking, I would cut across his front lawn and head over to his neighbor's house to make my next delivery. He didn't like it when I did that but it saved me from having to push my bike back up his neighbor's long uphill driveway.

It was just starting to be morning and I turned and headed downhill on his lawn. The lawn was wet though from the morning dew or maybe he'd been up early that day and had already watered. It was a little steep and I wasn't all the way familiar with the new gears and brakes on the awkward bicycle I'd borrowed for the morning. When I squeezed the lever, the brake pads down on the tire rims engaged but because the lawn was wet, the metal rims were wet, the pads had no grip, and the bike didn't slow down a bit.

I was headed downhill on a man's lawn, where I should not have been in the first place, squeezing as hard as I could on the brakes and picking up speed. If I continued the way I was heading I would soon come to the sidewalk and then to a steep drop off onto the neighbor's gravel driveway and eventually to the street below. There were cars parked there. Without a miracle of incredible balance and bike riding skill and maneuvering of newspaper bags full of heavy newspapers, I would surely hit and disfigure a car or worse my body or my face on one of the cars on the road down below me. I decided that if I acted quickly, I could turn left and duck under the leaves of a tree where the man's front lawn remained more level. There was no path in that direction though, only wet, slick, green grass. I was pretty sure I could slow down if I could make that turn. Maybe if I stopped there at the top of the big hill in front of me, I could get off the bike and dry off the rims and the brake pads with my shirt or something else dry, so they would work better.

 I did it. I turned to the left and ducked down. Somehow, I kept control as the tires swerved and picked cold water from the grass and sprayed it up behind me. I saw, to my left, for only a second that the old man I had dropped the paper off for was standing on his porch in his bathrobe watching me, frowning. There was a moment too, a second at the most, as I was hurdling across this man's wet front lawn that I could see that the leaves I was ducking down to avoid were hiding something behind them. They looked all innocent and they were fluttering and twitching in the early morning breeze, but I could tell there was something else there, something hidden.

 By the time all of the necessary danger warning synapses had fired and my nerve impulses had begun to communicate from my brain to the rest of me, I smacked hard into a hidden branch squarely, solidly with my shoulders and part of my chin. My bike kept going but I did not. It hurt too. Papers and rubber bands and leaves were combined in a brilliant moment of impact and very near unconsciousness. In another instant I found myself lying on my back on the wet grass with newspapers under me and all around and my big canvas bags twisted and tying me up in some kind of knot. My bicycle kept on going too. It somehow managed to ghost ride itself across the wet grass and down the long driveway before it wobbled and tipped over the edge of the curb between two cars parked on the street below.

 I had bumped my head pretty hard and I wondered if I was okay. I laid there on the man's lawn for a few minutes thinking about standing up. I was already wet all over; I thought that jumping up would not help that. So, I laid my head back down on a part of my newspaper bags behind me and I didn't do anything. I closed my eyes and rested my head and heard the old man in the bathrobe ask, "Son, you took a big spill there. Are you all right?" I opened my eyes and I looked up at him. All I could think to say was, "Good morning sir, I'm sorry I'm late this morning." It was the first time I saw him smile.

 For the next three or four days I begged my dad to wake up with me and drive me on my paper route in his dark brown Lincoln Mercury Marquis. I folded the papers in the back seat and Dad got out of the car and placed them where they needed to be. I don't think he bothered with throwing papers over the man's pool until he got one right at the base of the sliding door or the whole Chris Sadler "Sorry I'm Late" greeting.

 But Dad got the newspapers delivered. When I went to school and told Chris the story about the tree branch and the old man in the robe, he laughed so hard I thought he was the one who had maybe bumped his head.

 Looking back on the time I spent on my bicycle as a paperboy, it's pretty clear to me that I learned a lot of important things I would remember for the rest of my life.

SIX

Junior Varsity Football

It was 1974. The President of the United States was about to resign, and Hank Aaron had just broken Babe Ruth's record by hitting his 715th career home run for the Atlanta Braves. My friend Paul had convinced me to play football with him for the La Jolla High School junior varsity football team. It had been a long season and we were about to play the final game of the year. We only ended up winning this one game all year long and, truth be told, we didn't really deserve it either.

We scored our only win of the football season on a fluke when their long snapper hiked the ball almost into outer space, way over the head of their quarterback. A guy on our team ran like the wind and scooped up the ball and juggled it and then dropped it. It bounced into the other team's end zone where every player on the entire field threw themselves into a huge pile of arms and legs and cleats and sweat. Somehow one of our guys was on the bottom with his arms wrapped so tightly around the ball that he could have popped it. It was a beautiful, completely inglorious touchdown, but we got six points. We missed the extra point but still somehow ended up winning the game 6 to 3.

I watched the whole pile up in the end zone from our bench. I wasn't in the dog pile in the end zone that day because I was a sophomore on the third string team. I was still deciding if I liked to play football and maybe that's the reason I wasn't in the game. I played defensive back and sometimes, very rarely, in practice, I was a punt returner. I don't think I had actually played in a game yet that whole year. We called my friend Paul "The Ogre" because he liked to scream when he got excited and once, on the bus ride to an away game, he fell asleep and drooled on himself. It was Paul who had convinced me at lunch one day, near the beginning of the season, to try out for the team.

Now, I was on the third string team not just because I had joined the team late but mostly because I am more of a gentle soul and not keen on fighting or drooling. I've heard it said that to compete well on the football field one has to have a bit of an anger problem. I was never sure about my willingness or ability to muster up enough hatred for the other team to be a starting player. I've always naturally been on more of an even keel, even if the people around me got frothy and upset. During this particular game, though, for some reason I felt a little bit more ornery.

Although I had not played organized football before that year, I had watched plenty of it. When I was about ten I sat with my best friend Sandy as Johnny Unitas of the Baltimore Colts lost to Joe Namath and the New York Jets in the Super Bowl. None of us saw that one coming. A year later, my family had moved from Washington, D.C. to San Diego and I crowded onto our yellow couch with my dad, my brother, and Uncle Mark as Lenny Dawson, the quarterback of the Kansas City Chiefs, led his team to victory over the Minnesota Vikings.

We also talked a lot about football in my family. My dad played football for his high school and then as a freshman for the University of Washington. He told me once about how in a practice he stepped up to tackle the first string running back who had the ball and was cutting into the backfield on a practice play. Dad had been the star on his high school team in Fullerton, California sometime in the 1940s. This was when football helmets were mushy and cardboard-like and when there weren't any face guards on them. Dad told me that he stood his ground in the backfield as this first stringer came careening through the defensive line. He told me he was the only person left to try to bring this guy down. The runner's name was Hugh McElhenny. It turned out that he became an All-American. Dad said he jumped up right into McElhenny's way, and planted his feet, and closed his eyes, and threw his shoulder as hard as he could at the big first stringer.

He hoped to bring him down. He wanted to wrap his arms around Hugh McElhenny and knock him off balance and show the coaches and the rest of the boys how he was tough and how he could play with guys like Hugh McElhenny. And he did it. My dad stepped up and braced himself and launched his body wide-eyed and with all the strength he could muster into the full barreling force that was this local football hero. But the moment of glory that my dad hoped for never materialized. It was not even close. Dad says now, when he thinks about it, that he bounced right off of Hugh McElhenny like there was some unknown force repelling him.

Mr. McElhenny was a brute. He was a once-in-a-decade force of nature. He was a natural. He could not only run fast, but he was strong. He was stronger and more rugged than anyone my dad had ever conceived of. My dad's tackle, or attempted tackle, was over before it even began. It ended with my dad dazed and lying on the field wondering what had happened and Hugh McElhenny continuing down the field as though he had swatted him aside like a mere annoyance. "It was just sheer brute force and a completely different level of football than I had ever been involved in," Dad told me once.

I thought about my dad and Hugh McElhenny as I stood by our third-string quarterback. He was a small sophomore kid who had never played in an actual game either. I stood next to him on the sideline and caught the ball for him like the pros do to warm up. It was late afternoon. The field was a mix of green grass and mud and our coach was yelling at the offensive line that had huddled up around him. It was winter and a thick fog was slowly making its way from a few blocks down the street where the ocean lapped at the shore. The few family members in the crowd who had showed up for our game were talking and buying candy and Hostess Twinkies from a folding table by the field that was being used as a snack bar.

Our opponent was a small school from up the coast. It was the very first year that their school was open. They didn't have a football tradition. They were a brand-new school and they hadn't had the time to develop any traditions. Once the game started, I was surprised at how quickly their boys started yelling at us and taunting our players out on the field. I had friends who played in the game who came off the field and yanked their helmets off and complained that the other team was just mean. You could see players out on the field squirming to get out of the pileups that happen when plays are over. Guys on our team would jump up out of the scrum and hold their hands up wide complaining to the referees about getting their fingers twisted or getting punched down where the refs can't see at the bottom of the pile.

I could feel my eyes narrow and my jaw clench as I became more and more angry. It was one thing, I thought, to beat us. We got beat a lot that year. It was another to have to cheat to do it. My dad had always taught me that only losers resort to cheating. He said it was because they weren't good enough to win on their own. I sat on the bench and stewed. It wasn't fair. It was definitely wrong. I stood up and started yelling at my team to get fired up. This wasn't like me either. Normally, I took my place on the sideline and tried to support my friends after they came off the field and sat down. Now I was screaming at them and shouting at the kids on the other sideline, although I don't think they could hear me.

The game was almost over now but I jumped and pointed and yelled at the other team. I even convinced my friend, The Ogre, to get up off the bench and start yelling too. It was quite a commotion as one by one players from our side stood up off the bench and started yelling and taunting the other team. I ran around slapping them on their helmets and shouting that we could beat these cheaters. It was like I was transformed from a mild-mannered high schooler into a rabid lunatic.

As I was yelling and slapping and jumping up and down, I heard our coach, who I wasn't sure even knew my name at that point, shout out, "Nielsen!" I looked up. "Nielsen!" he grunted. I couldn't believe it. I scrambled around to find my helmet. I stuttered and my eyes darted back and forth wondering why he was calling my name. I grabbed my helmet and threw it on my head. When I did, it jammed down over one of my ears which folded down painfully so that I couldn't hear very well. I tried to snap my chinstrap on as I nervously ran over to the head coach. When I got there, he put his hand on my shoulder pad and shouted something that sounded like "punt return left!" in my ear. Normally, a team that was losing wouldn't punt on the last play of the game. Maybe they were backed up against their end zone, or maybe it was just junior varsity coaching—I don't recall the details. My coach slapped me on the butt and I ran out onto the field.

I ran up to the huddle. Everyone was crouched down staring at me, waiting. I took a knee in the middle of the circle and I shouted, "Punt return left!" like I was in charge. We all clapped our hands and then everyone got in place for the next play. I was to stand way back, field the punt when the other team kicked it, and then run like my life depended on it toward the other team's end zone. I looked out through my white plastic face guard and I clenched my fists together and tried to stand there with confidence like I imagined Hugh McElhenny would. I knew this was my moment. I didn't have time to think about it too long either because as soon as I took my place alone, way back near my own end zone, the other team had lined up. They leaned in and then hiked the ball to their kicker.

I couldn't see over the line of my teammates and the kicker's teammates pushing and shoving and running in the mud. The next thing I knew the ball was sailing up into the sky. It was a beautiful kick. It arced up into the air above everyone and sailed right toward me. Everything seemed quiet at that instant. Maybe I was concentrating. Maybe I was scared to death. I moved toward the ball, all the while thinking, "Please catch this ball; please catch it!" I squinted into the sky and I saw the big brown football dropping. I was focused and deliberate. I set my feet and I watched as closely as I could as the ball floated down through the air.

Once in practice my coach had told me to focus on the ball as it sailed toward you. He said I should try to read the writing on it as I got ready to make a catch. So that's what I did. I watched it …just like he told me. I stood there alone in the quiet of all that mayhem and I tried to will the ball into my hands. I got right up under it and felt it hit my hands and I grabbed hold of it tightly. I had caught it! I was thrilled. Then I looked out in front of me and I could see eleven angry, hate-filled, cheating players from the other team running straight for me as if no one had touched them. I was alone with the ball and everyone on the other no-good team wanted a piece of me.

One guy was on me the instant I looked back down at the field. I jumped to my right more out of instinct than some strategy. Then I started to run as fast as I could up the field. There was no one from my team anywhere on my entire side of the field. All I could see were the red and yellow uniforms of the enemy and they were all coming after me. I was sure I would die. Or at best I thought I might be maimed.

I was running hard when I noticed one of my teammates standing over on the left side of the field like he was waiting for me. Then I remembered the play I had called when I was kneeling in the huddle. It was punt return left. "Left" was the key word so I bolted to my left like my very existence hung in the balance. When I did, I saw a guy on my team move between me and one of the enemy and knock him down. I looked over and saw my whole team lined up in an arc to the left side of the field. They had listened in the huddle! I ran as fast as I possibly could and the blocking line held. I gasped and ran and pushed my legs until they burned and my heart was pounding inside my black and red uniform.

I ran as though this was the Super Bowl and I was Joe Namath or Lenny Dawson. I ran to avenge my dad for the hit that Hugh McElhenny had laid on him. The play was working perfectly, just the way it was designed. One by one, the players from the other side were getting smacked into the mud and I was still running toward the end zone. I could feel my shoulder pads flapping up and down as I ran. I knew if I could just get around this last guy, I would score a touchdown. It would be glorious and a great story to tell if I could actually score a touchdown the only time I ever touched the ball in a real game.

It wasn't one player though, it was two. I had used up all my blockers and they had the angle on me. I was scrambling down the other team's sideline at the end of the game, trying to not step out of bounds and find a way to get away from these two hulking, cheating, finger twisting guys from the other team as they ran toward me. I decided that it was inevitable and it was probably going to hurt so I just lowered my shoulder and I braced myself and I tried with everything in my 15-year-old frame to run right through them like this was practice at the University of Washington and they were my dad and I was the All-American running back.

Even though I had lowered my shoulder and braced myself, the moment of impact came and my dance with the sideline and my daydreams about junior varsity glory were obliterated. These two opposing players apparently had similar dreams and we collided with such force that for a minute I could not breathe. All three of us were flying for a second. There was a terrible sound of sudden impact and pain. I instantaneously lost track of where I was or how the field was aligned underneath me. I was spinning and flailing, and they were too. Somehow in all the crashing, I held onto the football. The ball and I ended up looking up into the clouds from the grass and the mud by the other team's bench. The game was over. I distinctly remember wondering why I had ever wanted to play football in the first place.

In a second I was surrounded by their team. I could hear them as they leaned over me and frothed and screamed and shouted at me. I couldn't see them until I untwisted my helmet. It had ended up sideways on my head from the force of the tackle. When I could see again, I thought they looked like they hated me, like they were ready to twist my fingers and punch me under the cover of the angry mob of players surrounding me.

I was ready to jump up and scream back and go *ogre* on them, but when I looked up through my helmet and saw them standing over me, I felt weirdly like them. I felt like I was one of them. Maybe I got hit a little too hard, but for a second, I felt like I saw myself laying on the other sideline wearing a Falcon uniform instead of the one I had on. It was a weird metaphysically threatening instant but for a flash I could tell that my team, the Mighty and for this one day triumphant La Jolla Vikings, would have done exactly the same thing. They would have stood there and yelled and shook their fists and screamed and drooled with righteous indignation. They would have felt no mercy, none.

It was freaky and I didn't know what to do. I lay there on my back looking up feeling a very odd kinship with my tormentors. They continued with their collective anger issues. I looked up and made eye contact with the biggest loudest one of them and I smiled. When I did, he stopped. For a second, he looked confused. Then he looked around and pushed some of his teammates out of the way and he reached down and gave me his hand and helped me up. He yelled something at me but I didn't understand him and then he turned me toward my sideline and he nudged me away from his teammates back toward where my team was celebrating our only victory of the year, like we had just won the Super Bowl. I can tell you for sure that none of us had seen this win coming.

I walked away toward my friends on the team thinking about what a teeny difference there is sometimes between winning and losing, having an anger problem and not, taking the blame and trying to give it. I was moving slowly across the field toward my team. The game was now over and we had won. It was in the books. I watched my team as they celebrated on the sideline. To be completely honest, I think the celebration came more from relief at not having gone the whole season without a single victory than it was from a feeling that we were the better team.

Don't get me wrong—we deserved to celebrate. We deserved all the cheering and reveling we could do that day. This rag-tag team of young teens who had either not been judged good enough to make varsity, or did not yet have the right amount of fire in their bellies, was not going to end up winless. That knowledge was, for us at least, more than enough to celebrate.

The other team was subdued. They took off their helmets and started to crowd around their coach in the same end zone where we had recovered the winning fumble. They listened, I imagined, as he tried to wrap up their effort and tell them not to hang their heads.

I liked the feeling of having won. I enjoyed competing, being in the game and running with the ball until I almost actually scored a touchdown. I could see how some of my friends might look back on high school as "the glory years." It was fun, in my mind at least, for that one day, almost being the hero. I could only imagine what it might be like to actually do it. After it all was over, though, my very favorite memory was when I was down on the ground realizing I wasn't hurt and their meanest, cheatingest player reached down and helped me get back up. He surprised me by helping me up and shouting something I couldn't make out into the ear hole of my helmet. I imagined it was something like "good game" or "you guys won fair and square." I guess I'll never know what he actually said. It might have been something bad but, I didn't hear it and it rests better in my memory this way.

SEVEN

Getting Attention

I stood alone on an old stage in a creaky theatre in La Jolla High School's main building. I was 17 years old. There was an insanely bright spotlight shining down on me from somewhere across the room. It was so bright and hot that I couldn't see anything except a little oval of brightness surrounding me on the soft, scratched, wooden stage. Wherever the light touched me I felt it hot on my skin, like I was an ant and there was a giant little boy hovering over me with a magnifying glass, trying to see if I would burn up from the intensity of it all.

The stage I was on was around a hundred years old. It was painted a flat black color and it had scuff marks on it from a century of Converse tennis shoes or Clark Wallabees, or whatever shoes young people used to wear back when the school opened. I'd heard the old theatre had been condemned because it could no longer pass California earthquake standards.

I stood in this circle of light trying to see out into the rows and rows of mostly empty seats to get an idea who my audience was. I couldn't see anything, though. If I could have, I would have seen only a handful of high school friends and my 3rd period drama teacher, Mr. Morales. I don't remember him very well. It's been almost 40 years. I'm not even sure I've got his name right. But I do remember that I thought he had a certain daring about him. It was a 1970s kind of boldness. He would speak with words and phrases and gestures that all said that he was a dreamer. He really believed that any one of us in his class could one day be a great actor or lawyer. He thought we could change the world. He thought one of us would one day be president. He didn't just talk about it either. He *knew* it. He truly believed that he could teach us how to turn things from make believe into reality.

 I didn't want to get up on the stage that day but he made me. He made all of us. The assignment he gave us was to come up with a short 2 or 3-minute bit that had no words, only movements. He wanted us to go out on stage alone, in front of everyone, and communicate something important about ourselves. We could have music playing, he said, but nothing else.

 A few weeks before, I'd gotten up on the same stage to try out for the play *Up the Down Staircase*. I didn't make it into the show and I wasn't that surprised either because I was sick when I tried out. I felt dizzy and tired and extremely disoriented. I remember trying to remember the lines I had been given. I stood there and tried to summon up some fire, some gumption like I thought an actor like Al Pacino would. I wondered if Al Pacino had ever tried out for a school play. I'd heard that Cliff Robertson and Raquel Welch were alumni of La Jolla High. I thought they had probably tried out for something on that same stage once.

 The day I tried out for *Up the Down Staircase* I felt awful. I remember looking around the auditorium and seeing Mr. Morales. He told me a couple of times to begin but I didn't feel like it. I felt slow that day like I just couldn't muster up anything. After an awkward couple of minutes, I heard Mr. Morales ask, "Peter, Are you okay?" I told him no, I didn't think I was and he had my friend Chris Sadler take me to the nurse's office where I felt even more sick and they had my mom come and pick me up and take me home early from school.

This time though, as I stood in the circle of burning light and waited for my cue, I felt much better. I'd brought a black vinyl record of my dad's called "Soul Flutes" and I'd given it to my friend Chris who was sitting on the bottom rungs of a ladder manning the "sound system" which was really just a small record player and a microphone. I couldn't imagine Al Pacino, or Cliff Robertson, or Raquel Welsh ever doing a pantomime like this with a sound system like the one we had, or ever submitting to Mr. Morales or any other drama teacher.

I couldn't believe I was going to do it. It wasn't like me. I stood there in the light wondering if I'd be able to move when I heard my cue. I wasn't nervous exactly; it was more like I was already embarrassed. I did not feel loose and relaxed. Instead, I felt extremely self-conscious. The thought that I was going to stand up there and reveal something about myself only using movement felt like I was about to dance for everyone. I was pretty much an expert at working my way out of tense or awkward situations with my friends, but now…here…out on the stage…I was all alone, with the ridiculous spotlight blinding me and reminding me that there were people out in the audience that I could not see, scrutinizing my every move.

Before the music started I tried to collect myself. I took a deep breath and sat down at an old desk I'd dragged out from the back of the stage and into the light. I looked down at the desk like I was studying or reading and the flute music started crackling out over the public-address system. I tried hard to channel my inner Al, or Cliff, or even Raquel, and I focused on what I thought I looked like when I was home at my desk studying. I pretended to read my book as the soft beautiful music pushed its way out of the big Fender amplifier on the corner of the stage.

I sat at the desk like the book was boring me. I yawned and stretched and rubbed my eyes. I'd made a book cover out of a brown paper grocery bag and I'd written the words "Drama - Period 3" on it in with a black felt pen. Then I closed it and I sat up and acted like I was thinking of something other than school. I acted like I was thinking of Bjorn Borg and the grass courts of Wimbledon. Thinking about Bjorn Borg and trying to act like him was almost second nature to me in high school. To me, he was an amazing Scandinavian gentleman tennis player who was understated, quiet, and humble, even though he absolutely ruled the world of tennis back then. It seemed like every year he ended up playing his foil, John McEnroe, in the finals. McEnroe was a brash, awful, spoiled American who embarrassed me.

    I stood up from the desk and toed the imaginary service line. I bounced a pretend tennis ball and then I started to serve it to John McEnroe. I could see him waiting with his floppy curly hair sticking up out of his headband and his East Coast-looking tube socks pulled up almost to his knees. I knew exactly how Bjorn Borg served the ball. I'd watched him do it a thousand times on TV. He took a little step with his right foot when he tossed the ball up into the air. I reached up in the air with my right hand like I had a wooden Donnay tennis racquet in it, just like my hero's. I pretended to serve the ball right at John McEnroe and I watched as it landed right on the line and the dust of the brown grass poofed a little into the air. McEnroe was helpless. He didn't even have time to move and the ball was past him. It was an ace on match point! I fell to my knees like Bjorn did each of the seven consecutive times he won Wimbledon. I could almost hear the crowd roar. When my knees hit the grass, I held my hands up in amazement. I could feel the English sun and smell the grass and hear everyone clapping.

    The music rested for just a second before the flute song went into its last final echoes. When it did, I looked up again from my knees like I had just realized I wasn't Bjorn Borg and I wasn't on center court at Wimbledon. I looked like I knew it was just me winning Wimbledon in my mind, all alone in my room. I looked around to see if anyone was watching me pretend and then I picked myself up and dusted myself off and shrugged like I wondered what that was all about. I went back over to the desk and put my head on my book and acted like I fell asleep. The spotlight popped off and I really was in the darkness, alone on the stage.

The little group of students there that day and Mr. Morales stood right up and cheered like maybe I *had* actually won Wimbledon. My friend, Chris, who had been helping with the record player and the microphone started shouting, "Yeah Nielsen!" Girls in the class, pretty girls, came up and told me how well I'd done. Mr. Morales told me I should really think about getting more involved in drama. But I couldn't. I didn't have time. Every spare moment I had, I was practicing, trying to learn to play tennis.

A few minutes later, class was almost over. All of the students that were there, every one of us, were up on that old stage. Mr. Morales was down in about the third row. He had one arm resting on the top of the folding seat next to him and one double-knit pant leg folded over the other. He clapped his hands to get our attention and he told us he was going to give an extra credit "A" to whoever was up on the stage that could do something to draw his attention to them, and away from everyone else. Then he looked back down into a book he had open on his lap and acted like he was busy.

A boy stood right up front to the very edge of the stage and started acting like he was a rock star. He started screaming out some song by Three Dog Night or Rod Stewart. He jumped around the stage all spazzy like rock stars did back then and he screamed like the seats were full of fans. But Mr. Morales didn't even look up. A girl near the back of the stage started jumping around in circles and yelling out the words to a poem I'd never heard. One by one the kids in the class lost their inhibitions and screamed, or sang, or jumped. They started pushing and shoving. There was a chaotic tangle of young men and women moving up on stage like a mob toward where Mr. Morales was sitting. They were at full volume and maximum drama-soaked commotion.

Everyone was doing everything they could think of to get Mr. Morales's attention. He let it go on for 4 or 5 minutes. Then, with every bit of the dramatic style he had in his system (which was endless) and without looking up from his book, he held his hand up in the air. One by one the kids in class noticed and started to quiet down. When he felt like he had enough of the attention, he stood up. Everyone stopped and looked back down at him from the stage.

He took his glasses off and rubbed his eyes and then, with the frames of his glasses still in his hand, he pointed at me. I could not imagine why. I'd been sitting on the ladder the whole time, minding my own business near the back on the side of the stage. I felt like I'd already performed, like I didn't need more attention. As everyone else had tried in absolute vain to get him to look at them, I just sat there looking down on them all from where I was sitting on the last couple of rungs of the ladder. I was minding my own business, not moving or saying a word. When Mr. Morales pointed at me he paused for a second. Everyone was listening. Everyone was leaning in waiting for him to say something important, something profound. He paused and then he said with great emphasis, pointing straight at me, "He gets the A!"

Mr. Morales got up before they could move and he strode toward the stage. He told them that they had been loud and wild but he said it was all very much the same and it was all very predictable. He complained that everyone pretty much did exactly the same thing whether it was a guy in front playing a pretend guitar and screaming out the lyrics of a song, or a girl jumping around and yelling. "It was all just noise," he told us, "and it was unremarkable." "But," and again he pointed right at me, "the quiet boy on the ladder found a way to be different!" It took me a second to look around and realize that there was no other ladder and I was the only boy anywhere near it. Mr. Morales said I had been different from everyone else. He said I had found a way to stand out from the crowd. The weird thing to me was that I'd been trying to *not* stand out. In fact, I didn't think I was even in the game. I wasn't jumping or yelling and I had kind of checked out. He said he was aware of all that, but, he said, I was the one who got the attention, and the A.

EIGHT

Bats in the Attic

After Kathie and I were married, we were finishing up at school and we lived in Provo, Utah. Sometimes, usually on the weekends, we went down a few exits on the freeway to Payson, to see my Grandpa, "The Doctor" (everyone called him that) and his wife, Janice. For some reason, he always called me "Pierre of the Plains." Over the years, as he got older, he got tired of my long nickname and he called me "Pierre the Plains" or just simply "Pierre." I was never sure why he called me that. I always thought he'd made it up. I'm sure there was a story he once told me that went with his calling me that, but if there was, I can't remember it. Regardless, to me he was "The Doctor" or "Grandpa Doctor." To him, I was "Pierre" or "Pierre the Plains."

The Doctor and Janice lived in a brick house with a steep wood shingled roof so the snow would slough off in the winter. It was next door to a little store called the Milk Depot where you could buy milk and ice cream. There was also a sign in the window of the Milk Depot that said "Night Crawlers," which was some kind of a worm that people used for bait when they went fishing. Between the ice cream/bait store and the house was a huge apple tree. I swear it was twice the height of the whole house. Grandpa told me once that he'd planted it when he was young. He'd just graduated from medical school in Chicago and brought the family home to Utah and settled in Payson.

Back when he built the house, the main north-south highway, later bypassed by Interstate Highway 15, ran straight through town. Cars traveling to Nevada or California from up north would have to slow down at each one of these towns and stop at the stop signs and drive down Main Street past the shops and past my grandparents' red brick house.

The house had old steel radiators in every room and a creaky oil heater down in the basement that thumped loudly sometimes. Back in the 1930s he'd built the house so that it could serve as a home upstairs and a small hospital below in the basement. At that time, it was the only hospital anywhere near Payson. Grandpa told me he was convinced that he'd removed hundreds of tonsils in that basement hospital. He said it had all the latest technology back then and that it was the "finest operating room south of Salt Lake City."

Outside by the apple tree, there was an old red garage down a long concrete driveway. I was climbing around in it one day when I was a boy and I found a dusty old saddle and bridles and bits, and other ranching equipment I was not at all familiar with. I also found an old metal and glass cabinet with white scrubs, a stethoscope, and one of those round mirror things that doctors used to wear on their heads to make it easier to see when they were examining someone.

It was an old house by now, but it was always immaculately cared for. Except for the things he'd long since forgotten about in the attic, the house was always perfectly neat and clean. I think we all knew that was Janice's doing. My mom grew up in that house. Her bedroom window looked out to the backyard and the giant apple tree and, for as long as I remember, a small garden just below it. When I was 17, on the night before I left home for my freshman year of college, I lay in a sleeping bag under that apple tree by my Uncle Mark and we talked until it was late and we both fell asleep.

One Saturday, shortly after Kathie and I were married, we drove down from our apartment in Provo to see The Doctor and Janice. Kathie set to work with Janice in the kitchen canning peaches. They worked for hours, just the two of them. I wasn't in the kitchen but anyone could see that Janice and The Doctor loved Kathie. They even told me once that if things for some reason didn't work out between the two of us, they wanted her. I was glad they loved her like they did. I also assured them that it was going to work out. At the end of the day, Kathie balanced a brown cardboard box on her knees as we drove off to Provo. Three or four or five jars of freshly canned peaches were in the box. Janice told Kathie that she should take them with her to put them on our ice cream when it was cold outside and peaches were out of season.

While Kathie and Janice were working away with the jars and the peaches in the kitchen, my grandpa, The Doctor, was lying on his little single bed in a room filled with dark-colored furniture that I'm sure he had bought before World War II. There was a glass top, or cover, on the top of the dresser. In between the wooden top of the dresser and the hard, clear, glass were small black and white photos of The Doctor as a young man with his surgery whites on and a mask covering his face. It looked like he was just about to start on some surgery to take someone's tonsils or something else out. There was a picture of Uncle Mark holding his trumpet and one of him in his Payson High School football uniform (except for his helmet so you could clearly see his face). He had the ball tucked under his arm and his other hand stabbing out into the air so he looked athletic and dashing. There were pictures of my Uncle Jay and my grandpa holding up the head of a deer they'd just shot. They were kneeling in the snow grinning from ear to ear holding the animal's head up by its giant tangly antlers.

My grandpa had had knee surgery a few months before and hadn't recovered very well. Janice told me once that she thought he had been "poking around in his own medicine cabinet." It was more like a closet and it was full of every drug

I think you could buy and probably some medicines that were long since de-certified or whatever the medical community did to get doctors to no longer use certain drugs. There was an old ether bottle in that drug cabinet. I didn't know what it was the first time I saw it. My mom saw me looking at it when I was younger and she told me it was a doctor thing and that it really worked well to clean her shoes when they got scuffed.

Just off the hall, by the drugs in the closet, there was the little room he was "recuperating" in. It was the room with the old furniture and the old pictures. He used to lie there on the little bed and not move. It seemed like he lay there all day long. Before his surgery, when we went over to see them on Sunday afternoons, he would get up out of bed and throw an old blue bathrobe over his long, one-piece thermal temple garments, and he'd limp into the front room using an old wooden cane. He'd sit there and tell us stories about my mom, or about medical school in Chicago, or deer hunting in the mountains with his boys, or what the oddest surgery he'd ever done was. He told us some of the stories three or four times. He was always consistent with his facts, too.

After they cut into his knee, he was either in too much pain or he was completely free of pain. Either way, he wouldn't come out of that little room. We'd go in and sit by the bed and he'd pull on my ears and laugh and tell us one of his stories again or he'd go over and over and over how he wanted me to be a pallbearer at his funeral and who would be the speakers and where he was to be buried, etc.

That Saturday though, at Janice's request, when Kathie and Janice canned the peaches in the kitchen, I climbed up a big ladder they had out by the apple tree in the backyard and squeezed myself through a little louvered door into the attic above everyone. My job was to climb around in the attic and figure out a way to make it so that, when springtime rolled around again and the bats came back from wherever they go in the winter, they would not be able to get back into the Doctor and Janice's attic.

Janice told me that every summer ugly brown bats swirled around their attic and made their homes up there "like it was a kind of a bat hotel." She looked at me and pointed her arthritic finger right at me and with every ounce of seriousness she possessed she said, "Peter, I'd sooner see a mountain lion walk across my kitchen floor than I would see one of those dirty bats fly in here!" I told her I would see what I could do. So, I leaned this super tall ladder they used to pick apples with up against the outside wall of the house and I climbed up it until I could creak open the little louvered door. It was right up in the angle of the eaves where the very top of the two sloping roofs came together. When I pushed on the little door it creaked and opened inwards creating a hole in the wall just big enough for me to poke my head and shoulders through and squeeze the rest of myself in.

    I fell through the opening onto some old blackened and dirty boards. It was dark and so dusty that when I waved my hand in front of my face I could see particles and dust and smoky, dirty flecks dancing around in a murky swirl against the shaft of light from the opening in the wall. It felt like I was on the moon, all grey and shaded. I had an old flashlight with a dim bulb that cast an eerie orange glow where I pointed it. I stood up on one of the old boards and balanced. The bulb in the flashlight was making every effort to bring some light to the thick darkness surrounding me but it seemed for a minute like the darkness was winning, like the bulb might just slowly wind down and give up once and for all.

    I fumbled around by the louvered opening and found an old light switch that I didn't think had been touched for years and years. It was covered with cobwebs. I brushed them off and pushed one of the buttons on the ancient switch, all but sure that nothing would happen. But I was wrong. A light bulb in a very old porcelain fixture that was nailed to the ceiling turned on. It was probably the first time in 50 years that the bulb had been on and this attic had been exposed and out of the darkness.

    When the light went on I could see the attic of my grandfather's house clearly. It was full of old wooden beams, like the one I had fallen on. They were lying across the joists that the lath and plaster clung to. Random nails poked up through the boards with years of dirt and infection on them, waiting for me to make a wrong step. I was lucky when I fell in that I hadn't been stabbed by a nail or broken through the ceiling of the room below and landed on my grandfather as he planned his funeral.

The inside of the sharply pitched roof pushed down from outside with more nails poking in to hold the shingles above and keep out the rain, snow and light. I had to hunch over a bit to be sure not to snag my head on one of those little fangs. The whole thing seemed oppressive and dark and at the same time delicate and precarious. I had to be careful of the old nails above me while balancing on the boards, careful not to step through the plaster ceiling onto Grandpa in his bed or Kathie and Janice canning their peaches below.

As I looked across the jangle of wood and nails and old dirty insulation, I could see giant mounds of dirty, dusty, crusty guano from years and years of bat infestation. There were no bats there right then. It was fall and too cold, but the attic was literally full of piles and piles of their poop. I could see very clearly where the bats got in. Back in the 1920s or 30s, when the house was built, a mason had carefully laid the bricks together to form the walls. These walls pushed up to form brick peaks in the middle for the top of the roof and pitched down sharply on either side. Roofs were steep in this area so that, in the winter if there was a heavy snow, it wouldn't be able to accumulate. It would pile up a little and then slide off the roof as soon as it got a little weight.

I could now see that the problem for Janice and The Doctor was that each brick laid to form the pitched angle of the steep roof formed a small triangle-shaped hole where it met the fascia board, and each hole was just big enough for a flying critter to wiggle through. There were literally hundreds of these little triangular points of light where the bats had and could squeeze through as they pleased. I turned back and poked my head through the louvered opening on the side wall. I wiggled myself through the little door like a rodent would and I grabbed hold of the apple picking ladder and twisted myself out of the attic and down onto the back driveway. When I got down, my grandfather was there holding the ladder in his blue bathrobe. He had an old tin bucket and a shovel and he told me to get back up there and start shoveling.

I must have filled twenty or twenty-five buckets full of fifty years' worth of bat guano. I lowered each bucket down to my 90 year old grandpa who stood at the bottom of the ladder, took each bucketful of bat poop, untied the bucket from the rope, and limped over with his bucket in one hand and his old cane in the other and poured the guano out on his tomato patch.

One time I found a dead bat and I laid it on the top of the guano in one of my bucketfuls. When I lowered it down he saw it and started to laugh. I was looking down from the opening in the wall, and I saw him pick up the dead bat in his old weathered hand and look at it closely. Then he got an idea and he looked toward the house and shouted, "Mother! Oh Janice...I've got something for you!" Janice and Kathie came from the kitchen into the backyard. The old doctor lifted his creaky arm when Janice approached and showed her his stiffened, dirty, ancient little bat. Janice's face turned red. She pointed at him with a tenacity that I'd expect if she were defending an innocent child. She said something like, "Don't you take another step!" She stared him down like I'd never seen and said, "Stop right there!...I am not pretending here…I will march myself right over, right now, to the judge this very morning and file for divorce right now so help me God if you do not put that filthy thing back down in that bucket!"

"I'm putting them on the tomatoes!" he said. "I thought you might like to see one." "No! I want nothing to do with it. I am not kidding you!" said Janice. You would think that my grandpa would take her not at all subtle hint. I hung my arms out of the opening to the attic and watched as he held the bat out in front of him and started limping towards her. She looked at him like he may as well have been the bubonic plague incarnate. She said, "Come in, Kathie," and they went back inside and locked the door. It was the only time I'd ever known them to lock their door. He was laughing like he was so clever. He laughed himself all the way over past the old apple tree to the tomatoes where he buried the dead bat at the base of one of the tomato plants under a bucket-full of guano. Janice swore that even if those tomatoes were the finest in the whole county, she would not touch one this year.

    I spent the whole day filling up buckets and lowering them down to my grandfather, if he was there, or I'd squirm out of the opening onto the apple ladder and down to dump the guano in the trash. The next day I showed up with a friend named Gary. I'd called animal control when I got back home and they told me that in order to keep the bats from coming back, we'd have to shut them out. Gary and I stopped down at the hardware store/feed shop and bought some mortar that we mixed up in what was the guano bucket from the day before, and we crawled around in the attic and slapped the mortar down with our bare hands into all of the little holes we could find. We smooshed and pressed the slushy mortar into every nook and cranny of that attic until our hands were raw and the moisture had been completely sucked out of them by the cement.

    Finally, after two days of digging around and balancing and smooshing both concrete and bat guano, we had cleaned up as much as we could and stuffed up every hole in the attic. Finally, we replaced the screen on the inside of the louvered doors on each side of the house, wiggled back around and out onto the ladder, and knocked on the backdoor that Janice had since unlocked. Janice thanked us profusely and gave Gary some of the peaches. The Doctor appeared at the door of his room and peered through the doorway into the kitchen. He took a toothpick he'd been chewing on out of his mouth and said, "Pierre the Plains, come on in here. I've got to show you something." Gary and I walked in with our peaches as The Doctor was lying back down on his bed. "Well...I think you've surely earned your pay today!" he said. "I don't think the bats will be able to make it back up into the attic, and I surely thank you for that. Janice will also be very thankful about it come springtime." We nodded and told him it was no problem.

He laid down with his head on the pillow and he looked straight up at the ceiling right above his head and said, "But what do you think about that?" He pointed up directly above him, right where his eyes would naturally rest as he was relaxing and recuperating. There was a long rusty nail I must have stepped on in the attic poking down through the plaster ceiling, like it was pointing at him. He laughed and said that he thought we ought to get about fixing that, now shouldn't we?

I went back a few days later and pulled the dangling nail out and fixed the hole in Grandpa's ceiling so he didn't have to look at it as he lay there and worked out plans for his funeral. We had to wait, though, to see if the bats came back. It was a good thing we had Janice and Kathie's peaches to help us as we studied in school and waited for autumn to come to an end and for the cold, snowy winter to be over and for springtime to come so we could watch as the bats tried to get back in. When spring finally did roll back around, the bats swarmed around the top of the house for weeks, confused and frantic every afternoon as it was getting dark, trying to find even a teeny hole they could squeeze themselves through. After a while they stopped and gave up. Janice was relieved and felt like the old house was hers again.

Occasionally, over the years when I would visit them, I would hear something in the late afternoon that sounded like it could have been a bat or two flapping around outside. Of course, it could have been a sound emanating from their oil heater down in the basement that was much older than it should have been allowed to get. I felt good when I went to see them because I knew that I had done what I could to keep the bats out for good. I'd had a part in helping them stay warm, clean and protected from things that, if you don't watch out, can wiggle their way in like those bats.

NINE

The Wizard of Westwood

What follows is an attempt to explain the complicated reasons that I am a fan of UCLA basketball. Even though I don't know anyone who ever played there and I've only been on campus once or twice in my whole life, somewhere deep in my subconscious there lies a rabid, crazed, loyal fan of the UCLA Bruins.

It may have started way back on a Saturday night when I was a student at Muirlands Junior High School. I lived in La Jolla, California in a tract home in a new part of town with my mom and dad and brother and sister. It was a brand-new housing area carved into the side of a hill with wood framed houses popping up all over the place. Everyone who lived there was new to the neighborhood. After dinner each night, I'd just walk out of my house and look around for a friend and we'd figure out something to do. I ended up spending a lot of time with a kid up the street named Roger who liked to take apart his bike and put it back together over and over again. It was complicated and we had no manual or teacher. We just kept working at it. Sometimes I brought over some of the tools my dad had laying around in our garage and we'd try to figure out how they worked and how we could use them on a bike.

One night, I came back home and my mom told me that the Smiths, our neighbors from across the street, had asked if I could babysit for them. I don't think I'd ever babysat for anyone before and I kind of always thought of it as "girl work." Mom assured me I could do it. In fact, she said, there really wasn't anything to it. She told me I'd go over there around dark as the Smith's two girls finished their dinner. I would play with them for a half an hour or so, read them a story, and then tuck them into bed. Then I'd go downstairs and wait for their parents to come home. When Mr. and Mrs. Smith came back home, they'd ask me how things went. I would tell them everything went well and go home. She told me they would pay me $2 an hour and I thought that sounded pretty good. The Smith girls were both in elementary school, around 8 or 9 years old. I remember my mom telling me to call her if anything strange happened. She said she'd be right across the street.

At dusk, I rang the doorbell. I would do things just the way mom told me. She told me to introduce myself to Mr. and Mrs. Smith and to look them in the eye when I did. She said I should ask them to show me around the house, which I'd never been in before. She told me to make sure I called them Mr. and Mrs. Smith whenever I spoke to them. Honestly, I can't imagine anything else I would have called them. Mom told me I should also introduce myself to each one of the girls, whose names I can't remember anymore.

I did it all just the way she said. Mr. and Mrs. Smith introduced me to their daughters and then told me when to expect them back. They told me they'd find a phone and call me at some point during the night to make sure everything was okay. Then they hung around for a while. Mom also told me they'd never left their children with a sitter before so they might be a little uncomfortable. They were formal and they were extremely adult-like. I remember them speaking a little louder and slower than they normally would so they could be sure I would understand. They lingered at their door a bit longer, like they were getting up the courage to leave and then Mr. Smith said, "okay then…" and they walked out and closed the door.

So, there I was standing inside on the tile by the front door, looking at these two little girls in their pajamas. I reached into a backpack I'd brought with me and I pulled out my favorite book from when I was about their age. It had a tired old brown cover with the white cardboard insides poofing out of it on the worn-out corners that I had turned over a million times.

I pretty much had the book memorized. It's about a boy who can draw his world and, I think, he travels all around and then, in the end, he draws himself back at home. I told the girls I would read it to them if they wanted and I said it was my favorite book. Their eyes widened and they had me follow them upstairs into their room where I sat down against the wall in between their two beds and read them the story. Before I even got to the last page, they were both asleep. It was so adorable how much they trusted me and just fell asleep. It was only six o'clock or so and I wasn't even close to tired so I turned off the light in their room and, as quietly as I could, tip-toed downstairs to the family room. I left the light on upstairs in the hall in case one of them woke up and got scared.

I sat down on a white couch that had a footrest. I kicked my feet up on it and stretched out and thought how this was a pretty sweet gig. I could just sit there if I wanted to. Most likely the girls were asleep for the night. I stretched out on the couch and tried to relax. It felt weird being alone in the Smiths' house trying to figure out something to do. I didn't think I should go to sleep. They didn't have any magazines lying around. I'd left my homework back on my own desk across the street on purpose.

I got up and started looking through the books on Mr. and Mrs. Smith's bookshelves but they were all boring-looking, about science, technology, engineering, or something else I couldn't have understood even if I had had an interest. I picked one up and flipped through the first few pages. It was precisely the opposite of the book I'd just read to the girls. It looked exacting and hideous and it had symbols and charts and things that looked like they were written in a different and excruciatingly boring language.

I thought about getting something to eat from their kitchen but that didn't seem like something I should do. I wasn't hungry anyway. So, I sat back down on the couch and rested my feet on a little square footrest. The thought struck me that maybe the reason I hadn't done very much babysitting was because it was so boring. I just sat there and tapped my fingers on the armrest.

I thought about how my dad and I had spent that Saturday afternoon hooking up a set of speakers that he'd bought for me down at Radio Shack. He had me fish speaker wire up through the wall behind our HiFi stereo system in the living room into and through the attic all the way above the long hallway and then down the wall at the end of my room. I was up above, crawling through the rafters and the insulation, stapling my wire down to the tops of the dry, greying wood structure while dad was down below inside the house. We were yelling back and forth so I could hear him telling me where to drop each end of the wire so it would be able to pop back out like a miracle, right where it needed to be. I played Neil Young's *Harvest* album on those speakers until it was almost worn out. I liked to listen to Johnny Cash, Herb Alpert, Tommy James and the Shondells, and Herman's Hermits. It was fun building the whole thing but it was most fun that Dad and I did it together.

Now, though, I was here sitting on the Smiths' poofy white sofa tapping my fingers, waiting. What I was waiting for I was not sure. There had to be something to do more than try to read boring books and daydream about crawling around the attic. I took my feet off the footrest and sat up when I noticed that they had an old black and white TV. I was just getting up to turn it on when I saw, or thought I saw, a shadow by the door into the family room. I sat up, suddenly more alert, thinking maybe someone was out in the hallway. I wasn't sure I had actually seen anything, but I had a hunch.

I *almost* saw it, like when you're telling someone something and right in the middle of your sentence you can't remember a word. The meaning is there in your mind, ready to be expressed, but it can't quite find a word to jump onto. I felt like something or someone was out there in the hallway even though there was no noise and no change I could see, since I had walked through there on my way back from the girls' room, just a few minutes before.

I sat there silently trying to hear everything I could. I stood up and crept slowly toward the hall as if all the lights were out and I was afraid I might bump into something. I even held my hands out in front of me and I walked slowly, my eyes darting around every corner, searching for the nothing I thought I might have heard. I turned on every light I passed until the downstairs was bright and glowing. I walked the entire area until I was satisfied that I'd made the whole thing up, and I turned to walk back into the family room.

"BOO!"

The two little girls were sitting on the stairs next to each other, smiling and impish. I nearly fell down and had some kind of seizure, I was so startled. I never expected them to be there. They were cute and all, but cunning and mischievous too, and I had not expected that at all. I think I blurted out some unintelligible grunting exclamation that was half word, half moan, and I know I stumbled back into the very well-lit hallway.

My first instinct was to bark at them and wave them off and tell them to get back to bed where I had put them. In the few seconds since I'd recovered the recollection of my name and realized I had not wet my pants from this near-death experience, I paused and smiled and waited for my brain to catch up. I nodded at them and said something like, "Ohhh, you guys *got* me!" They giggled and ran back up to their room. I followed them, peeked around the corner, and mouthed the word "Boo!" back to them. They giggled again and I told them something about staying in bed this time. They nodded.

I turned on their black and white TV and collapsed back in the poofy chair downstairs. I was rattled. I needed something to calm me down. Maybe there was a show or something on TV that could do that. Back then, there were no recorded shows or "set-top boxes" or premium disk channels, or ESPN. I hoped I could find something worth watching to distract me for a minute. My heart was still thumping so loudly I wondered if you could hear it outside my body. I was still a little spooked and I left all the lights on downstairs.

There was a basketball game on whatever channel the TV turned on to. I was going to watch it no matter what because I didn't want to get up out of the chair and change the channel. It was a UCLA game. I remember their guard was a guy named Henry Bibby and they had a forward named "Silk" Wilkes. Bill Walton was on the team that year. He was from San Diego somewhere and he was lanky and tall and he had a funny-looking shot. He was all over the place too. The game was really close and exciting.

I watched the whole thing and I decided that even though I was only about 5'6 or 5'7, I would practice every day in my driveway so I could play. I knew I had no hope of playing like Bill Walton. He was a real athlete. Nobody could stop him. He could pass and block shots and he was quick. He could have slam-dunked the ball all the time, but there was a rule against it.

When Henry Bibby or "Silk" Wilkes threw the ball to Bill Walton, even if he was wide open under the basket, if he wanted credit for a basket and wanted his team to score two points, he had to jump up. These days, everyone in the building would expect him to dislocate the rim and hang onto it and kick his feet in ecstasy and pound the ball through it with brute animal-style force, but back then, he couldn't. He was constrained by the rules to hold the ball just above the hoop and then release his hands away from it almost daintily and leave it there in the air so it would just float down into the net.

I sat there alone on the floppy white couch with all the lights on and the game glowing back at me. In those few minutes, I realized I had become an all-out UCLA basketball fan. I don't know why that game connected with me. Maybe it was the feeling of losing myself while watching. Maybe I felt like it was partly responsible for saving my life from what seemed to be lurking in the shadows. I don't think Bill Walton or UCLA basketball have really had any concrete effect on my life, and I don't have any idea why I remember the slam dunk rule. But, deep down inside me, even though I really haven't had anything to do with UCLA at all (except that I live in the same state and I root for them whenever they play USC in anything), there is a part of me that is a dedicated, loyal fan.

My new obsession with UCLA basketball surprised me. It didn't fit with my normal pattern of rooting for the underdog because they were never underdogs. They absolutely dominated college basketball in every way for over a decade. They won 10 NCAA championships in 11 years. I started watching at the tail end of their complete and utter dominance. Bill Walton was their last great center. Even after the string of unbelievable successes was over, I still followed the team.

A year or two later, when I was in high school, I remember lying on my back looking up at the upholstered roof of my mom's station wagon as we drove home from Utah. We'd gone there to visit my grandfather and now we were headed home to San Diego. I had begged her mercilessly for days for us to leave at another time so I could lie on the floor in my grandpa's house and watch on The Doctor's new color TV as UCLA played Louisville in the semi-finals of the NCAA basketball tournament. Mom said no, though, because we had to get back. So, I lay down in the back seat of her Oldsmobile and I listened, with her, to the game on the radio. It faded in and out as we drove down Highway 15 through southern Utah and into Nevada. I lay in the back seat and asked her again and again to turn the volume up at the good parts.

I imagined I was there in the arena watching the game. It was exciting. The game was a close one. In fact, it was tied and went into overtime. As I remember, Louisville had it in the bag with only seconds remaining. But their free throw shooting star, a guy who had not missed a free throw all year, missed two in a row at the end of the game. Then, a UCLA player hit an outside shot and sealed the game. By the time it was over, Mom and I were cheering and giving each other high fives. I recounted the last 5 or 10 minutes of action to her as if she hadn't been sitting right there the whole time, listening to it with me. It was the most exciting game I'd ever seen or listened to.

Now they were on to the finals to play Kentucky for the championship. I loved their team that year because Bill Walton and the other big stars of the team had graduated. The guys that were left were sort of unknown, at least in the crowds I ran around in. The dynasty was ending. John Wooden had announced that the final game would be the last one he would coach for the Bruins. Their roster that year had a couple of stars like Dave Meyers and Marcus Johnson. They were good but they didn't have a Lew Alcindor (Kareem Abdul Jabbar) or a Bill Walton, who the press and every basketball fan in America had heard of. They had journeyman players like Pete Trgovich, and Ralph Drolinger, and Dave McCallister. Their games were always close like the Louisville one, but they seemed to win and now they found themselves in the finals.

The championship game against Kentucky was being played a few days later, right near my home in the San Diego Sports Arena. I decided that afternoon that I would drive down and see if I could buy a ticket from someone and go in and watch it for myself. I hadn't been able to watch the game against Louisville so I thought I should try to see the final game in person. I bought a ticket from a scalper about a half hour after the game had started, for half price, and I went in and found my seat way up in the highest possible section. I mean, these were the cheap seats. They were probably the worst seats someone could possibly have, but I didn't care. Even though I was up there in the nosebleed section by myself, I felt like I was watching history.

John Wooden, "The Wizard of Westwood," was retiring and everyone knew that this would be the last game he coached. He was a legend. He used to sit on the bench with a rolled-up program in his hands. He was proper and respectful and he demanded excellence and discipline. I felt excellent and disciplined just looking down at him from my seat in the millionth row. I don't remember many details about the game except that UCLA won, which was fine with me. It would have been wrong for Kentucky to win John Wooden's last game.

Right after the game ended, I walked down as close as I could to the court. I wanted to get a glimpse of these players and their historic, incredible coach. All the players were standing out on the court hugging and shaking hands with each other. I stood right down by the court just out of the way so reporters and other people could get by. They kept coming down the aisle right next to me. They would make eye contact with a very bored looking security guard wearing a blue double knit blazer. He'd barely look up. They flipped open some kind of ID and then he waved them on and they walked right past me, and stepped down onto the court where they got to talk to the coaches and players. I mean, UCLA players like Dave Meyers and Pete Trgovich just stood there and talked to these reporters. I was so close that I could almost hear what they were saying.

I watched a reporter approach Dave Meyers out on the court. He showed him his press pass but Dave Meyers didn't really bother to look at it. They started talking and I thought to myself how the press passes looked a little like my La Jolla High School ASB card. I couldn't believe I was doing this but I took my ASB card out of my wallet and I showed it to the security guard. He was still there holding a rope to keep people like me off the court. He looked up at my card with zero enthusiasm, waved me past and then I stepped down onto the court.

I couldn't believe it had worked. I ran to the first UCLA basketball player I could see. It was Dave Meyers, a lanky forward with an excellent outside shot who I had kept track of during the year. Watching from the cheap seats, when all the players were down on the court playing next to each other, they all looked normal sized. As I sat up there in my seat, I thought that, if I worked really hard, maybe I could play like they did. Not like UCLA, but maybe I could play for my high school or something. When I walked up to Dave Meyers, I was behind a TV news broadcaster who was holding his microphone up asking a question. Dave was answering something about John Wooden, I think. I waited until the interview was over and then I stepped forward. I think I only came up to his chest; he was so tall and just plain big that I could not believe it. He was still sweating from the game and he looked down at me. I reached my hand up and he grabbed it and shook it. I squeaked out the words "Good game!" and he said thanks. He looked at me for a second like maybe I had a question, but then someone shouted something and caught his attention and he let go of my hand.

I was amazed at how huge his hand was. It was nearly double the size of mine. If you've ever shaken the hand of a toddler and noticed how their hand fits right into your palm and when you grab hold you grasp their whole hand and part of their forearm, that's what it was like for Dave Meyers to shake my hand. College basketball, I thought, is played on an entirely different scale. They were all giant men and I felt like a toddler around them.

I bounced around the court reaching up and shaking the hands of UCLA players like Marques Johnson and Ralph Drolinger and Dave McCalister. I got swept up in their interviews and their celebration. I could not believe I had finagled my way down on to the court where they had just won their 10th NCAA basketball championship.

I saw a couple of Kentucky players, who were equally tall, walking slowly toward the exit. A crowd of people who didn't have press passes, or ASB cards that looked like press passes, gathered in the first several rows of seats up in the stands and cheered for UCLA. I was thinking I had shaken everyone's hand I needed to when I saw John Wooden, the Wizard of Westwood himself, standing off by the team bench next to some other guys in suits. I couldn't believe no one was talking to him. Maybe the press had already gotten their quotes. Maybe there was just a lull when the reporters were all fighting to speak to other people. I don't know. But I walked over and held out my hand and said, "Good game." He shook my hand and looked me right in the eyes and quietly said, "Thank you."

That night, on the way home, I thought about how John Wooden was such a monument to coaching. He did all the things that, in my opinion, qualified people for hero status. He was disciplined and yet soft spoken and he was confident but thoughtful and kind. He had just won his tenth NCAA national championship and he took the time to look me in the eye and thank me. I was just a high school kid who should have never been down on the court where he was in the first place. I should have been thanking him. I also thought about Dave Meyers and how big his hands were. I drove home and remembered listening with my mom to the Louisville game as we meandered through southern Utah in her station wagon. I hadn't expected the UCLA players to be so graceful and nice after they'd won it all. I was surprised, and impressed at how they all talked to me, including their coach, as if I actually belonged out there on the court after the game.

Time passed. In fact, a lot of time passed. I grew up and got married and had a family. I still rooted for UCLA when their games were on TV. But they had struggled since Coach Wooden retired. They had some good players and even some stars. I think they even won another national championship, but it was not the same.

Years later, when my son Jeff was in high school, a friend gave me some tickets to a game up on the UCLA campus in Pauley Pavilion. I picked Jeff up from school and drove through stifling traffic from Orange County, where we lived, to Westwood. We arrived a few minutes early and found our seats. The Bruins were playing Arizona State that night. The players looked so young I couldn't believe it. They were all out on the court with their oversized bodies acting like they didn't care that much, shooting warm up shots, and making practice layups. There were cheerleaders dressed in light blue and yellow outfits following exact choreography as a band sitting next to us in the stands blasted out fight songs. There were popcorn vendors shouting and fans socializing. Tuba players revolved their bodies back and forth in unison and blurted out their bold tunes as the crowds began to settle into their seats.

    I was just sitting down when I saw, across the parquet floor, a few rows up from the court, a line forming for autographs. It must be a movie star, or a famous singer in a rock band, I thought. I stretched my neck and looked past the line and saw a frail old man with grey hair and a pointy nose. He looked older to me but I recognized him immediately as John Wooden, "The Wizard of Westwood." He looked old and frail but he sat there patiently signing autographs for anyone who would wait in line. I'd heard that his wife had passed away and it was said that he had never been the same after that. It looked like the years had worn on him since he shook my hand. Of course, he had just won the NCAA national championship back then so maybe he was a little less reserved than normal.

    I'd heard that he came to UCLA home games and sat in the same seat and signed autographs before every game but I had forgotten about that until now. He was the same coach I shook hands with after he won his last game. I wished I could have sat down next to him and told him how he had inspired me. Now he came to every home game and watched a new bunch of players who probably weren't even born when he was coaching.

    My son, Jeff, was down on the floor watching the cheerleaders. I shouted over the tubas and trumpets, pointed at John Wooden, and told Jeff to go get in line for his autograph. Jeff shouted back to me over the crowd noise, "Who is he?" I thought for a second about shouting back something about 10 national championships and Coach Wooden's "Pyramid of Success" and Bill Walton and that night on the court in San Diego after the big game, but the crowd was going wild and the players were heading off the court for their final pep talk in the locker room before the game started. I just pointed at John Wooden in the stands and told Jeff to get in line and get his autograph.

Jeff was playing freshman basketball on his high school team back then. He absolutely loved basketball but he was struggling to be able to play as well as he wanted to. He'd never heard of John Wooden or Bill Walton, much less Dave Meyers or Pete Trgovich. I didn't have the time to go through the whole thing with him and the crowd was screaming and the band was crazy loud, so I just pointed to John Wooden and the line. Jeff couldn't imagine why he'd want this old man's autograph, but he stood there in line anyway like I told him. John Wooden really didn't look that impressive, I admit. He was reserved, even back when I saw him coaching in real life. Now, I imagine, he came to the games because he didn't have anything else to do. Still, he was honored and revered by everyone there. Jeff waited in line and, still not knowing who John Wooden was, handed him his ticket stub and a pen I had found and thrown to him.

The old coach looked up at Jeff and smiled. I smiled to myself as Jeff smiled back at him. Jeff was about to ask for his autograph when Coach Wooden asked, "Do you play basketball?" Jeff, thinking of his freshman team at school, said, "Yes, I do." Coach Wooden signed the back of the ticket stub and handed it back and said, "You look like a basketball player."

What a great comment. To me, Jeff looked like a typical freshman in high school. He had a mess of curly hair on his head and he was young. But back then he just wanted to be on the team. Inside him beat the heart of a great player. If wanting something badly enough ever had anything to do with it, then Jeff was a basketball player. I don't know, but I believe that John Wooden saw that in him.

Jeff came back across the floor to where I was sitting, eating popcorn. He sat down next to me and told me about their exchange. He asked me who the old man was and I told him about Bill Walton and Lew Alcindor and "Silk" Wilkes and Pete Trgovich and the 10 national titles. The crowd screamed and the band roared and the current crop of UCLA players ran out of the tunnel next to us, back out onto the court. We were screaming as loud as anyone. I was even more of a fan now.

Incidentally, Jeff continued to struggle on the freshman team. His high school coach was the opposite of John Wooden. He was a ridiculous disciplinarian who believed if you yell and swear at kids enough, they will win. One day after practice, Jeff was walking off the court toward the locker room when he passed this young coach. The coach looked at Jeff disdainfully and muttered, "Who ever told you that you could play basketball?" Now, I would have been crushed when I was a kid if a coach spoke to me like that. I may have punched the coach in the nose if I'd been there and heard him say that to any 14-year-old boy like Jeff who was trying with all his might to just make the team. But Jeff stopped and looked back in the coach's eyes and said, "Well, actually, John Wooden told me once that I look like a basketball player." He said the coach was speechless and then he went on into the locker room with his friends.

TEN

Crushing It

It had to be 1974. I know that because I had just received my California driver's license at the DMV in San Diego. I was the first one in line early in the morning of my sixteenth birthday, right when the DMV opened for business. On that day, the day I got my license, I felt like I'd been untethered, like I was a grown up. I felt like I was ready for whatever the world was going to throw at me. It was about time, too. Whole new parts of my life were about to unfold at my feet.

I had also developed an all-consuming, life-and-death teenaged crush on Debbie Moncrief, a beautiful, wonderful girl who lived in Pacific Beach and went to Mission Bay High School. Or maybe she wasn't in high school yet. I don't remember. All I remember is that we went to the same church and that I thought she was pretty and for some reason, no matter how hard I tried, I just could not stop thinking about her.

Mind you, this wasn't my first crush. When I was about fourteen, I'd fallen completely and instantaneously in love with Janet Lynn, the little blonde Olympic figure skater: I remember watching her skate across the Olympic ice on my family's brand new color TV. I also remember paying rapt attention when she fell down in Munich during her ice skating routine and then, amazingly, she got back up and still won the bronze medal. I sat there without making a sound. Something was beginning to fire inside of me. I was pretty sure I liked it but it felt like it was completely out of my control.

But all of this was nothing compared to the pull I felt from Debbie Moncrief. To me, she was as pretty as any of the Olympians, but she was different from them. She was a real person that I knew in real life. I'd overheard her talking to friends. I'd watched for her in the halls at church. I tried not to stare at her when she sat with her family listening to the sermons on Sunday. For reasons I knew I didn't understand, I felt like there was a tractor beam pulling me in her direction. I was powerless to resist; the thought never even crossed my mind. I knew I really "liked" her and I didn't care or think about anything else. I felt self-conscious around her and a little intimidated. I had no idea what I was doing, but for some reason that didn't matter to me at all.

One night I shared my new obsession with my friend and church mate, David Hansen, who was also sixteen. He assured me that Debbie Moncrief not only knew of my existence, but that she "liked me back." I smiled and felt pleasantly strange when David shared this news with me. I was excited, scared and confused. It felt completely illogical, like I was in totally over my head. I felt at least a million times more pleasantly strange when David added this news: Debbie Moncrief needed a ride to the dance on Saturday night.

This was the 1970s, just before the disco craze, with its relentless, thumping party music, its new style of dancing, its women dressed in silky skirts and its men jammed into tight-at-the-top-and-swishy-at-the-bottom bell bottom pants. This was before all of that had made its way to where we lived in San Diego. Actually, it's hard to explain the impact of the disco boom to people who weren't born when it seemed to drown the world, submerging everyone, all at once, in the pounding falsettos of The Bee Gees and images of a young

John Travolta ruling the dance floor in the movie *Saturday Night Fever*.

For the record, I liked the early music of The Bee Gees much more—songs like *"I Started a Joke"* and *"I've Gotta Get a Message to You."* To me, their later monster disco hits were hard to stomach, let alone stomach more or less constantly for years and years and years.

But that's a different story for a different time. This is the story of Debbie Moncrief and the time she needed a ride to a totally non-disco dance. This dance was part of a series of youth events organized by local churches in different parts of San Diego. They had them every Saturday night back then. There were maybe 10 of us—my friends and I—who went and danced every Saturday without fail, no matter where they were.

This particular Saturday night, as usual, there were only two of us who had driver's licenses and cars to drive—one was my friend Matt and the other one was me. Matt's car was a lime green VW Beetle that he had spent countless hours polishing and tweaking. It shined and hummed when he drove it. Mine was a pale blue 1963 Bel Air station wagon. It was about the same size as an aircraft carrier but not as easy to steer. It had been my grandfather's car until he got too old to drive it safely. I felt very cool that I also had a car that I could drive. I felt like I had arrived, like I was "all that." I felt, when I sat behind the wheel of that giant car, like I was *crushing it*, like I had everything.

Back then, Matt and I drove everybody everywhere. One week there would be a dance at a church in Point Loma and we would take everybody out there. Then the next week the dance would be in El Cajon or Poway. We drove to them all and we always had fun too. And no matter what, on the day of the next dance, like clockwork, Matt and I would always get a ton of calls from friends looking for rides.

I loved the Bel Air. It had a V8 engine, two huge cloth-covered bench seats, and a cavernous storage area behind the seats that everybody called "the way back." I'd like to say it was both sleek and powerful, but it was definitely neither.

The power it once had had long since been compromised by a tired automatic transmission that slipped and popped whenever I tried to shift its gears, and it had never been even the slightest bit sleek. Anyway, on that night when Debbie Moncrief needed a ride to the dance, I sat down in my Bel Air wagon full of excitement, pulled the old metal shifter on the steering wheel, put my foot on the gas, and prayed that this would not be the night that the gear box finally fell apart. Fortunately, after spinning and grinding for a second, the gears caught hold of each other and the old car jerked itself forward, out of the driveway, and onto the street, while I hung on tight to the steering wheel.

I remember exactly where I went first that night. I headed up the narrow streets that wound to the top of Mt. Soledad. Then, I drove down the other side to David Hansen's house. David was a wiry, smart-alecky kid with a razor wit and a constant willingness to use it. He was also one of those rare young men that people tended to believe, even when there was reason to think he might be lying. His was a sense of humor laced at times with a subtle cruelty. I'd once spent an entire weekend driving around with David in the Bel Air—windows rolled down and the radio booming—while he convinced me that the title of the then-popular song "Evil Woman" was actually "Pete is a Woman!" Part of me knew he was being ridiculous, but David gradually wore me down, riding in the passenger seat and talking non-stop. Before the ride was over, he'd actually made me believe that "Pete is a Woman" was in fact the title of that song. Fortunately, after I dropped him off and the fog of his words began to clear, I realized he'd been playing me. He'd made the whole thing up.

I picked David up that Saturday and he slid onto the passenger seat and immediately announced that he was repulsed by my choice of music. My dad had just helped me install a fancy new 8-track tape player in the enormous glove compartment of the Bel Air and I had "The Best of Bread" playing when David sat down. I liked this music. It was mellow and soothing, and my 16-year-old brain thought the words were "deep." But David hated it *because* it was soft and relaxing. He said something about how this was no way to start a Saturday night and without asking or even thinking, he reached in the glove box and turned it off. Then he flipped a big AB switch I'd installed next to the tape player which caused the sound to switch and come from the radio instead.

A song by Barry White was on the radio when he turned the switch. David blasted it and began to wiggle and squirm around in his seat like a slow-motion version of Mick Jagger, pretending he had a microphone and a deep voice and that he was a sexy love machine on the prowl. He stopped several times in the middle of the song and told me he was sure tonight was my night. I wasn't sure what he meant until he said he knew that I liked Debbie and that she liked me. He said he could feel something in the air. I couldn't tell if those were David's words or if he was somehow channeling Barry White. Actually, I knew the part about Debbie was from David, but all the rest was the blur of a loud, pulsating, psychedelic Barry White groove, David's ridiculous dance moves, and the scratchy rev of my car's engine in the night.

There were several other kids we were supposed to pick up that night also. I had promised them all a ride to the dance. But first, I knew I was going to Debbie Moncrief's house to pick her up. She was all that I could think about, in part because David kept trying to set the mood by singing along with Barry and wiggling like Mick Jagger. As we drove down the hill past Kate Sessions Park and into Pacific Beach where Debbie lived, I yelled at David to turn the music down. It was annoying me and making it hard to think about what I'd say to Debbie when she opened her front door.

It was dark as my big station wagon crept up to the curb in front of her house. I stopped the car, shifted it into park, and stepped firmly on the emergency brake. Then I hopped out and ran around the front of the car and up to the Moncrief's front door. David waited alone in the front seat of the car listening to the radio. I was all ready to be smooth and clever, I kept telling myself. But I was very nervous as I rang the doorbell. I was looking back out toward David in the car when the Moncrief's front door opened. When I turned back I was ready to smile and be gallant, but that optimism vanished when I saw that it wasn't Debbie who had opened the door. It was Debbie's dad. No need for the smiling and the gallantry, I thought. After all, to put it very mildly, talking to Debbie's father involved an entirely different skill set than I was ready to use to greet Debbie herself. I did my best to switch out of "I'm the coolest guy in the universe" mode and into "talking to the Dad" mode without looking like a deer caught in the headlights, but before I was halfway through saying "Hello Mr. Moncrief," he started shaking my hand, absolutely crushing it with a vice-like grip that got tighter every second. I was still expecting to see his daughter come up behind him, smiling a "yes I like you too" kind of smile. But then, while still squeezing my hand so hard it made my elbow hurt, Mr. Moncrief stared me down like a policeman would look at a pickpocket, or the town drunk, or both. "Could you come inside for a minute, Peter?" he said.

 He was tall with dark hair and, as I remember, he had a very serious, almost accusatory look on his face. I glanced back at Dave, who was still in the front seat of my car. But he was too busy keeping the beat with whatever was on the radio to know I was looking his way. I turned back around and followed Mr. Moncrief into his living room, where he directed me toward his couch. I sat down immediately, not knowing what to expect. I half expected him to tell me that there had been some kind of terrible accident, but he just kept looking at me. Then he cleared his throat, put his hand on my shoulder and glared down at me. "What are your plans for the evening, Peter?"

 I had spent a lot of time that week daydreaming about what might happen at the dance. I can absolutely assure you that zero percent of that daydreaming time had involved answering questions from Mr. Moncrief. So, I just shrugged and smiled at first, nodding my head in a lame effort to suggest that I thought what he had just said was interesting (and not terrifying). Meanwhile, inside, my thoughts raced back and forth in a panic, trying to think of something to say.

Mr. Moncrief wasn't giving me any wiggle room, either. He just looked at me and waited. I sat there in his family room, half smiling and half praying, still not sure what to do besides try to return his steely gaze. I knew I was absolutely unprepared for a conversation with anyone holding a gaze like that, let alone Debbie Moncrief's dad. At that moment, I wasn't even sure I could remember his question. I didn't have any plans for the evening besides driving everyone to the dance, dancing, and then driving everyone home again. But I was convinced that that would be a disastrous thing to say. So, I just kept sitting there, racking my brain.

The first time I tried to speak I felt so intimidated that I stopped in mid-sentence and went back to smiling and nodding. Mr. Moncrief kept staring at me. I'm sure he was a little confused by my inability to answer simple questions. "We're just going to the dance," I finally spit out, trying hard to smile. Mr. Moncrief nodded silently, looking like he might just decide to lock his daughter in her room and have me executed on the spot. Then, to my surprise he spoke again, "So, what time do you think you will be bringing Debbie home?"

Oh no, I thought, he's asked another question! I had barely been able to force out my answer to the first one, and now he wants to know something else. The evening had barely begun and I was totally freaked out already. I was wilting right in front of him. This conversation with Mr. Moncrief had become a full-blown crisis. It took all the strength I had to blurt out when the dance would end, and then to solemnly promise that we'd come straight back after. Mr. Moncrief glared at me. I was sure my answer hadn't satisfied him in the slightest.

Thankfully, that was when Debbie walked in the room. Now, as this is a story about young love and its perils, I should include here a paragraph about how Debbie walked into the room and completely took my breath away with her dazzling grace and beauty. The truth is though, that I really don't remember how she looked or what she did except that she told her dad to stop grilling me. She looked at him as sternly as he had looked at me. She said something about how I was only giving her a ride to the dance. He stopped and smiled, and then he told her to have a good time and walked us to the door. As we turned and headed toward the car I could still feel the soreness in my hand-shaking hand. I could tell he was glaring at me the whole way down the walk. I could feel his eyes on the back of my head.

When we reached the car, I noticed that in the two or three minutes I spent in the house—by the way, it felt like two or three hours—David Hansen had cleaned up the front seat and stopped dancing and wiggling around. He'd even reached into the glove compartment and switched back to the 8-track, filling the car with the music of "The Best of Bread." Then, he stood next to the front door of the car, holding it open for Debbie, smiling and nodding like he was a chauffeur as Debbie walked past him and sat down in the front seat.

I was stunned and more than a little suspicious. David raised his eyebrows at me over the roof of the car before I sat down in the driver's seat. Then, and I definitely was not expecting this, he sat down next to Debbie. She didn't expect it either and she moved over across the big bench seat next to me. David, of course, acted like he needed lots of room. He wiggled into his seat and filled up more and more of the bench area of the front seat, gradually and obviously pushing Debbie closer to me.

Debbie and I both did our best to ignore David's actions. I felt awkward but excited. We drove away, our heads jerking backwards as the transmission finally slipped into gear. I tried to make conversation with Debbie as we drove from her house to pick up our other friends. I think there ended up being seven kids crammed into my car that night: me, my not so secret crush and David in the front, and four other friends in the back. It was a long way out to Poway, or maybe it was El Cajon. I don't remember which it was, although I do remember driving on Interstate 8 past what we then called Padre Stadium.

I was trying hard to be smooth and relaxed and effortlessly pleasant, when the inside of the car started to smell funny. It smelled a bit like burning rubber but I wasn't sure, and I wasn't going to waste the evening worrying about whether Grandpa's '63 Bel Air would make it to the dance and back. But I thought the smell was growing steadily stronger. Nobody else had noticed yet but I was becoming aware that something inside my car was burning, in or near the engine.

I said nothing about it to my passengers, even as I started to worry that something awful was about to happen. Maybe a bad oil leak was about to kill the engine. Maybe a tire was about to explode. It was only the hint of a smell. It was almost not noticeable. But something was up with my grandfather's old car.

David, still in the front seat, was in rare form that night. He had twisted all around and was telling everyone in the back seat a long, funny story about some gross thing he'd eaten once. Everyone in the back seat was laughing as David kept acting out how he had almost thrown up. Then he found some paper in the front seat and crumpled it up and started throwing it at the people in the back. They batted it back at him, still laughing. Once, when David ducked, the crumpled wad bounced off the dashboard or the inside of the windshield and hit me in the face. I shook my head to get it off which caused me for a second to bump heads with Debbie. I smiled at her. She smiled back. I drove without saying anything, while David, oblivious, kept sucking all of the attention and energy in the car in his direction. Everyone was laughing and yelling and throwing whatever they could find lying around the inside of my car. It was chaos.

Finally, we had arrived and I parked the car. Everyone, including Debbie, piled out of the car and went into the church. I sat in the front seat for a moment, alone in the dark parking lot. I was a little shaken but mostly relieved that everyone had survived the long drive and the flying wads of paper and the mysterious burning smell. After everyone was out of the car, I sat back and closed my eyes trying to gather myself and summon up all of my energy to go into the dance.

I realized I could still smell that smoky rubbery smell and I looked around for a second to see if I could tell why it was happening. It was a dull dirty smell, like melting tires. I pulled a latch to unhook the hood and the car jerked briefly forward. I realized that the latch I'd pulled did not unlock the hood. It was the parking brake that I had set all the way back at Debbie's house and forgotten to release as I drove all around picking friends up and then taking them out to Poway, or wherever we were.

Once again, I felt relieved. I was also glad that I had been the only one in the car when I figured out the cause of the smell. David was already acting a bit crazy and I knew this would make him crazier and maybe even a little meaner. He would have ridiculed me all the way. I was sure that the back seat would have roared with laughter. Then I smiled to myself, took another deep breath, locked up the car, and hurried into the dance.

It was dark inside and kids my age were everywhere. What the world would soon know as a "disco ball" hung overhead, with lights bouncing everywhere off of its round mirrored surface. There was a live band playing dance music on the stage. Kids were dancing, but only some of them. Most of them were standing around the edges of a big dance floor, talking and trying to look cool. Back in the seventies, at one of these dances, if you wanted to dance, or even just talk to a person of the opposite sex, you had to catch her when she wasn't dancing and ask her if she wanted to dance with you. It was an unwritten rule. I'm not sure who made it up but everybody followed it. If the person you asked said yes, you would walk out onto the floor and, if it was a fast song, you would dance that way, trying to be funny or stylish. If it was a slow song you stood close together, trying to think of things to say.

One night at a different dance, my friend Greg saw a girl across the room and almost fell over. He told me she was the most beautiful girl he had ever seen. I nudged him and told him he should ask her to dance. He looked at me with a kind of confidence that I don't think I'd seen before in him. I told him to walk over and talk to her immediately, thinking that his confidence might fade before long. But he told me no; he said he was waiting for a slow song. Greg had never met this girl. He'd never even seen her before. But he didn't take a step while the fast songs were playing. Then, just before the first slow song, he started walking across the floor, not taking his eyes off of "his" girl the whole way. Later he would tell me that she never took her eyes off him as he walked toward her. It was like something from a movie or a romance novel, but just before he got to her, another boy walked in front of him and grabbed her arm and pulled her away to dance.

It was dark and I could barely see him, but I watched as he stood there where she had been standing and waited for the song to end. When it did and she came back, the band played another slow song, which felt like a miracle. Everyone knows that a good band would never play two slow songs in a row, but that night they did, and when the second one started Greg asked this girl to dance. I don't remember anything else except that when that dance was over, Greg told me he had asked her to go to his high school prom with him and she'd told him she would. I told him that was nuts, that he didn't know anything about her, but he was soaring by then.

On the night I forgot and left the emergency brake on, I spent a little while standing there, quietly recovering from what had very nearly been a total fiasco. Then I spent the rest of the night dancing and talking. I danced with Debbie a few times and she seemed to be giving me indications that she really did like me back. But back then, I had no idea how to read those kinds of signals, so I just tried to be funny and thoughtful. It seemed to me that things were going well when the singer from the band announced that they were about play their final number, which turned out be "Moondance," which everybody liked. As soon as the song started, we all scrambled, looking for someone to dance with.

I danced with Debbie Moncrief. I can't remember what we talked about or even if we talked about anything, but when the dance ended and everyone flooded back out into the parking lot, I realized that I had forgotten how many friends I'd driven there, which meant I didn't know whether they had all returned to the car, or whether the ones who had climbed inside were the same ones I'd driven out. But Debbie was there, still interested and smiling and laughing at my jokes in a way that had really begun to make me nervous. David was there too, still in the front seat, still pushing Debbie up next to me.

Part of me thought things were going well. But another part of me was silently evaluating every word I said and everything I did—even what I thought about that evening. I tried to stop, but a little obnoxious part of my mind just kept on relentlessly critiquing, to the point where I would laugh and immediately ask myself if I had laughed too loud, or not loud enough, or maybe for too long.

I think I appeared to be a smooth and relaxed guy during that ride home and it probably looked like I was thrilled to have Debbie Moncrief next to me, leaning on me, the whole time. I tried to keep talking and keep things comfortable. I told myself again and again that things had indeed gone well. Debbie was still sitting next to me, smiling and laughing, and probably sending signals I did not know how to read. I found it hard to focus in part because I had absolutely no idea what to do next. It didn't help at all that David was again throwing things all over the car, or that the people in the back seat were loving it. They were all yelling and bumping each other around and trying to find things to throw back at David. As wads of paper and other things flew back and forth between the seats and David yelled, I felt like total and complete chaos was about to break loose again.

I kept telling myself that I should be more like Greg. I decided that it was time to "walk across that dance floor," like Greg had done, and try to put my arm around Debbie and see what happened. I can't tell you why I thought the timing was so perfect for such a romantic gesture. I guess I was oblivious to everything else and only seeing the pretty young girl sitting right next to me. I was convinced I could do it. I told myself that as soon as we passed a school that was up ahead, I would smile a little and, acting like I was in complete control, I would reach up and just place my arm around her shoulders and see how she reacted. I was pretty sure she would respond well and lean in and I would keep steering the car with my left hand and never move my right arm again.

We passed the school. My hands never even began the slightest movement from where they were on the steering wheel. I could see the school getting smaller in the rearview mirror and I thought, *There is a mailbox box ahead...when we get to the mailbox I'll put my arm around her then.* I was really going to do it this time, too.

Then David turned the radio up so far that it was deafening. The song that blared out at us was the theme from the *Poseidon Adventure*, a movie about a cruise ship that capsizes and sinks, but not before Gene Hackman and Ernest Borgnine lead a group of innocent vacationers to the top of the capsized hull, where rescuers cut through it and lead them to safety. David thought the song was sappy but he started singing it anyway, bellowing to the backseat crowd and resuming his Mick Jagger/Barry White routine, which didn't come off as well because White and Jagger do not sound anything like Maureen McGovern did. But the back seat roared with laughter anyway. I slumped a little in my seat as we drove by the mailbox and neither one of my hands even for a second loosened its grip on the wheel. Now I was getting irritated, even though I was still determined not to chicken out with Debbie.

Come on, Peter! You can do this! I told myself. I thought about promising myself that I would do it when we passed the next driveway but then I caught myself. I sat up and I thought that there never was going to be a "perfect time." I thought that if I was ever going to do it, it was going to have to be on impulse. I would just have to reach up and do it...without thinking about it or planning it. I was going to put my arm around Debbie Moncrief. I was going to be bold and impulsive and I was going to do it right NOW!

Without any more thought, I pulled up my arm up like a real man would. I did it fast and I was decisive. It was such a quick and sudden maneuver that I almost didn't know I was doing it until well into the arm swing motion. There was a problem though. In my haste to be romantic, it turns out that I didn't aim quite right. While I was yanking my arm up and around Debbie I hit her hard with my elbow right smack in the nose. Her head jolted backwards from the impact and everyone in the car gasped.

 I wanted to disappear or go away. I wanted to get out of the car and leave everyone there and just run. But I knew I couldn't. I had to do something. So, I turned to Debbie and squeaked out a feeble "I'm sorry" and she looked at me and said, "it's okay." To my horror, David had seen the whole thing. This was too much for him to pass up; it would have been against his best instincts to not say anything. Instead, his eyes widened and he exploded in loud and hysterical laughter. He was pointing at me and shouting to everyone in the car, "Did you see that!? Nielsen!" he squealed, "You are so stupid!"

 Then he laughed until he was almost crying. He reenacted the whole thing for anyone in the back seat who had not seen it. They were all roaring and almost crying with pure teenage joy. After a while, David was no longer able to speak he was laughing so hard. "Oh, my gosh!" he gasped. He pointed at me and screamed with laughter. He was leaning over Debbie, right up in my face. The paper wads had stopped flying. They had been completely eclipsed by the absolute hilariousness of my blunder. The old car itself bounced up and down as people squealed and laughed so hard they could not speak.

 Debbie was holding on to her nose with both hands. Her eyes were watering from the whiplash caused by the blow. She bent over a little holding her face in her hands trying to say "It's okay!" but she was also, I think, trying to decide whether she should cry from the pain or laugh hysterically with all the others. I slammed my foot on the gas pedal. I'd like to say that I recovered well and acted like a poised gentleman would, but I did not. I can't really even say that I drove safely the rest of the way. In fact, I am sure I was pushing the old Bel Air to reach maximum velocities and scream through the fabric of time and space to get to David's house as soon as humanly possible and kick him out of the car.

Debbie kept covering her nose with her hand, her eyes were still watering and she kept saying, "It's okay! It's really okay." After I screeched to a halt at David's front door, I couldn't get him out of the car quickly enough. Even after he got out, he walked toward his front door continuing with loud spasms of hideous, and very objectionable, pure and absolute teenage hysteria. He almost couldn't breathe he was laughing so hard. At one point, he spun around and looked back at us. Everyone was staring at him like he was a rock star. He was like Mick Jagger or Maureen McGovern the way everyone was waiting in the palm of his hand. Even I was watching and I was pretty sure I hated David at this point. In slow motion, he moved his right arm up and around and then pretended to bump someone in the nose. The crowd inside the confines of the back seat of my car roared again. I stepped hard on the gas again. The old car hesitated as the engine revved and then it popped into gear and lurched ahead and down the road away from David's house.

After I'd dropped everyone else off, I slowly rolled the car to a stop at Debbie's house. I looked at her next to me. She looked back at me through her hands. She got out and I watched her walk the few steps up the curb to her door. She opened the door and stopped for a second and turned and waved goodbye.

On my drive home, I turned the radio on loud and listened to the music. I rolled down my window and let the air blow through the car. I decided that I could not just move on socially from such a hugely public romantic disaster. I made a teenage calculation that, for no good reason but to rescue any fragment I had left of social standing, maybe Debbie Moncrief wasn't the girl for me after all. It didn't hurt that my other friend Matt who owned the lime green Volkswagen gave Debbie a ride to the next dance a few weeks later. He was light years smoother than I, and they seemed to hit it off quite well.

ELEVEN

Kathie

It's hard for me to write about my wife Kathie—probably because it's a delicate subject. I feel like I'm getting close to something inside me that is tender or vulnerable. I've always felt that she saved me from what would have been a mediocre life. I've tried to write about her several times. I've started, and stopped, and started again, but either because I was afraid I would not do her justice, or because I was walking so close to things that really, really are important to me, I felt like the writing came out all stiff and lifeless. I decided to try again. What follows is a little bit about when we first met and how she nudged me forward to a better life. Because of the role she's played in my life, this book would be incomplete without a few words about her.

I remember the first time I ever saw her. It was at a picnic. Really, it was more like a family gathering at a park. Kathie was 15. Her father and step-mother had moved in near us and brought their newly combined family with them. I had met one of Kathie's older sisters earlier that year in my high school physiology class, but Kathie and her little sister, Leslie, didn't live with them yet. They stayed with their mom up in Los Angeles after her parents divorced. The other girls, and there were five of them (not including Kathie or Leslie), moved into a house up on the hill a few miles from mine.

It was a clear day with blue skies and we were all sitting around a concrete table by a big eucalyptus tree. Kathie's father was a PhD from Stanford University. He was always soft spoken when he wanted you to listen to him. You had to lean in to hear him. That day he was almost whispering as he talked to us all about some unique part of history.

I don't know, honestly, if I was bored or confused, but I leaned in and tried to listen and be open-minded. As I did, I looked around. I'd met everyone there I thought, except there was this new girl, I didn't know her name. But she was clearly part of the family. She was younger than me and she was listening to her dad closely. I remember that she asked her dad a question that I would have never dared ask. It wasn't a threatening question. It was thoughtful and sweet, but a little challenging. It was more a question that most 15 year old girls don't have the presence of mind to ask. He smiled at her like he was proud of her and then he answered it honestly.

She had curly brown hair. She was wearing a striped shirt and some canvas overalls that she'd embroidered with the logo for the band "Chicago." I remember wondering who she was. She was quiet mostly, but not afraid. Kathie has never been afraid.

I don't think it was love at first sight, or that the stars aligned causing me to jump up and immediately know in my heart that it was our destiny to be together or anything like that. What I do remember is seeing her that day. I remember noticing her sitting there across from me.

The next time I saw her I remember more vividly. It was a few weeks later at a youth activity down at the church. I was never in on the planning of these activities. It's a good thing too because I think I would have had everyone just bring their tennis shoes and play basketball every week. The adults that did plan our activities sometimes invited other adults to come in and help us figure out what we would do when we grew up, or teach us about a skill or a craft. One time, a man came in who worked for a company called Photomat which was a drive through place where people went to get film from their cameras developed. That night he told us all about photography, and dark rooms, and how to develop film into pictures. It was a night just like that, a few weeks after we learned about dark rooms and Photomat, that someone thought it would be a good idea to have a youth activity to teach us all to swing dance.

They took us all in a big room in the church and started by telling us how much fun we were going to have. I was not enthusiastic at this point because, I thought, if they had to start off the night by telling us it was going to be fun, it probably wasn't going to be. I waited, trying to look cool as I got in one of the two lines they had us form. One of the lines was for boys and the other one was for girls. They had the lines face each other and they told us to pair off with the girl we ended up standing in front of. I hadn't done a lot of dancing before then. They turned on some 1950s sounding music and showed us how to hold hands a certain way. Then they showed us how to move around in a circle to the beat and do a basic swing dance step.

The girl I was dancing with was named Kim. She was blond and pretty but dancing with her was a struggle. We tried to move around like we'd been taught. But we ended up just kind of smiling at each other and tripping. They had us go around in circles holding hands like that for a few minutes. My hands were sweaty and I tried to be smooth, and relaxed, and make it seem effortless. We pulled each other around until it got a little easier. Then they stopped the music and told us to get back in our lines and switch partners.

Swing dancing had been around for quite a while by the time we were learning. Everyone who did it now dressed up like they were from the '40s or the '50s and the good swing dancers were really amazing. The good ones could spin, and flip, and hop, and do all kinds of moves that really looked cool.

This time, I did purposely maneuver my way around in the line. In fact, I switched places with two of my friends so that the next girl I was facing turned out to be Kathie. She put out her hands and I held them. When they put the music on we started to dance. The whole experience was immediately different with Kathie. It felt more like dancing really should. Neither of us knew entirely what we were doing but I could tell right away that she was a great partner. We spun around the floor pretty effortlessly and right on the beat of the song. After a little while, we learned some intermediate swing dance moves. We learned that the basic step was just to set up other really fun moves that involved Kathie spinning around and jumping in the air and whipping our arms around so fast that even some of the instructors were surprised. I'd never thought of myself as a dancer before. But swing dancing was definitely cool. I mean, I knew I had been totally wrong. This was absolutely fun.

The next afternoon I was at school walking in the science building past a long row of old wooden lockers in the hallway across from my physiology classroom. I saw a hand painted poster on the wall that said "La Jolla High School '50s Dance Competition." When I read it, I remembered how Kathie and I danced together that night at church. I thought for a second and then I decided I would ask Kathie if she could go with me and we could dance in the contest. I was pretty sure that '50s dancing was the same as swing dancing. I knew that none of my friends could do anything at all resembling swing dancing and if Kathie and I practiced a couple of times before the dance, we might actually have a chance to win. I didn't really care that much about winning though. I knew it was just a really good excuse to see her again.

When I got home from school that day, I sat down in my dad's leather chair behind the big wooden desk in his study and I closed the door. I took a few minutes to get up the nerve and then I dialed her number. She was still pretty new to town. She was young too, in 9th grade. I was a little nervous when I finally reached out over the big desk and picked up the old black telephone receiver and held it to my ear and pushed the plastic buttons to dial her number. I got right to it once she answered and I told her about the poster I'd seen and asked her if she wanted to go to the dance competition with me.

She was nice and polite but she told me that they had a rule in their house that they weren't supposed to go out on dates until they were sixteen. I had never heard of a rule like that. I don't think my family really had rules except for obvious things like don't fight with your older brother, but that seemed more like a safety tip because he was older and stronger anyway. I was anticipating that she would have to say no, but then she told me I needed to talk to her dad. The sixteen year old dating rule was his rule, she told me.

A few days later, on a Saturday morning, I went over to Dr. Kent Lloyd's house and I sat down at his dining room table. I was sitting there when he came in and sat in the chair across from me. He was official. He never smiled the whole time and he was definitely in charge. He leaned forward and took off his reading glasses and then slowly, for maximum effect, folded them together and set them down on the table in front of him. Then he folded his hands together and rested his elbows on the table and peered down over his folded hands at me. He didn't say anything for a long time. I mean there were entire minutes of silence. I just swallowed and tried to smile.

Finally he spoke to me. He did so very quietly and I had to lean in closer to hear him. He was serious, almost like he was breaking the news about some horrible accident or tragedy. I leaned in further and heard him tell me to relax. That was one hundred percent impossible. Even though he said I should relax, his gaze was gravely serious like he'd just caught me doing something bad and was considering which would be the harshest punishment. I tried to relax. I took a deep breath and I leaned in to hear him.

When he spoke it was slowly, calmly, and quietly. He said that he had made a deal with his seven girls. He'd told each one of them that they could go on six dates before they were sixteen years old but that was it. Once the six dates were used up, they had to wait until their birthday before they went out with a boy again. He'd reminded them, he said, that they only had six and that they should be very choosy and careful who they decided to go with. I took this as hopeful, but I couldn't square the good news I was hearing with the gravity and seriousness of his delivery. Then he looked at me over his folded hands and told me that it was Kathie's decision. I had to convince her he said. He thanked me for coming over, walked me over to their front door, and showed me out.

Kathie told me much later that she used all six of those pre-sixteen-year-old dates on me. I'd never counted, I just kept hoping after each time we went out on a date that she still had some of the original allotment remaining, or that if necessary, her dad could grant her some kind of a special dispensation, and extend the number to seven or eight.

A few nights later, on the night of the dance competition, I showed up at Kathie's house dressed like I thought people did in the 1950s. I had on converse tennis shoes and a pair of Levis I had rolled up a little around my ankles. I wore a white T shirt and I tucked the little box from a deck of playing cards in the cotton sleeve on my shoulder so they looked like cigarettes. There was a Rexall Drugstore in downtown La Jolla that I had delivered papers to for years and I bought some hair goo there on my way home from school. Then night of the dance, I slicked back my blond hair until it felt stiff and gummy.

I drove over the hill in my mother's Mustang convertible and rang Kathie's doorbell. She opened the door wearing a felt poodle skirt and white tennis shoes with little socks rolled down around her ankles. She was cute. When I saw her there in the doorway I got excited and I couldn't think of anything to say. She looked at me and then smiled and said something like, "Let's go win this contest!"

We went down to the high school gym and we got out on the dance floor and danced. Kathie seemed to know right what I was thinking. I would only gently pull on one of her arms and she followed around and twisted up and spun out across the dance floor. It was really fun. We were actually better than I had remembered. We danced until we were winded, and sweaty, and hot, and then we kept on moving and dancing.

I remember swinging her around and under my arms during the song "Surfin' Safari." There's a part in that song where the Beach Boys are singing about great surfing spots and they say, "All over La Jolla, and Waimea Bay, everybody's gone surfin', surfin' USA." We were doing some spin, or turn, or lift right when they mentioned La Jolla and the timing was such that I couldn't tell if all the kids in the gym were cheering because the song mentioned our home town or because of some cool dance step we'd done. It was fun, and exciting, and amazing how we were so in synch and so smooth.

The dance finally ended and the lights were still turned down low. The crowd was cheering. I didn't let go of Kathie's hand. They had a spotlight pointed at a person talking into a microphone. She was walking around the front of the gym twisting and untwisting herself from the long black microphone cord as she talked. She thanked everyone for coming, and she thanked the ASB dance organizing committee. Then she said she was going to announce the winners. She said that the second place winners were two friends we had made a couple of weeks before the dance. Then she announced that the first place prize went to me and Kathie. They gave me a new black plastic comb and declared us the winners. I wish I still had that comb.

We drove to the dance in my mom's Mustang convertible. I had put the top down. It was cold but I thought it looked cool. I liked Kathie. I knew I did. I knew she was different than the other girls. I didn't know back then that she would become the love of my life but I knew she was special, and I felt like in some hidden part of my heart, there would always be a place for her. I hoped she felt the same way too.

I knew, when the dance ended that I would have to drive pretty quickly to get her back home so she wouldn't be late. Her dad, who I mentioned before, used to set an alarm clock in his bedroom for midnight, which was her curfew, and then he would go to sleep. It was Kathie's job to get home before the alarm went off and sneak into his room without waking him up and turn the alarm off. If it ever rang and woke him up, he would be waiting at the door for us both when I finally got her home.

We sat down in the car. It had been a great evening. I pushed down on the clutch and turned the key, expecting to hear the Mustang's engine come to life, but nothing happened.

I just smiled. I knew nothing about fixing cars or getting them to start when they didn't want to. After trying again a few more times, I finally asked Kathie if she had ever driven a stick shift and she said no. So I explained how she had to hold the clutch down and turn the key while I opened up the hood to look and see if there was anything I could do to help the engine get started. It was dark and I opened the hood and leaned in over the engine to see if I could do something. Kathie climbed over behind the wheel and held her foot down and turned the key. I really had no idea what I was even looking at. I was not a car guy at all. I had not had time to even touch anything but when Kathie tried it, it started right up like nothing had been wrong in the first place. I walked out from under the hood acting like I was wiping grease off of my hands, and smiling like I was a car genius.

I came around and showed her how to put the car in neutral so she could take her foot off the clutch and move back over into the passenger seat and I could drive her home. I told her how I really hadn't even had time to do anything when she started it up and we both laughed. The whole "fixing the car" process had actually taken some time and we rolled up to her house late and definitely past her curfew. I could see her dad inside waiting. I was ready to wave hello but he never made eye contact with me, so I got back in the car and I drove over the hill to my house.

The next day was Sunday. I went to church and sat down alone in one of the pews near the front of the chapel. I was minding my own business waiting for the service to begin when Dr. Kent Lloyd, who I think I had only spoken to once before, came in, and saw me, and sat down right next to me.

He was almost squishing me he sat so close. He leaned in even further to where I thought I might have a hard time breathing. I knew whatever he was going to say to me was important. I could see that some of my friends had noticed and were watching carefully from all the way across the room.

Dr. Lloyd leaned over me trying to act like he didn't notice he was doing it, but I am sure, with full and complete awareness. Just as the bishop stood up at the pulpit to greet us all and began to speak, Dr. Lloyd cleared his throat in my ear and said, "I heard you had a bit of car trouble last night." He looked at me without a tell. He was one hundred percent impossible to read. It wasn't that I was experienced at all in reading people at that point in my life, but I am telling you that if he looked at me again today the same way, all these years later, I still would have no idea what he was thinking. I answered, and when I did I probably spoke so loudly that everyone in the room could hear. I said, "Yes, really; I promise we did. The car wouldn't start."

Now it seemed like everyone was looking at us. He studied me carefully, weighing whether I was telling the truth or not. I guess I convinced him because he sat back and rested his arm on the wooden bench behind me and looked up at the speaker for the rest of the meeting as if sitting next to me was something he did every Sunday. Even though he was cool and hard to read, I got his message loud and clear.

Months later and a few days before my high school graduation, I was in a history class at the high school when a voice came over the public address system announcing that the faculty was looking for students who would be willing to speak at commencement on graduation day. The voice declared that anyone who thought they could, should write a speech and then show up at a certain place the next day and audition.

I never took public speaking and I don't even think we had a debate team at school. For some reason though, I thought I could do it. I felt that speaking at graduation would be cool. So, the next day I showed up in one of the small rooms in the old main building. I don't think I'd ever been in that room before. It had to be a teacher's lounge or some other place that students never went. There was a small panel of faculty members sitting on one side of a big soft wooden table. I stood up when they called my name and I gave a speech that a friend's mom helped me write the night before.

    My drama teacher, Mr. Morales, was there exuding dramatic belief in the future. So was the teacher who taught public speaking. He had straight blond hair and long bushy graying sideburns that reminded me of the bad guy Bill Sikes in the movie "Oliver." I can't remember his name but he was sitting next to Mr. Eiler, who was the Vice Principal for student discipline. Fortunately, I hadn't ever been in the kind of trouble that would have sent me to Mr. Eiler's office and I didn't know him very well. Although he looked nice enough, some of my friends who had been called before him had told me stories that he was not a man to be trifled with.

    When they called my name, I smiled and they nodded. I had practiced my speech in the bathroom mirror a bunch of times that morning. When the time came, I stood up and tried my best to look serious and collected and give my speech. After I was done, Mr. Morales and the other teachers huddled together and talked. I was across the room trying to act like I wasn't listening. After a minute or two, the debate teacher with the long sideburns popped his head up and told me that they wanted me to be one of the speakers.

    I did it. I stood out on the football field in my black robe and my black square graduation hat, with all of my classmates sitting behind me, and their families and friends up in the stands, and I gave my speech. The debate teacher had been assigned to give me some tips about speaking in public and he taught me to speak slowly, and clearly, with inflection in my voice. I remember standing up when it was time, and walking to the wooden pulpit, and clearing my throat. When I did the crowd got quiet. I could feel them listening and watching. When I finished people clapped, and I went back and sat down in the front row next to the valedictorian.

After the ceremony was over, I was walking in my cap and gown on the field over by where the end zone and the snack bar would have been on football nights. After I was done speaking and the ceremony was over, I saw Kathie walking towards me. She wasn't in my class and I can't remember if I invited her to hear me speak, or if she was coming to see one of her older sisters graduate. She walked over and hugged me and she said something like, "That was really neat." Truthfully, I don't I remember many other things as clearly from that day as I do her hugging me and telling me she thought I'd done a good job.

I always hoped things would work out for us, although I wasn't really sure what that meant. When I left for two years to go on a mission to Guatemala, there was no promise that she would wait for me or anything like that. I wrote her letters, though, and sent them airmail from the old post office in Guatemala City. She wrote back. Once, I got a small package from Kathie. The day I received it was a day off when all of us missionaries got together and went out to a baseball field somewhere in Guatemala City and blew off some steam and played ball.

The weather was perfect. I could see why they call Guatemala City "the land of the eternal spring." I was feeling anxious though, and homesick. It was very hot where I'd been living out on the coast. I was feeling homesick and run down and afraid. Some things I'd seen in Guatemala had turned out to be a bit grim and I was struggling. It was hard. I couldn't shake this dark cloud I was carrying around with me and it made me feel pretty bad.

Being in the capital that day was a little bit of relief because the weather was so nice at the baseball field. I got out of my mood and tried to get into the game. I ran around cheering for my friends, acting funny, and making people laugh. I was sitting on a bench cheering for my team when Elder Farr, a tall skinny missionary from somewhere in Utah, handed me mail he'd picked up for me at the mission office, including Kathie's package. I opened it and there was a cassette tape inside it. I couldn't play the cassette there at the ball field so I put it in my shirt pocket and waited and wondered what was on it.

Later that night, when I was back in the jungle on the coast, I pulled it out and put it in my tape recorder. The second I pushed play and heard Kathie's voice from back home, I felt relief, like I wasn't sitting on my little army cot out in the heat but instead like I was with her somewhere. The anxious thoughts that I'd been fighting against for weeks slipped away for a few minutes. I heard Kathie on the tape talking and saying hello and telling me she was thinking about me. It sounded like she was almost there. She talked for a while about how she thought it was a great thing I was doing. She didn't say anything she thought would make me homesick. She was cheerful and optimistic.

At the end of the tape she said she wanted me to know what was going on in the music world, so she turned up the volume of a radio that had been playing in the background so I could hear the song. The only music that made it down to Guatemala then was the BeeGees on the soundtrack from "Saturday Night Fever." It was everywhere. I heard the BeeGees on buses, and in people's houses, and coming from big speakers on the sidewalks outside of stores in town. I didn't own their album but I knew every word of every song, in English and in Spanish. I was sick of the BeeGees.

I'd never heard the song on the tape Kathie sent. I knew that Kathie had randomly turned it up so I could hear. I knew she hadn't picked it out to send some kind of message to me. But the song said, "I'm gonna love you till I die, 'till we both break down and cry, I'm gonna love you 'till this fear in me subsides."

I imagined, for a second, that maybe she felt that way. I knew it was too advanced for what we had back then. As the next few days went by though, I thought about the song a lot and I decided that my job, for as long as it took, was to get the fear in me to subside. It knew it wasn't a rational fear. Some scary things had happened, but this feeling of exhaustion and the gnawing pain I felt had to go. So I started to try to believe. It sounds a little strange to say but I really think that's what I did. I started to believe that all of the things I was doing did matter and that I should try to step up and be noticed. It's difficult to describe this to someone who's never felt it, but I felt like I needed to get up and make a difference and just face the things I was afraid of or didn't like.

A few weeks later I got another letter from Kathie. This one had a picture of her in it. I put it in my shirt pocket by my identification and kept it there for the rest of my mission.

I remember coming home after my mission was over and then eventually heading up to BYU to continue my studies and to try to sort out the last two years. It was late September and I drove my old car up through Nevada and Southern Utah. When I arrived in Payson, which is a few miles south of where I was headed, it was late in the afternoon. I got off the freeway and drove down the main street slowly feeling a bit like I was in a dream. The air felt crisp in the late afternoon and the mountains were starting to turn all kinds of red and orange with the coming fall. As I rolled up to the old house where my grandfather and Janice lived, I saw Janice standing out in front working in her yard. She was cutting some flowers up near the sidewalk in front of their home. I pulled the car over quietly to the wrong side of the road so I could lean out of it and say hello.

The car crept over the gravel and I approached slowly. I was so close I could have touched her now. I leaned out of the window and I said, very casually, "Hey Janice." She didn't look up at first and she said something about her front yard and how it was getting to feel like fall. Then she looked up at me and I smiled. Her eyes widened and she smiled bigger and said, "Peter, you better climb out of that car and march yourself over here and give me a hug!" I did and she told me to come inside. She said The Doctor was down feeding the animals but he would "shorly like to see you!" She assured me that they would do something big, like "kill the fatted calf or something" if I would come for dinner on Sunday. I told her I would. She told me I was a sight for sore eyes and she couldn't be happier to see me standing there. I told her I had to head on up to BYU and find a place to live for the next semester but, I would be back.

A few months later I stood outside late one night in the street. It was cold and snowing and I couldn't believe it. It was so quiet and clear. The street was covered with a few inches of white slick soft snow. I stood out there for a while with my eyes closed and felt the snowflakes fall on my face. I had on an old worn pair of Levis and a grey T-Shirt. It was very cold outside that night. But I didn't care. I just wanted to stand there and breathe in the crisp night air and feel the quiet all around me. I was starting to feel like I was all the way back home.

When I stepped back inside the creaky kitchen door of the old house where I was renting a room, I heard the phone on the wall ring. It was Kathie's step-sister, Susan calling. She lived in a small apartment down the street with a bunch of other girls. I was a little surprised to hear from her. We were friends but we didn't talk that much. She asked me if, when Kathie got home from Spain, I thought I would like to come over and see her. There was no hesitation whatsoever and I said, "Yes!" Then she said that Kathie had flown in that day and she was there in their living room. Susan asked if I had time to come over. I said, "How about if I stop by right now?"

I felt like there had been a lot of buildup in my mind about this relationship with Kathie. I knew she'd always been important to me, but I was guarded. I told myself that I had grown up and changed and that she had probably changed too. I wondered if with all these changes, and all the time that had passed, she would still feel something for me. I told myself to not expect anything, but I was hoping. I hung up the phone feeling excited and turned to go out the door and get in my car, when my roommate, David, said something like, "Was that Kathie Lloyd?" I told him it was her sister. He said that he had gone on his mission to Spain and he wanted to talk to Kathie too. He made some comment about me "not owning Kathie Lloyd" and asked me if it was okay if he went over also.

I looked at him wondering if he was for real, and knowing that he was breaking a cardinal roommate rule. I couldn't believe he was doing this but I told him that that was more of a question to ask Kathie, than it was for me. Before I could even move for the door, he grabbed his coat and jumped in his car and swerved it down the snowy street toward Susan's apartment. I got in mine too, a little amazed at how this reunion seemed to be happening. I drove over to Susan's and I parked out front just in time to see my roommate jump out of his car and run up the concrete stairs and ring the bell. I walked a little slower because I didn't want to arrive at the exact same time and because I thought he was being a jerk. He knew how I felt about Kathie. I think everyone did.

So I waited for a minute or two until he was inside, and then I went up and knocked on the door. Susan answered and told me David was already in their living room talking to Kathie. I told her I knew and I would wait. I didn't think he would take that long. So I sat down in the kitchen. I couldn't see anything in the living room but I could hear him talking about Spain and laughing and asking her about places I'd never heard of like "Santander" or the *"Plaza Mayor."* I didn't think he would keep going on too long, especially when he knew I was there waiting. But he did. I strained to hear her voice from the kitchen, but all I could hear was David laughing and talking about Madrid like he and she were the only ones who had ever been there.

The longer David talked and laughed, the more discouraged I got. Maybe something had happened after I left and she liked David more than me. Maybe I should just go. I'd been waiting for a long time. I didn't think I could compete if I went in and tried to chime in on a discussion about Spain and Madrid when they had both been there. David would definitely have the conversational advantage. I couldn't imagine leaving without seeing her again though. So I waited.

I was wondering if over the past two years I'd built this relationship up in my mind to be more than it was. I was also trying to figure out how to smoothly get rid of David and go in the room and talk to Kathie. That's when Susan quietly slipped back into the kitchen. She came over to me and got up real close. She whispered with emphasis, "Peter, Kathie doesn't want to see David. She wants to see you!"

That was all I needed. I stood up and without thinking any more about it I walked into the living room. I saw David there and I interrupted him and said something like, "Oh…hey Dave." then I looked at Kathie. I could not believe she was sitting right there in front of me. I felt sure of myself and I said, "Kathie, do you want to go for a walk?" She said yes and I helped her put her coat on and I walked her out the door past David, who had stopped talking and was just kind of staring. Susan was still in the kitchen smiling.

We walked all around campus until very late that night. We talked like no time had passed since I'd said goodbye two and a half years before. I felt like it was just right, like things were where they were before, only now they had a real chance of getting serious.

Months later, after many more long walks in the snow, we struck up where we'd left off what seemed like a hundred years before, and in a park in Provo, Utah I asked her to marry me. She said yes right away. I felt happy, and nervous, and sure deep down in my heart that we were definitely doing the right thing.

TWELVE

The Pasture

Every summer for as long as I can remember, from when I was a boy until I graduated from college, I traveled with my mom, and sometimes my dad, to visit my grandpa up in Payson, Utah. By the time I grew up, he was old and wrinkly. He had bowed legs and he limped and walked with a cane. He was old, but there were still old people like him living outside of Payson in even smaller, more rural towns like Thistle, or Benjamin, or Mona, Utah who refused to see any other doctor until the day they died. He had a little black bag with instruments that looked as old as he was. Whenever someone from one of these places called, he would grab his doctor bag and limp out to his truck and drive out to see them. Everyone in town called him Doc or The Doctor. I bet some of them didn't even know his real name.

In his spare time, he was also a rancher. He raised cattle and sheep on a flat piece of land he owned in the valley between Payson and West Mountain. My mom told me once that she thought he was more successful ranching than he was as a doctor. He was always an opinionated, hard-working, stubborn man who was admired by some people and disliked by others.

His first wife, Lola, my grandmother, died of cancer when I was very young. I only have vague memories of her. My Uncle Mark, who is the youngest of my mother's brothers, still lived at home when my grandmother, his mom, died. He was still living at home later when my grandfather met and married Janice, a widow with a fear of bats, who lived in town. By the time Janice married my grandpa, I was just a boy and starting to become aware of who all these people were and what was going on. I knew that I had a blood grandmother named Lola, but really, I decided that Janice was the only real grandmother I knew. She was the one in our family who started us all calling him "Doctor" because he was her doctor. He called her "Janice" or "Mother." I guess that's because, when she married my grandpa, she brought her three children, Kay Marie, Jay Russell and Debbie, with her.

It was her son, my uncle Jay Russell, who completely captured my interest when I was young. He was what I wanted to be. Every year I would spend all my time in Payson following him around. He wore a pair of old cowboy boots and he had a cowboy hat that was made of straw and was bent and discolored from sweat from all the days he spent out on the pasture helping my grandpa with the cattle and the sheep.

When I was ten he taught me to shoot a gun at some tin cans he'd lined up on a bale of hay out in a field somewhere by Utah Lake. He was about seventeen that summer. He could drive, he had an old truck, and he didn't mind taking me with him to run his errands. I loved it. We drove around in his truck with his friend Max and he'd turn up the volume on the tape player until, he said, "the speakers were good and hollerin'." I am not kidding; he actually did talk that way. That's the way people from our part of Payson talked back then.

It was the late 1960s and I was an innocent Herman's Hermits fan. I loved Herman's Hermits because their lead singer was blond like me and I liked their songs. My favorite song was "Mrs. Brown you've got a lovely daughter." Jay didn't want anything to do with it, though. He didn't say that, he just wasn't interested. Instead, he put a tape in the 8-track player and blasted some Led Zeppelin louder than I could ever imagine it could be played. I remember one summer day, on my 11th birthday, eating a very sloppy hamburger from a drive-thru on what used to be the only highway that ran through town. I was riding in the passenger seat waving my hand in the air listening as Robert Plant from Led Zeppelin screamed out, "Wo-man…you need…love!"

One day we were sitting in the back of my grandfather's truck and I asked Jay what happened to his real dad. He told me that he'd died when Jay was young in what Jay called a "grain elevator accident." I had no idea what a grain elevator was and I couldn't imagine how you could die from one. Jay told me that his dad was standing up on top of one of the silos on a grain elevator and he tried to jump from the top of it through the air to the top of another silo, but he didn't make it. He fell. Jay was very matter of fact about the whole thing. Then he said something like, "Well, we better get back to work," and he jumped up and brushed off his shirt and walked over and started doing something. I had never known someone so close to me who had faced the death of a loved one before that day. It seemed so abrupt and unforgiving. It took me a minute to get up and start working again.

On another day that same year, Jay and his friend Max took me down into an area everyone I knew called "the pasture." It was an area outside of town where all the cattle and sheep were. They pulled the truck over along a dirt and gravel road and they asked me if I wanted to "go fishin'." I told them yes and they explained that they had a "surefire way of catchin' a fish." They showed me how to straddle an irrigation ditch that was about two feet wide and two feet deep. Then one of them handed me a crossbow (as if he handed people crossbows every day). I don't know where they came up with a crossbow. They must have just driven around with one in the truck in case they ever needed it. I don't think I'd ever even seen a crossbow before then. It was black and solid and heavy. Jay put an arrow in it and cocked it for me and told me to look real close at the water, watching for a carp to swim by. If I saw one, he told me I should pull the trigger and shoot it. I thought maybe he was messing with me, but I trusted him so I stood there looking down into the muddy water and waited.

Eventually I thought I saw something move. I wasn't absolutely sure but I went ahead and I pulled the trigger. The instant I did, water and mud splashed up all over the place and all over me. This full-sized arrow that was designed to fly for about a hundred yards had exploded downward and sailed right on through the poor fish and then continued several yards into the murky, shallow water beneath both of us. I had sticky, black mud all over me and I looked up at Jay Russell and Max as they roared with laughter. Jay came over and he pulled on a wire or line that was attached to the arrow and now stuck with the arrow deep in the ground. He reached down and pulled it back up and then laughed and told me I was not a bad shot. He said the fish would make good bait for another day. We all laughed and then got back in the truck and went home.

Jay's bedroom was downstairs in my grandpa's house, off to the side of a long dark hallway. It was a basement room with one of those window wells that let the light in. If you looked out of it though, you could only see people's feet if they were walking up on the walkway outside. Jay's bed was an old metal hospital bed. Someone told me later that his room had been a recovery room and that the whole downstairs of the house had been the town's only hospital.

Over the years, Jay taught me how to wear chaps and he told me why. I learned how they protect your legs when you haul hay (among other things). I learned to pick up a huge bale of hay with chaps on and kick it with my knee up to the back of a moving truck where Jay would grab it and stack it on top of other bales until they wobbled and swayed high in the air above the truck. I chased herds of sheep all over the fields and tried to head them off and keep them from going in the wrong direction.

I don't remember talking about much with Jay Russell, but I loved standing there next to him in the bed of the truck holding onto the wooden truck rail, looking out over the top of the cab with the gravel kicking up behind us. The one thing Jay Russell taught me was that a cowboy's life was relentless. No matter how hard you worked one day and how tired or sore you got, the animals still had to be fed the next day. It didn't matter if it was 100 degrees or -30. Every day when I was visiting, and every other day too, Jay Russell and my grandpa were out there opening the gates and feeding the cows and the sheep.

I went home each year in between and I carried on the life of a city boy. I did get a job as a paperboy, which I thought was easy compared to lifting bales of hay and running around chasing sheep. I would almost forget the lessons I had learned "up to the pasture" as Jay Russell used to say. But then every year, just as I was beginning to think of myself as an all-out California city boy, my mom would tell me we were going back to Utah for the summer.

When I went away to college, I chose BYU. It was only about 15 miles away from my grandpa's house in Payson. I used to try to go down to Payson on the weekends, as often as I could, and help out with the animals and the chores. I felt like it was a part of me, like it was in my blood. I was strong enough by then to actually contribute more than just opening up the gates and chasing the sheep. One year just before final exams, I asked The Doctor, if there was any work I could help them with down at the pasture to help me get my mind off of my studies. He told me they could use the help, but I would have to hustle, it would be a full, tiring day. Jay Russell said he wasn't sure it would be a good idea if I came. He said, "They was about to commence de-horning some of the cattle."

I don't think most people are familiar at all with farm work, cattle, or large animals and, to be truthful, except for the short time I spent visiting each year, I didn't know that much either. For the most part, I'd grown up in a suburban middle class part of San Diego. I used to go to the beach or play tennis in my free time. Nothing could have properly prepared anyone who grew up like I did to help out my grandpa and Jay Russell work with the animals that day. I'd never done anything like it. I'd never even thought about anything like it.

It was chilly that particular morning. It must have been springtime. I tried to stand in the back of the truck and face into the wind as The Doctor drove us out of town, but my hands and face stung from the cold so I ducked down low to get out of the wind. Jay had an old dog named Jethro who used to ride in the back of the truck with me. Even when it was cold, Jethro seemed calm like he might fall asleep as we rolled down the dirt road to the pasture. When we arrived, I heard The Doctor yelling at me from the sliver of space where he'd cracked open his window. He told me to jump on down and untie the gate and then go get the sheep from the other end of the field.

I hopped out onto the hard ground and unlatched the gate. Then I called to Jethro who had been sitting next to me in the truck bed. He barely bothered to uncurl or even look up at me at all. My grandpa watched me in the rearview mirror as I tried to coax the dog away from the truck. He had a bothered look on his face. Then he rolled his window down one or two more inches and made some kind of half growling, half yelling sound and directed it at the dog.

I don't think Grandpa had actually even made a sound; I think he was still clearing his throat getting ready to, when Jethro sat up. It was almost like the dog and my grandpa spoke the same language. Jethro's grey and brown ears pointed straight up like they were at attention, ready to hear and obey. He went from "couldn't be bothered" to perfect sheepdog attention in a second. All at once The Doctor yelled at the dog and then whistled so loud it hurt my ears. Jethro instantaneously jumped straight up into the air, sprang out of the truck bed, and bounded across the field where an innocent group of sheep had gathered.

I watched Jethro barrel toward the sheep with his tongue hanging out like this was the best moment of his life. Then I looked back up the side of the truck and saw my grandpa staring back at me. He looked annoyed and he gave his head a nod, or a jerk, to let me know that I should be running too, just like the dog. It was morning and it was cold, but I hopped out of the back of the truck and ran after Jethro into the field. That old sheepdog was ahead of me from the start. I had only taken a few steps when he was circling around behind the sheep bumping them and nipping at their heels.

The sheep were panicked. They complained and bounced toward me to get away from him. I kept running until I heard my grandpa whistle at me. He'd moved the truck a little closer and rolled his window down about half way and was yelling something at me and waving his arm out the window. "Get away! You're in the sheep's way!" he bellowed. I could hear him, but just barely, and I turned and ran toward a nearby fence made out of bent grey wood posts and wire. As I leaned up against the fence post and got out of their way, the sheep bustled across the field right where I had been, to get away from the dog. I stood by the fence and watched Jethro work. The dog and Jay and my grandpa clearly had a system worked out that kept Grandpa warm in the truck and Jethro running around herding the sheep in the right direction. After only a few minutes, the sheep were all standing, wondering if they should try to make a run for it. They were stuck there in a corner of the field with rusty barbed wire at their backs and an old sheepdog stalking them on the other side.

Grandpa drove slowly over to the sheep and stopped the truck. Jay jumped out almost like Jethro had and worked his way over and grabbed one of them and twisted the poor animal until it fell on the ground. Jay held him there and stapled a tag of some kind to his ear and applied a painted brand on his rough outer wool. Jay didn't hesitate or flinch, ever.

Next came the cattle. They were much bigger and louder and smellier than the sheep. Grandpa told me that the cattle were different. My job with the cattle was to wave my arms and my cowboy hat and anything else I could in the air to scare them out of the field they were in and into a corral. Grandpa told me that they wouldn't want to go, but if I insisted and if I could be stubborn enough with them, they would eventually do what I wanted.

There were a lot of cattle that I chased, blocked, and waved at that day. After they were all in the corral and I was winded from jumping around, I stopped to rest. My grandfather was still seated in the heated cab of his truck. I came over to him and rested against the hood of the truck. He unrolled his window and said my next job was to get each cow to walk into a little opening in the corner of the corral that led to a narrow chute. The chute led to a large metal contraption that grabbed ahold of the cows and squeezed them so hard they couldn't move. They were squeezed so tightly that I was surprised they could even breathe. When each cow stepped into this metal trap, Jay pulled on a long metal bar. The sides would clamp down on the cow until it wasn't able to move at all and it was helpless, moaning and waiting.

I jumped around chasing cows one by one into the corner of the corral. My grandpa shouted out from the front seat and told me to be careful because they were huge animals. He said something about them being more scared of me than I was of them but, to be honest, I was no longer paying attention. I was too busy waving my arms trying to make sure he was right. He also told me they were expensive and he didn't want any of them to get hurt.

Once a cow was secure in the squeeze, I would just watch. I absolutely could not believe the things they did to them. They first looked them over to see if there were any sores or wounds that had to be treated. If there were, the treatment consisted of spraying a red, gooey animal disinfectant directly on the wound. It must have stung because the cows would groan and moan like they were dying. Then they cut and tagged the cows' ears and took a branding iron out of a fire somewhere, where it had been getting hotter and hotter while I ran around trying to get cows from the corral into the chute.

The Doctor's brand was a diamond and a half, sort of shaped like an angular fish. I had heard of branding and seen it done in the movies and I thought they would have a brand shaped like a diamond and a half. I don't know whether my grandpa was cheap or whether the simpler version somehow worked better, but the actual glowing red hot instrument was only shaped like a small right angle. Jay would get it hot while the cow was struggling in the squeeze and then he would take the glowing brand out of the coals and press it firmly against the cow's ribs. It would sizzle and smoke would ooze upward into the air and stink. The cow would make a primal noise that sounded like complete anguish and suffering. Then Jay would have to go back and reheat the iron three times and reapply it on the groaning cow again and again and have it stink and smell each time. Sometimes, if it could move at all, a cow would kick into the metal bars that were pressing down on it. After the brand was burned into the cow's hide, I thought they would release the poor animal, and they did for some, but for others, the ones with horns, they told me they needed to do one more thing.

I'm sure all of this was somehow necessary. The gooey stingy spray probably kept a cow from getting a horrible infection later in the year. The brand established who owned the cow if it got lost, and the tagging and cutting, well I'm not sure what that was for. I turned away and didn't look when Jay castrated a young calf. It skipped off afterwards over to where the other cows were with their clipped ears and sore hides.

Once a year, though, they also dehorned some of the cattle. After a day of cows squeezed tight into the press, Jay reached up under the seat of the truck and pulled out a thing that looked like nunchucks—that karate weapon—except where the little connecting rope between the nunchucks would be, there was a hinged, looped blade that was supposed to be maintained razor sharp. The idea was to take it and loop it over the cows' horns and snap the two handles apart which caused the blades to come together around the horn right where it attaches to the cow's head and slice it off.

The cows did not like this at all, and hence, the need for the squeeze. They moaned and complained like this was really something awful. I felt weak and completely grossed out. The horn that got cut off would pop off and land on the field somewhere and the wound would bleed until Jay could get over to it and squirt it with some of the red goo disinfectant.

The tool they used for dehorning was supposed to always be sharp, but I don't think my grandpa ever thought about it except each spring when he got around to dehorning the cattle. It sat somewhere until then, neglected. Over the years, my grandpa's dehorning blade became very rusty and dull. He'd remember on his way out to the pasture each year that he should have sharpened it, but he always just gave it to Jay anyway to do the work. This meant that for the big cows, Jay had to practically stand on the bars of the squeeze and with all his might, squeeze down and yank on the handles as the cow's head was forced in the other direction. He would lean in and push and shove the blade deeper into the cow's horn and head, until the horn finally gave up and fell off and the cow got sprayed with the goo and cried like a cow baby would.

I just stood in the corral and stared the first few times this went down. It was like the underbelly of ranching, I thought. It was something I'd never even conceived of. It was nothing to the two of them, like they'd done it a hundred times, which I'm sure they had. Jay was all about just getting it done and my grandpa never left the cab of the car. I was exhausted, more from watching them dehorn the cattle than I was from chasing around after them all day.

Finally, when all the horn nubs were laying out on the dirt by the cattle squeeze and their can of red goo disinfectant spray was nearly empty, Grandpa whistled for me and shouted "Pierre!" from the cab of his truck. He rolled down the window and told me that he only had one more task for me and then we could call it a day. He squinted at me, like he was deciding if I was up for it. Then he said I needed to chase their bull from the field into the corral and then into the chute that led to the squeeze. I told him I would, not thinking that it would be any different than shooing the rest of the cattle in there.

He said something as I was walking away and I turned around and looked at him, but by that time he'd rolled up his window again. He lowered it a crack and shouted to me through it, "If the bull decides to chase you, don't come anywhere near the truck. It's new. We wouldn't want it to get scratched." Then he put it in gear and drove away from the bull and me, about 50 feet down a narrow dirt road.

I hadn't noticed the bull before that very instant when I turned and saw him staring at me. He was huge and black. If something can be both sleek and muscular then this bull was. It looked much more stubborn than I. It also looked like it had no intention of going into the corral much less the squeeze. I could tell just by looking at it that it wouldn't even twitch in the face of my jumping around. I waved and yelled, trying to make the same kind of sound Grandpa had used with his sheepdog Jethro earlier. I waved my hat in the air and I moved toward it like I had done with the other cattle. It didn't move. It clearly had no intention of moving. This huge animal stood there emotionless, absolutely certain that I was nothing more than a mere annoyance. The bull was like a living, breathing, rippling statue staring me down as if he was wondering if hospitalizing me would even be worth the effort.

I hooted at it and waved my hat some more and I got a little closer to it. With each wave of my hat it was daring me to step closer. My grandfather watched me from his car like this was some kind of a test of my manhood. Jay stood there on the other side of the old fence and hung his arms over it and watched closely.

I don't know what it was that triggered the bull, but this brute of an animal slowly moved its head up and around. I must have poked my hat the wrong way into the air or shouted something that caused him to lose his cool because, without warning, he lunged toward me. His muscles contracted, he narrowed his eyes, and he snorted like humongous bulls do just before they charge people, and trample them to death, and leave their bodies to rot in the field right where they take their last breaths.

By the time this evil bull had given even the smallest micro indication that he was the slightest bit annoyed, I bolted. I turned and ran as hard and as fast as I could. The problem was that I ended up running away from the animal, into a wide-open field. I knew as soon as I looked up and saw the endless expanse of sagebrush and dirt ahead of me that I was probably going to meet my demise there in the next few seconds. I saw my grandpa in his truck all warm and safe and I ran toward him like I was a sprinter in the Olympic time trials. He looked confused for a second and then he put his truck in gear and drove it away further down the little dirt road so it wouldn't get scratched by the charging black monster that was directly behind me now, and gaining fast. For the briefest second, there was a complete disconnect as I realized that the truck was moving away. I don't know how it was possible but I ran even faster.

I could hear it behind me now, digging into the hard ground and snorting as it reeled me in. I was feeling panicky and I ran much longer and faster than I ever thought I could. Finally, I leaped in the air toward the top rail of the old fence. It was smooth wood on top. I didn't have time to consider the risks of whether the top of the fence would hurt more than being mashed by the bull, so I threw myself toward it. My arms were outstretched. I swear the big bull was only a step or two behind me when I reached up and grabbed at the top rail of the fence. It was my only remaining chance.

I wish I could say that I was graceful and acrobatic and that I deftly caught hold of the rail and swung upward and did some kind of gymnastics maneuver and landed on my feet at a safe distance on the other side of the fence. But I can't. The fence was covered with fresh manure from all of the frightened cows I had been cajoling. It turns out that the fence was slippery and disgusting and I tried to grab it, but I only accelerated through the air when I did, my arms and my shirt and pants now covered with the only thing the cattle had been able to leave behind. This all happened in the blink of an eye.

Before I knew it, I heard a very sticky sounding thud-like noise and I found myself lying on my back in mud and cow manure. It was in my hair and on my back and all over my clothes. I would have been disgusted but I was far too relieved that I was still alive to think about anything else. The bull had run away once it saw that I was out of reach. I was so relieved that I found it impossible to be grossed out. I looked up and saw Jay Russell waving his cowboy hat, running across the field in his cowboy boots, and chasing that bull away. I stood up and shook the gunk off of my hands. I looked over to my grandpa who was still sitting in his warm, shiny, unscratched truck.

I don't think it is possible for an old man to laugh any harder. He had the truck door wide open now and was doubled over crying with hysterical, gasping, uncontrollable laughter. I mean, I thought he might hurt himself, he was laughing so hard. It cannot be good for a man so old to laugh so hard. It took him several minutes to be able to speak. When he was finally able, he whooped and then he smiled so big I thought he might permanently stretch his face out of shape. He shouted at me and said, "Oh Pierre the Plains…that was a moment for the ages!"

Somehow, while I was watching my grandfather laugh, Jay had chased the bull into the squeeze by himself. The bull was not happy at all. In fact, as I remember, the giant animal flexed and kicked and almost broke the whole machine as Jay squeezed him in there even tighter and began to look him over.

I don't remember this with any sense that I'd been wronged, or even embarrassed. I am sure that neither Jay Russell nor my grandpa, The Doctor, did either. It just seemed like part of life out taking care of the animals. I'm sure that my grandpa didn't think I was ever in any real danger, and Jay was probably just waiting until he had to before he stepped in and chased the bull away. I don't know why but I'm also pretty certain that every cowboy worth his salt goes through similar experiences all the time down at the pasture.

Older brother John, sister Kirsten, and the author

The author, riding horseback on his grandfather's ranch

The author, a student at BYU

Left to right: Jeff, Emily, Kathie, Peter, Sara

THIRTEEN

Jupiter Bowl

I was shaking when I stepped up to wait for the chair lift that would take me to what was, at the time, Park City, Utah's most feared peak. I can't remember if it was that I was afraid or that I was cold. Now that I think of it, I am sure I was both of these things, scared and cold. My college roommate, Marty, stood next to me. He had grown up near the Wasatch Mountains and was the kind of effortless, beautiful skier they make extreme adventure movies about. I'm sure he had appeared, or at least he should have appeared, in one of those movies where a helicopter and a super stabilizing zoom lens would be needed to film as he gracefully made his way down a near vertical descent, in waist deep powder, making perfect, glorious, effortless turns with the sun setting behind him in the sky. I, on the other hand, was an advanced stem christie skier with a tendency to lean back instead of forward when the run started to feel too steep.

I was cold that particular morning. I was so cold, in fact, that I buttoned my down ski parka all the way up around my chin and I pulled the hat my mom had forced me to knit a few years before over my ears and as far down as I could to cover what was still showing of the bare skin on my face. The wind at the base of Jupiter Bowl was icy cold, which made waiting for the metal chair seem to take forever. Also, I was fairly certain that I was completely out of my mind for even considering going down this run. It was only after a long negotiation that Marty had convinced me to do it. I said no to him about 15 times but he kept at me. He finally won me over by telling me that even if I fell the whole way down, I could still go back to the dorms and start sentences with girls using the phrase: "The other day, when I was skiing down Jupiter Bowl…."

I told Marty that I didn't have the skill required to actually ski down it and for that reason alone I thought the phrase "skiing down Jupiter Bowl" would not be true. Marty thought about that for a second and then he assured me that even if I fell at the very beginning of the run, way up at the top, and ended up bouncing the whole way down, it would still actually be true, if only for a nanosecond, that I had skied on Jupiter Bowl. He said that there was a fine line between skiing *on* Jupiter Bowl and skiing *down* Jupiter Bowl.

Many people ski Jupiter Bowl and fall at some point and then get up and finish, he told me. In fact, he was sure that some of the world's greatest skiers, with names like Stein or Jean Claude, had in fact skied down Jupiter Bowl. It only stood to reason that one of them had probably fallen once. If they could ski down Jupiter Bowl and fall and get up and ski the rest of the way and still say that they had skied it, then, he said, I could too. He told me it was only a matter of the time and distance they spent falling. Whose job was it after all to tell us how much of a run had to actually be skied, and not fallen down, in order for what we were doing to be called *skiing* and not *falling*? He assured me that even if I fell the whole way down, I would still be able to make a fairly compelling case that I had skied it.

I made him pledge to never correct me if I started a sentence with a girl that way and then, against every single logical thought I could possibly come up with, I agreed to do it and I slid into the next spot in the lift line. Marty slid in next to me to wait for the chair like his name actually was Stein or Jean Claude. People probably saw how smoothly he moved into the lift line and thought he was from a European country and spoke with the thick accent of a romance language like French or Italian.

    He stood next to me in line and gently bit into the middle finger of the outside of his leather glove and yanked it off so he could reach into his pocket and grab some Chapstick and put it on. He had exactly zero worries about our pending near-death experience as he applied the lip balm and he shook his hair around in the icy wind. The chair spun around and bounced a few times before it ground towards us. I knew at that point that there was really no way out of this. I was going to do it. I couldn't jump away from my position in the lift line without causing the lift operator to have to push an emergency button and stop the cables from moving, stranding everyone above me in the frigid air, and bringing myself total abject embarrassment. Marty ran his skis in the snow next to me, telling me about how it was a perfect day to ski Jupiter Bowl. It was sunny and beautiful, but I was looking through my goggles at the steep face of the mountain in front of us. I was trying to convince myself that Marty had any idea at all what he was talking about. I told myself that his now-feeble argument—that I could make it down what I was sure was a quintuple black diamond run—had to be true at some level. Maybe if I got very lucky, I told myself, I could make it down.

    The chair arrived behind us and we sat down. It pushed behind my knees and yanked me up almost vertically into the air. It was really more like an elevator than a ski lift. In only a few seconds, we were dangling high in the sky, way above the valley floor. We were bouncing and swaying inexorably higher in our little metal chair. Marty barely noticed that I was about to meet my demise. He had no worries at all. He told me about a girl he liked named Darla. He said that he liked the way she parted her hair on the side. It showed her individuality, he said. He also told me how much he hated the University of Utah. He said most of his friends from high school didn't go to "the U." They instead went with him to BYU. I wanted to listen, because I liked the way he always told a good story, but I couldn't, I was too busy trying to look down to see if it was remotely possible that I could survive a fall from these heights.

Marty kept talking as I searched the cliff face below to see if I could chart an easier way down. He continued about Darla and college rivalries. I couldn't see the face of Jupiter Bowl because there were too many signs bolted to the grey metal posts holding the chairlift onto the granite, snow-covered, windy, jagged cliffs. The signs all said things like "Extreme Avalanche Danger" or "Never ski this area alone!" My favorite said in small, almost clinical, unfeeling, matter-of-fact letters: "There is no easy way down!"

The wind blew the chair so it swayed in the bitter winter air. When it did, little shards of ice snuck off the trees and into the seams of my ski clothes. I remember thinking I was so cold that I may as well have been completely buck naked up on that lift. I curled up in my seat into as much of a protective ball as I could. Marty hooted like he was actually enjoying the ride. I just closed my eyes and waited for the wind to stop and the chair to settle down.

When I was in the sixth grade, my parents took us on a skiing vacation for the first time. It was a budget vacation. We stayed at my grandfather's house down in the valley in Payson. Each morning we'd pile into my dad's dark brown Lincoln Mercury Marquis and he'd drive us to a different ski resort. It was fun learning to ski, but it was much more fun to *think* of myself as a skier. My dad would put an 8-track tape of Simon and Garfunkel in the tape player and my brother and sister and I would climb into the extremely spacious leathery back seat. We would listen to the music and look out the windows until we were in the mountains and we had every word of every Simon and Garfunkel song memorized on a cellular level. That was how we would arrive at a different ski resort every day.

We went to Snowbird on the day it opened. I don't mean the day it opened for a certain season either—I mean the day it opened for business. They had a huge tram that seemed like it held hundreds of people. We all boarded and then stood, holding our skis and poles, and wearing our bulky ski boots, our poofy down jackets, our knitted hats, and our goggles. I thought that tram was the latest in technology back then.

    Another day we went to Park City. There was a T-bar lift by the side of an old ski lodge that has since been torn down, that took beginners up a little "bunny" slope. I don't think we moved from that bunny slope all day long. We also went to the Sundance ski resort in Provo Canyon. I think Robert Redford had bought it by then and changed the name from Timp Haven to Sundance. It rained the day we went to Sundance, but Dad had paid for the whole day so we were required to ski all day, rain or shine.

    On the way home, I sat by mom in the front and she told me about how when she was in college, if the weather was right, she and some of her college friends used to throw their ski equipment into the back of a car and drive from BYU up the same canyon. She had a friend named Junior Bounous who they would drop off where the canyon began. He would strap on his cross-country skis and race their car up the winding road to Timp Haven. By the time we took our family vacation and went skiing in the rain at Timp Haven, or Sundance, he had become the ski school director there.

    The chair lift bumped and shimmied as it rolled over one of the cold iron posts protruding from a rock outcropping. Marty was still talking. He was telling me about how he thought BYU actually had a chance to win the Western Athletic Conference in football next year. He told me there was a new quarterback they had recruited named Jim McMahon who was supposed to be really good.

    I wasn't listening anymore and Marty's voice faded into the wind. I felt like Gandalf the Wizard when he and one of those Hobbits looked from the walls of a great castle across the giant expanse, knowing that an epic battle would be upon them soon, and they were unlikely to survive. That movie had not come out yet and I had not read the books, but if I had, I would have known that this moment on this chairlift next to my ski-god friend could not possibly end well.

There is something incredible about riding a chair lift. All around you, the glistening snow pushes down on the tree branches and the air is crisp and clean and bright. It's incredibly quiet, except if you have a friend with you who likes to talk. I would say the view from the rising chair was incredible that day, but all I could see was danger signs and the face of the vertical cliff in front of us. I would have liked to be able to just sit back, relax, and enjoy the view like Marty and not worry so much, but I was bundled up in a ball on my side of the chair trying to stay warm and not think of things like falling and certain death. Marty was telling me about Darla and how he thought she was from California somewhere, when a sign attached to a frozen pole came into my field of vision. It said: "Keep your ski tips up!" I knew we were nearing the end of our ride and I uncurled from my protective, warm, fetal position. I wiggled my legs to try to get some blood flowing. I wondered if people approaching the top of this lift ever made the mistake of not keeping their ski tips up.

I imagined what would happen if you didn't and how you could catch the tip of one of your skis in the snow as the chair moved towards the landing spot. Once the tip of your ski dug in even a little bit into the snow, the chair would continue to shove your body forward. Without the ability to move your legs you would be thrust out and down onto the most vulnerable part of your body and your face. You'd end up in a pile of goggles and ski poles and knitted hats and snow. To make matters worse, you would land right where everyone behind you needed to also land. They, of course, would also be freezing cold and impatient to get off of the chair lift. The lift operator would frown and have to push the button that stops the whole lift and everyone would have to wait while you got up and grabbed your things, and checked your bones to make sure none were broken, and got out of the way. And, if the chair lift operator was not paying attention like he should be, the next chair would keep coming and dump its people right there and more people would ski off the chair into your pile of skis and arms and legs. I once saw something like this happen to a ski school instructor when his student had her skis pointed the wrong way and they got all tangled up and fell down together in a heap. The operator shut down the lift and they got out of the way, but it took a while.

Our chair finally shimmied to the landing spot and I pointed my ski tips up and made contact with the snow at the top of Jupiter Bowl. I made it down the little dismount area from the lift without any mishaps. Marty of course made it down too. He did some completely comfortable and smooth looking skating motion to climb up the hill to the very top of the mountain where he stood majestically balancing the very center of his skis on a small lip of ice and snow dangling between the ridiculous straight down death drop that was Jupiter Bowl and some thin red plastic tape that was fluttering in the wind behind him. There was a small cardboard sign stuck in the snow just a foot or two from where he stood that said "Out of Bounds." Another inch or two on the other side of the sign was oblivion. It was, over there, an abyss. It was lights out, total darkness, the gaping yaw, the mouth of hell, granite and ice and straight down, and true, unexaggerated, sure, instant, painless, falling death.

I knew how to do the same skating motion but I was happy having a couple of feet of mountain between the abyss and me. Marty adjusted his sunglasses and said something I couldn't quite make out and tilted his head downward toward the bottom of this run. He smiled and shouted, "Come on!" and then he was gone. Snow was schussing behind him in effortless, graceful plumes. He moved like he was almost part of the mountain, or maybe like he had actually come to earth for the sole purpose of skiing gracefully down this part of the mountain that very day. Without really trying, he stopped about halfway down. I could barely see him anymore he was so far down the hill now, but he waved at me to make my move.

This was it. I had learned from my classes in Junior Bounous' ski school that a skier's weight should be on the downhill ski. I stood there on the hill nervously pushing all my weight down on it until I thought the snow might give way beneath me. My other ski would have been right next to it on a normal ski run, but because the slope was so steep it was up by my knee. I leaned into the hill for safety and I contemplated what it would be like in the spirit world in a few minutes. Then I jumped into the air below me and threw my whole body downward in a giant heaving motion. I punched my scared to death fists straight down toward the valley floor and I leaned with all my might, like I'd been taught to do. I felt like I was diving from a diving board with my head down and my hands ready to pierce the white nothingness below me. In the blink of an eye, I had gone from a tentative guy hanging on the side of the mountain into a sleek, determined, fearless skier flying down the fiercest of mountainsides. For a brief instant, I felt like maybe my name should have been Stein or Jean Claude.

In one blinding moment, I was thinking about it and the next I was flying. I could see my social status climbing as I threw myself downward. I forgot about the bitter cold and all the danger signs posted above me and I left all of my tentative nature clinging to the side of the mountain. That moment when my balance shifted, I transformed from a scared intermediate skier on a hill that was way above my skill level into a crazed, rabid ski dog hurtling downward with the wind in my hair and icy snow crystals gently rising behind me as I slipped down into the open space at my feet.

It all happened in a flash of metaphysics or time melding, but it also felt like that flash of brilliant boldness caused time and energy to stand completely still. At the same time, the whole thing also happened in slow motion. I felt the movement of my hands pushing down and I could see every contour and dimple and fleck of snow and sparkle on the face of the run beneath me. It was a glorious moment when the sun was shining and the sky was blue and I had total complete control of my skis and my body. In that instant when I threw myself down the hill, I had conquered my fear. I had successfully looked it right in the eye and stared it into submission. I might as well have been an Olympic skiing champion the way I went for it.

My instructor at the Junior Bounous ski school had told me that if I could lean straight down a hill with all my might and not be afraid, my skis would follow me. He said I would be down the mountain in a snap standing at the bottom fielding questions from admiring onlookers. Actually, he didn't say anything about onlookers. I added that part. But he did say that the way to be most in control was to dive in without reservations. He told me to lean hard right at my fear and to go for it.

It all worked perfectly…for about a second and a half. That's when the inside edge of my uphill ski got caught for just a second on a chunk of snow, and suddenly I could feel my right leg not following me the way my instructor had promised it should. I heard myself grunt and then I realized I had hit the face of the slope with my body. There was a delay as my mind was still involved in the Olympic downhill skier vision I had experienced in the blink of an eye up above me; meanwhile my body was being pummeled by the mountain and streaking with no control whatsoever downward. It was not a graceful fall, but rather the kind of bumpy, bouncing, grunting, panicky total mind-body discombobulation that occurs when you ignore the laws of physics.

The thing about falling down Jupiter Bowl—and this was not something Marty had disclosed to me in advance—was that once you start to fall, once your ski tip is pointed the wrong way and you catch its edge and it goes even for a second in the wrong direction, you don't slow down until you reach the bottom. In fact, the usage of the word "Bowl" in the name Jupiter Bowl still irks me to this day. It conjures up images of gentle arcing slopes that, while they may indeed be a bit steeper than others, they form a bowl shape that gradually becomes less steep and more forgiving. This is not even close to the case with Jupiter Bowl. It is a sadistic, evil cliff that I am sure only had a light dusting of actual snow covering the jagged granite hidden beneath.

It turns out that, although I did actually ski for about a second and a half on Jupiter Bowl that day, I was now hurtling downward in a mass of snow and wind and confusion and blind raging twisted abandon. I bent one of my ski poles near the handle and my knitted hat exploded into the blue air somewhere. My skis, which had thankfully both disconnected from their bindings, were still attached to my legs by their "safety straps." They jangled and ricocheted around me wildly. I hit, and bounced, and flopped, and rolled, and planted my face in the snow, and twisted and finally slid down to the very bottom near the base of the hill where Marty and I had started in the first place.

I had snow and little crumbs of granite in my ears, my hair, my ski clothes, and even in places I don't think it actually had access to. I lay at the bottom for a second, blinking and wondering if I was actually done falling or if I had entered into the great beyond and my body and my spirit had separated in a process known as dying. I lay there in the silent twisted aftermath of my epic fall. Without moving, I could see the sky and the snow. I could feel the snow too, cold and stinging, and I knew I must have survived.

When I realized I was alive and that I was at the bottom of the mountain, I must confess that I was relieved. Even better, I realized that no part of my body was hurt. By some miracle of either sheer luck or divine intervention of a loving and all-powerful God above, I had not been harmed as I hurtled and crashed through the time-space continuum. I lay there, freezing in some places, and a teeny bit bruised, but alive and entirely free of traumatic injury. I slowly reached across the snow for my goggles, which were split clean in two and held together only by the elastic strap that had once secured them on my head. I scooped out some snow that was jammed into them and I looked back up the run for Marty. I could see a small dot on the hill that I could tell was Marty by the quality of his turns; he glided toward me like he wasn't really even touching the snow. I looked up from my rumpled and tangled pile of equipment and I could see he was coming at me hard. I thought he might run into me for a second but at the last minute he stopped like a hockey player would, and a huge arc of icy snow flew from his braking skis into the air and then down on top of me. We both laughed. He asked me if I was okay and then we picked up my stuff and got me back into my skis and I skied with him from there, with my bent ski pole, the rest of the way down the mountain.

Later that night, after Marty and I were back in our dorm room at BYU, we decided to head down to Heritage Halls where the girls lived. We were talking to friends when a beautiful girl named Sherry, who I'd only met once before, approached me and asked how I got the imprint of half a goggle on the side of my neck. I looked for a second at Marty and then back at Sherry, and I said, "Well, that's an interesting story. You see, I was skiing on Jupiter Bowl and…"

By the way, and for the sake of fairness, I tracked down my friend Marty and asked him to confirm my story. He remembers things a little differently but it's clear from his letter that this event did take place and was very memorable. For Marty's response, see "Figures" next page.

Peter Nielsen
2615 Burrier Lane
Tustin, CA 92782

Dear Peter

I received your letter detailing our trip to park city and how you fell down Jupiter bowl.

It was beautifully, artistically written. You have a real gift.

First off, let me say that I think you accurately and compellingly portrayed my skiing abilities. I'm not sure the whole "Jean Claude" and "Stein" thing is entirely accurate but I'll take it. Thanks. I also believe that you could have gone on a little more about the gap in our skiing abilities. While I've never been in a zoom lens stabilizer movie like you kindly imagined, I was chosen, after a very rigorous testing and qualification process, to ski out onto the Olympic downhill course up near my hometown in Ogden Utah; pick up the gates that the previous Olympic skier had crushed through in his quest for glory; replace them in their rightful locations; and then get back out of the way before the next tucked bullet-smooth downhill Olympian hurtled down the course. I am proud to say that I replaced all of the gates in time and the race proceeded without incident. Perhaps that could serve as a more apt example of my abilities than your reference to a zoom lens. I don't think stabilizing arms even existed when you and I were roommates in college. It's just a thought.

I must also say that I remember some other things a little bit differently. As I recall, the story really, truly starts the night before when you told me you were sure you could ski down any run in the entire state of Utah, and I told you about Jupiter bowl. You insisted that you were up for it. I warned you that it was not a run to be trifled with and that even the smallest, infinitesimal error could have grave and instantaneously frightening results.

Even in the face of my stern and serious warnings, you loaded your red Kastle skies, and poles, onto the ski racks of my old Volkswagen Beetle. Our discussion got a bit intense, as I recall, because you kept insisting that you could do it. Each time, and I think it must have been at least fifteen times, I kindly, but firmly replied that we should not go down Jupiter Bowl. I implored you forcefully and passionately to accept the fact that it would most likely prove to be too much for you.

It wasn't that you were a bad skier, Peter. In fact you were a good, even strong, intermediate skier. I was sure you could make it down almost all of the runs at Park City, but I was very uneasy about your abilities when it came to a run like Jupiter Bowl.

You say I spoke about a girl named Darla and you seem to have some strong recollections. As I remember, you were the one talking about a girl named Sherry. You even sang the chorus of the song "Sherry baby" by Frankie Vallie and the four seasons as we rode the gondola up to the

Figure: Page 1, Marty's letter

top of the mountain. I also feel the need to remind you that I was mad and had to open the small window on the door of the capsule we were riding in because you had stunk the place up. In fact, and this admission, has been a long time coming, but if I am being real, I must admit that your incessant talking about Sherry Haney and the ill mannered and potent farting on the gondola ride, were the straws that broke the veritable camel's back. It was there, bobbing up and down from a cable, desperately trying to only breath the hyper-chilled air coming in from the sliding window that I decided, I would, against my better judgement, relent and ski down Jupiter Bowl with you.

I feel also, that an apology, after all these years, is in order. I do believe that everyone on the mountain that day, and indeed, perhaps everyone in the entire state of Utah probably knew that you were not going to make it down without potentially serious injury.

So, we rode the chair lift up, and traversed the top of the trail. All I can say is that one minute you were right behind me and the next you were gone, vanished into the air. It was a silent departure. When I turned back to say "let's go!" You were no longer on the trail behind me. At first I didn't hear anything. Then came thumping, cracking sounds. They were stomach turning moments when the whole mountain seemed to know something was terribly wrong. It sounded like tree branches were failing, and big clumps of snow had decided to dislodge where they had clung securely all season and instead careen with you down the hill.

I, of course turned my skis immediately, straight down the face of the mountain, and risking all, maneuvered my way to your side, where I gave you sustenance and told you to hold on until I could summon help. You said something about how even if you had not skied all the way down Jupiter Bowl, you had skied "on" jupiter bowl. I thought these were just the ramblings of a young man who had lived through a near death experience.

Later that night, Darla and Sherry asked us about the bruises on your neck but you could not speak of it, both from the horror of it all and the fact that the goggles had apparently caused some distress to your vocal chords. I told them that you had "skied on Jupiter Bowl" that day. Sherry had never heard of Jupiter bowl but Darla, as it turns out was quite a good skier and had herself been down the run several times. It turned out to be a nice evening.

Those are my memories of the event in question.

Your pal,
Marty

Figure: Page 2, Marty's letter

FOURTEEN

Mission Calls

It was late one night after my freshman year of college. I was riding shotgun in the passenger seat of my friend Marty's dented and barely running Volkswagen Beetle. This was my roommate Marty, a guy who was at once the greatest skier I had ever known and at the same time a funny guy who could somehow get everyone's attention just by walking in the room. I'd met him one day on the 5th floor of Whitney Hall in the freshman dorms. He was moving in at the beginning of the school year and there was a small crowd of boys our age standing around listening to him and laughing as he unpacked his things. He could really tell a story. It didn't matter what he was talking about—everyone else there would be hanging on his every word.

That night in his little Volkswagen he was talking too, and I was listening. The car we were in was a one of a kind. It was the dull color of primer paint. It had only one bumper and to run the windshield wipers you had to reach around outside your window and pull a shoestring he had tied to one of the wiper blades to make them go back and forth and clear whatever was obscuring your view. Marty sat there with his right hand on the wheel. His window was rolled down and his left arm was hanging out of it in the summer air. It was August and the dry night air was blowing through the open window, ruffling my blond hair as it passed through the cab of the little car and then out the other side. We were up on Foothill Boulevard somewhere near the University of Utah in Salt Lake City. Foothill Boulevard sits up on what Marty, who was born and raised in Utah, called the "East Bench," a little way up the giant mountains that lie to the east of the city. I remember that the stars in the sky were almost as brilliant and shiny as the city lights were down in the valley. The radio, which only rarely worked properly, was on and a song called "Easy" by the Commodores was playing.

Marty was driving me up north to spend the weekend at the home he grew up in in Ogden, Utah. He was the son of Bob Newey, Ogden's Prosecuting Attorney, and Cammy Newey, a hometown beauty queen. Marty, their son, had developed an uncanny ability to fill space and time with words and stories and hold everyone spellbound for hours.

I listened as he told me how the Great Salt Lake and Utah Lake and some other lake were the giant areas down on the valley floor where there were no city lights. He said that where it was dark—where we couldn't see anything at night—that was where the lakes were. He told me how once, gazillions of years ago, there was a humongous body of water called Lake Bonneville that covered almost all of the entire state of Utah. I looked out my window as we headed north at the dark parts of the valley floor and started thinking about things.

Just a couple of days before, I had accepted an assignment to be a missionary for my church in Guatemala and I'd be gone for two years. I thought about home in San Diego as the Utah air pushed by me outside the window. I stuck my hand into the night and I pointed my fingers into the wind. I tipped my hand up and down like it was an airplane. When I tilted it up it got lift under my palm and flew up in the air and almost away into the night. I knew I wouldn't see my mom or dad for two years. I thought about my little sister, Kirsten, and how she was starting high school.

I told myself I was away from home in college now already. I wouldn't be too involved with her in high school even if I stayed home and didn't go on a mission in the first place. I knew I would miss her. My big brother, John, was up at Stanford by then. I already missed them all and I hadn't even left.

    Marty was punching the buttons on his car radio trying to find a song he liked. He was telling me about a friend of his who fell asleep in one of the display tents in a sporting goods store in the middle of her shift as a salesperson. I'm sure he'd been talking about it for a while, too, and I'd heard this story before, but I didn't mind. The details would change each time he told it. Plus, I liked the way he painted a picture with his words. I liked how animated and alive he got when he told a good story. I almost felt like I could see his friend lying there in the tent with the sales manager searching for her around the store.

    In between songs on the radio, the DJ announced that the "Son of Sam" killer had been arrested in New York. Marty stopped talking and turned the radio up for the announcement. We both looked at each other. Neither of us knew very much about this story, but we'd both heard that this "Son of Sam" guy was bad. Marty started talking about crime and murder and I tuned back out and waved my hand around in the air.

    Time was weird, I thought. It seemed like about a minute had passed since I graduated from high school in San Diego. Now, I was about to go away for two years and live in a country where nobody even spoke my language. I tried to imagine what it would be like. I saw myself living in a tiny upstairs apartment with a rickety set of wooden stairs leading up to it. In my imagination, it was always hot there. I let myself try to see it in my mind, but I knew full well I had no idea what it would really be like.

    I closed my eyes and heard Marty singing along with the Captain and Tennille, something about doing it one more time. He stopped singing long enough to tell me that where we were driving was once the main freeway through town before the big interstate highway went through. I wasn't sure that was true. I could never remember a time when the I-I5 wasn't there. But Marty had lived there his whole life and I'd only come up in the summers with my mom to see my ancient grandfather and his wife, my step grandmother, Janice. I thought about the two of them in their little house down in Payson, Utah. I always knew that my grandfather loved me but Janice was definitely the caring, nurturing part of that relationship. For every ounce of ornery he had in him, she always seemed to have more than enough kindness to make up for it. He was the original doctor in the small town they lived in and they had both lived their whole lives there. I wasn't sure if I'd see either of them again after I left for Central America.

 I thought about one summer day when we were visiting and my mom took me down to the only block in Payson's downtown area and bought me a wallet at Christiansen's Department Store. I was about ten or eleven back then and she told me to always keep it in my back pocket so I wouldn't lose it. When we left the department store, she made a stop at the drugstore and bought me a malt. The drug store looked the same as it must have looked the day World War II ended. A tall, thin man with short dark hair and a long white apron leaned toward me from the other side of the counter. He looked at us both and then said, "Well, hello Marilyn!" to my mom. "And who is this?" he said, pointing at me. She replied, "Hello Verle, this is my son, Peter." She ordered the malt as if she'd ordered them just the same way a thousand or a million times in the past, after school or on a date. On the way back to Grandpa and Janice's house, Mom told me how Verle was quite a catch in high school. I didn't know what she meant so I just sat there and sucked the thick chocolate malt up through a paper straw from the "to go" cup Verle had given me at the drugstore.

 When we got back home, I was wiping my mouth with the back of my hand and putting the malt cup in the trash can outside, when Janice threw the door open and hugged me until I almost couldn't breathe. She said something like,

"Where have you been?" as she squeezed. I told her that my mom had bought me a wallet. She said, "Well, gracious, Peter, I hope she took you up to Christiansen's and bought you a proper one!" I pulled the wallet out of my back pocket and held it up for her to see. When I did, her eyes widened. "Well, my lands! That *is* a beautiful new leather wallet." She reached out her hand and I found myself handing it to her. She was always so alive and animated. She pulled the wallet open and acted like she was trying to empty it. There was nothing in it though, which was her point. She said, "Well Peter, you can't very well carry a new wallet that has no money in it, can you?" Then she walked across the kitchen floor to where she had a cookie jar that was always full of Oreos and she looked in her purse and pulled out an old weathered dollar bill. She clipped her billfold closed again and then she folded up the dollar and put it in my wallet. Then she looked at me and said, "Now, wear that in your back pocket and see how it feels."

    I was brought back to reality when Marty stopped the car at a stoplight and idled. He turned down the radio and asked me when I thought he'd get his mission call and where I thought he was going. I told him it would be someplace like Korea or Switzerland. I told him I was sure he'd go someplace exotic like that. It would come in the mail any day, I said, maybe tomorrow. He started talking about the Swiss Alps and yodeling and something about lederhosen.

    Part of me didn't want to go. It was a very small part but, if I'm being honest, that small part has never been comfortable with change. This was no small change either. I was sure this would not be just a little different than what I was used to. This mission, I was pretty sure, would be completely life changing.

    I'd grown up in La Jolla, California and graduated from La Jolla High School in the mid-1970s. Somehow, back then, I thought that everywhere in the whole world was just like La Jolla. But then I went to BYU for my freshman year of college. Provo, Utah was definitely different from La Jolla. That's for sure. But I'd grown to love it and I'd made all kinds of new friends from all over the place. It was a lot colder than home, but the mountains were every bit as beautiful as the ocean.

I remember the radio announcer talking about how Elvis Presley was being laid to rest somewhere in Tennessee. Marty said something about how England Dan and John Ford Coley were better than Elvis ever was, as the song "In the Ghetto" started playing over the radio. Marty and I had little snippets of religious, doctrinal conversations. They came and went during the night. We were both thinking about it. Usually, it would start with something that reminded one of us of a class at school. We had taken a leadership development class from a young Steven R. Covey and a basics of philosophy class from Truman Madsen, a famous BYU professor.

After our first semester, I bumped into Marty one day down in the stuffy basement of our dorm building in Deseret Towers. He was waiting for a load of nearly cleaned clothes to stop thumping around and come out of one of the big metal dryers lined up against the wall. He was also studying a notebook-sized booklet with page after newsprint page of available classes and professors for the upcoming semester. He told me that his dad had told him, "You don't take classes in college, you take professors." So, we sat down at the little fiberglass folding table there in the basement laundry and, with the hum of the dryers in the background, we made a list of any professors we had heard of. The list had names on it like Steven R. Covey, Reed Bradford, Truman Madsen, George Durrant and others. We signed up for all of them and then we did everything we could to figure out a way to have them count for our general education requirements.

It was a great semester of eye-opening philosophical, leadership and doctrinal discussions. I loved it. I felt like these professors dove in deeply and went wherever our questions took them. Steven Covey used to look down from the lectern frowning, ask a challenging question, and sternly almost shout, "Think!" He wouldn't accept the pat answer either. He wanted us to learn to *really think*. George Durrant was funny and I laughed a lot. Truman Madsen never had to ask us to think. Our brains were straining so hard to understand the theories of guys like Kant or Plato, or all kinds of other famous philosophers, that it almost hurt. I remembered how Truman Madsen would walk into class with no notes—nothing but a piece of chalk in his hand. He'd flip it around a couple of times and then he'd go up to the board and just start writing. He'd quote guys like Descartes and Socrates as if he'd memorized every word of their original works.

As much as Marty and I tried to talk philosophy or religion when we were driving around that night, we couldn't do it like Steven or Truman or George. Our discussion wandered the same way our drive up to Ogden had. I didn't mind, though. Marty would throw out historical facts like about the giant lake that once covered the state, or he'd start talking about miscellaneous crime facts that he said were top secret that he'd learned from his dad. He told me about a crazy guy who picked up a girl who was hitchhiking and locked her in the trunk of his car and drove it off a cliff. Just before it went over the edge, he jumped out and walked away like nothing happened. The only problem, Marty said, was that the girl in the trunk somehow survived. In fact, for some reason, she wasn't really hurt that badly. She testified against the guy at trial in Marty's dad's courtroom and he was convicted. Hopefully, I thought, he'd be where they sent him for a very long time.

There was an update in the news that night about Gary Gilmore and how long he'd fought to be executed by a firing squad after the United States death penalty had been re-instituted after ten years of no executions. It happened in Utah at the Utah Federal Penitentiary. We'd driven past it earlier that night down by "the point of the mountain" where the freeway takes people up out of BYU country into the greater Salt Lake area. It had been several months since Gary Gilmore had been put to death, and I felt like the state of Utah had been put through the ringer. I believe they would have been happy to have some other state end the death penalty ban, but Gary Gilmore pushed the issue. It was weird how someone would fight for the right to be shot to death. The whole thing was dark, turned around, and backwards.

We drove around the East Bench for a long time that night. I remember feeling like I was on the edge of something, about to leave everything behind. I didn't know exactly what I was getting into, but I told myself it would be awesome and I felt sure it was the right thing to do. I'd dreamed about a mission as long as I could remember. That night driving along Foothill Boulevard with my best friend in his old blue Volkswagen Beetle is stuck in my mind as an important moment. It was just before I jumped, whether I was ready or not, toward adulthood. I don't know why but the people I'd met in Utah over the past year seemed less guarded and friendlier than people I'd known in California. I felt like they were my people. Although guys like Gary Gilmore got all the news attention, he was clearly the aberration. I didn't think he was from Utah in the first place anyway.

I waved my hand in the air some more and thought about how on my mom's side of the family, my roots went way back through small town Utah doctors and poor turkey ranchers and farmers, all the way back to English and Scandinavian immigrants who had fled the poverty of Europe in the 1800s on old wooden sailboats. They had come to Zion across the cold, grey ocean to New York. From there they made their way, mostly walking, across the American Continent to Utah.

Marty and I rolled into the comfort of his mom's split-level brick home on Ben Lomond Avenue in Ogden, Utah at about 2 a.m. We left our stuff in the car and went in through the door, which Marty's mom had left unlocked for us. I fell asleep on one of those Lay-Z-Boy Barcalounger-type chairs that was downstairs by Marty's room. It was still swaying back and forth from when I sat down in it and I fell fast asleep.

I had no plans for the next few days except to hang around with Marty and then go home to San Diego and pack up my new white shirts and ties and slacks and other missionary things and report in at the mission home. When I woke up the next morning, I was laying awkwardly on the recliner. Marty threw a pillow at me from across the room. I hadn't slept well in all the bends and folds and involuntary rocking of the Lay-Z-Boy, but I didn't care. We went upstairs to the kitchen. Marty's mom was up already, cooking. I remember the smell of her bacon and eggs; it's difficult to forget that smell.

She was very nice. She asked us all about our night. Marty told her how we mostly just drove around and talked. She listened and cooked breakfast. She had an unassuming way. After a few minutes, she asked what we were going to do that morning. Marty said he hadn't really thought about it yet. The only other time I'd been up here was for a double date to an Earth, Wind & Fire concert. The date was a bust. The two girls who had asked Marty and me on the date didn't talk. It had been like a contest how much we could try to draw things out of them and how little they could say in response. We finally ended up showing them home movies we'd made of ourselves. These were the kind of movies that only we and our moms could enjoy. We knew it, too, but Marty told me they deserved to sit through our movies because of how completely non-social they had been.

Marty's mom asked him, "Why don't you take Peter up the trail to Waterfall Canyon?" There was a pause while Marty swallowed his eggs and, for a second, we all just sat there. Marty's mom waited. I waited too. I had only been to Ogden once and it was Marty's turf and his decision what we would do. He stood up and pointed his fork at me and stabbed it into the air and said, "We need to go up Waterfall Canyon! Good idea mom!"

We drove somewhere up to the foot of the Wasatch Mountains around Ogden and found a parking place on a dirt road near the mouth of a narrow canyon. It was still pretty early when I shook out the remaining kinks from sleeping in the Barcalounger and I headed up the canyon with Marty. We hiked for a long time. It was uphill, strenuous hiking, the kind where you feel the burn in your quads and your calves. We talked about a lot of things that morning. We talked about girls we'd known at school and friends we'd met our freshman year that we both knew we might never see again. Marty told me what it was like to grow up in Ogden as the son of the prosecutor, a man who was a hero around town for some of the cases he'd tried and some of the bad people he'd brought to justice. He told me his dad had been a bomber pilot over Europe during World War II. He came home, married Marty's mom, and got his law degree from Stanford University. Instead of settling in San Francisco or Los Angeles or somewhere like that, he decided to go back home and raise his family in Ogden.

Marty told me he was sure that Ogden was the most progressive city in Utah. He also told me it was the least Republican. He said it was the most open to new ideas and the least narrow in its views. He said, for a long time, Hill Air Force Base and the IRS had been located there. Both of these places employed a lot of people and a lot of them came from other parts, outside of Utah. Marty loved Utah and he really loved Ogden. He especially loved Ogden, he said, because it was a little different. It didn't get stuck in its ways.

I told Marty what growing up in Southern California was like. I told him I thought we were a lot alike. My dad had joined the Navy during the Korean War. He graduated from the University of Washington and then became an officer. He was stationed in the South Pacific as part of the Naval Civil Engineering Corps, rebuilding runways from damage they'd incurred during the war. He came home and married my mom. She was also a small-town beauty queen from Utah. My dad studied at Stanford, too. He studied business and he went on to become the Assistant Secretary of the Air Force for Financial Management. He also eventually settled down where he grew up, in Southern California.

We blabbed all afternoon while we hiked up the canyon. I remember asking him what he thought Guatemala would be like. He said that, really, he had no idea. I wondered if I could learn to speak Spanish well enough to teach something as nuanced and incredible as why the gospel was important to me. He asked me again when I thought he would get his mission call. This time I told him I thought he would be called to serve in Russia. We both laughed hard and decided that if missionaries ever went to Russia it would be a sure sign of the last days, a sign that the end of the world was near. One of us said we thought it would be more likely that Leonid Brezhnev and Jimmy Carter would get in some kind of a standoff that would end with one or two atomic bombs being launched and a couple of cities exploding, and that really would be the end of the world. I told Marty that he'd know soon enough where he was going. We started talking about places like Korea, Venezuela and Switzerland.

We made it to the top of the canyon tired and sweaty and covered in dust we'd kicked up as we shuffled up the side of it. When we made it to the top of the Canyon, we got to a point where you had to inch forward on a big granite slab that jutted up out by the top of the trail. Marty told me to crawl up there with him. We slid ourselves up the last couple feet on our bellies until we reached the top of the highest point on the trail.

The view of the whole canyon below was expansive. I stopped and lay there looking out across open prairies, the city of Ogden, and part of the lake Marty had told me about. We could see things up there that I had only seen through tiny oval airplane windows. From where we lay on the warm granite, it seemed like we could see forever. We were above the trees, the clouds, the people, their cars, and the businesses down below. It was amazing. It was a clear day with a blue, blue sky and the horizon was far, far away on the other side of the valley in the distance. It was beautiful.

After a while I looked over at Marty and said, "This is so...beautiful." I told Marty that seeing things like this made me more sure about serving a mission. It made me feel even more strongly that there was a God somewhere. I couldn't really think of anything else that was worthy enough to say at a moment like that. I just crawled up to the top of the granite and looked at it all.

Marty, who was usually a very funny guy, who could wind up a story and wrap people up in it like no one else could, said in his Utah accent, "Peter, here's the *dil*. This is only His handiwork...You are His son." We sat there for a pretty long time just looking out over the valley from the top of Waterfall Canyon. This was the message I wanted to teach people, I thought. I wanted to tell them how everyone is important, how each life is important, how unique they are and how there is a reason we are here on earth. It's hard to describe how deeply I felt this.

Going back down the canyon took much less time that hiking up had. We made our way back to Marty's car and he found the keys where he had left them on the driver's side, under the wheel well, on top of the rubber tread of the front tire. We drove back to his house kind of reverently. I might be overstating—we were both only 19 years old—but that's how I felt. We didn't say much on the way to his house. We pulled into Marty's driveway and Marty parked the car. Before he turned off the key he saw his mom standing, waiting by the front door, smiling and excited. As soon as Marty saw her she smiled and nodded and he ran into the house like he knew exactly what was going on. She told him he had to wait until she got her friend Betty, who lived nearby.

Marty ran inside and found an unopened letter to him from the church on the coffee table in their living room. This was finally it. I'd been through this only a couple of weeks before and I could tell by looking at it that this was Marty's mission call. In a couple of minutes, he'd know if he was going to Switzerland, or Venezuela, or Korea, or Russia. It was almost impossible to wait for his mom to get Betty. Marty's mom and Betty came running in the living room wringing their hands and waiting to hear Marty read the letter. I stood in the back, by the kitchen. Marty, covered with the dirt of Waterfall Canyon, waited just a second like the natural showman he was. Then he unsealed the official envelope and unfolded the letter inside.

He told me later that as soon as he opened it, he saw the words "Anaheim, California" and he immediately closed it up again, hoping it would do some sort of Houdini trick and change to a place like Switzerland in the second he held it closed in his hands. When he opened it again though, it still said Anaheim, California and he read it to everyone. There was a pause. Then finally Betty broke the silence and said, "Disneyland! You're going to the Disneyland Mission."

For years since that time, Marty and I have kept in touch. Long after our missions were over, we would talk about how different they were. I went to a place filled to the brim with poverty, need, anger and hunger, and Marty went to Orange County, one of the wealthiest missions in the entire world. One day, after our missions were over, we met back up at BYU. We were telling each other stories of our times serving away from home. I told him about Central America and the collection of dead fleas I'd caught in various mattresses while I was there and how I had taped them to the first page in my missionary journal. He told me about knocking on Liberace's front door (Liberace, the piano player who used to perform in white tuxedos with huge crystal chandeliers on his grand piano). Marty told me they sat down in Liberace's living room, afraid to touch anything for fear that they might break something and put their families, or the church, in Liberace's debt forever.

I told him how I was sleeping on a straw mat one night, on a dirt floor, in a small village, and how I'd had to wake up and move my mat back under the eve of the roof so the rain wouldn't get me all wet. I moved the mat out of the rain and laid back down on it. When I did, I pushed a chair made from wooden slats and discarded soles from men's shoes that were all tangled up and riveted together. I pushed it into a dark corner of the room, causing rats, or mice, to scramble across the floor looking for another hidden spot. Marty didn't say anything for a minute. He just smiled and asked, "Have you ever been teaching someone about the gospel and gotten delayed for some reason, and missed the fireworks at Disneyland?" We could go on and on, and we did, and we sometimes still do whenever we get together.

So Marty got his mission call on the day we climbed up Waterfall Canyon. We'd spent the day and weeks before it imagining where he might go. He'd thought of all kinds of adventurous places. He'd talked about yodeling in the Alps somewhere, or learning to speak Korean, or Japanese and teaching the gospel in a foreign language. He ended up instead going to Orange County, California and talking to celebrities. It was funny. He was funny about it. After the first second or two, he knew he was going to a good mission, though, and he was completely on board. I've never forgotten about Waterfall Canyon and what Marty said up there. I remember how moved I felt by the thought that God was out there somewhere and that he cared about me.

FIFTEEN

Driving Home

The night after Marty got his mission call to the "Disneyland Mission," around midnight, on an impulse, we left Ogden and headed south on I-15 toward California. We decided to just leave and to drive as far as we could and stop wherever we ended up when we needed some rest. Actually, the original idea was that we would drive all the way, non-stop, through the night (except for bathrooms and gas), for 12-14 hours until we pulled into my family's driveway in La Jolla, CA. This was the 1970s. President Carter had just lowered the speed limit to 55 miles an hour on all interstate highways. It was tempting the whole way to drive faster than the speed limit. 55 miles an hour, it turns out, is an incredibly slow and boring pace. That night, as we drove south, the scenery crawled past us like it was in slow motion.

We had decided that we'd travel south as far as we could and then, when we were too tired and couldn't go any further, we would just stop right there, no matter where we were, and rest. The only time constraint we had was that in a few days I had to be home to give the farewell sermon at my church before I left on my mission. It was now just the beginning of the week. I didn't have to be home until Sunday. Even at 55 miles per hour, we could take our time.

Earlier that afternoon, when Marty opened up his mission call, he had looked crestfallen for a minute or two. Then he straightened up and smiled. His mom looked like she was disappointed for him too, for a second. I think she had to be relieved, though, that he was going somewhere in the U.S. where there were good hospitals if he got sick and good food and similar customs.

Marty's car was good for driving around in Utah, but we weren't sure it would make it all the way to California. My car was only a little bit better. I drove an Audi station wagon back then and it had been our family car when I was in junior high school. Now, it made a loud clunking sound somewhere by the back axle whenever it went over the smallest bump. I didn't care, though. I couldn't afford to fix it and, except for the rattling it made at any un-evenness in the road, it drove well. I figured I would fix it when it finally broke completely, whatever it was. I'm not sure why we felt the need to leave for California in the middle of the night. We didn't have a plan except that we had to be home by the time I had to speak in church.

Leaving so late at night wasn't a good idea at all, but we both thought it could make for a good story someday. We talked about it and we decided on some ground rules: neither of us would drive after that moment when we were just starting to feel the slightest bit sleepy. Whenever that happened, no matter what else was going on, we both agreed that standard nighttime driving rules would no longer apply. The driver would not be allowed to "tough it out" and fight through any nodding or fighting to stay awake. There would be no window rolls downs with the radio on loud and the driver screaming the words to songs on the radio. Those kinds of maneuvers to stay awake while driving, we decided, were on the forbidden activity list (at least for the night) because they wouldn't be safe.

We decided that whenever the driver even got a little bit sleepy it would be a hard and fast requirement, like a law, that he immediately pull the car over and stop. The other rule we made up was that no matter how soundly the passenger was sleeping, if the driver woke him up because he was getting sleepy, the first thing the passenger would do when he woke up would be to thank the driver and very politely encourage him to change places so the driver could get some sleep. This way, whoever was driving would never be nervous about stopping and we could take turns driving and stay refreshed and alert. Whenever the driver stopped, the passenger and the driver would both get out of the car. The passenger would do a couple of jumping jacks to jolt his system back to proper and responsible wakefulness. The guy who had been driving would stumble over to the passenger seat where he could get some well-deserved rest. There were no minimum times the driver had to spend behind the wheel. The only rules were that if the driver felt the least bit sleepy, the passenger would thank him for waking him up and they'd immediately switch places.

So, with all of this in mind, we started out toward Provo in Marty's car. It was midnight and we were both already tired. Marty drove first. I instantly fell asleep in the passenger seat with my forehead on the dashboard. We may have underestimated the amount of physical exertion we'd experienced going up the canyon or the level of excitement surrounding Marty getting his mission call. For a minute or two, as Marty started to drive, I was awake and the next minute I was in deep, deep REM sleep.

We drove down I-15 for about an hour and then Marty pulled over at our dorm building at Deseret Towers and we switched cars. He stopped in the parking lot and parked the car. Then he reached over and nudged me and I woke up. I blinked my eyes and things came into focus. I then untwisted from the crumpled position I'd assumed in my half of Marty's little car. I blew out a big breath of air and looked at Marty who looked very sleep deprived. I smiled and said, "Thank you, Marty, for waking me up. I would love to drive now!" I hopped out of the car, did a few jumping jacks there in the parking lot, took what I had out of Marty's car and threw it in mine and sat down behind the wheel of my old Audi. We rolled out of the parking lot around 1 a.m. Marty was asleep almost before we changed cars. I was kind of excited that our plan was working. I was awake. I had gotten my blood flowing jumping up and down a little and I was good to go. We were on our way home, moving down the road through southern Utah.

It was dark and cloudy as we left Provo. Except for the odd McDonald's or a gas station way out on the highway near whatever small town we drove past, there was absolutely nobody there. There was only the sound of the tires on the highway and wide open fields. Everyone in this whole part of the country was asleep. I followed the thin band of highway and tried to stay alert. We made it down to a town named Spanish Fork where I-15 splits into I-15 and Highway 89. I-15 is the fast way home but the Highway 89 is the beautiful way. It was night and I couldn't really see any of this but Highway 89 winds its way through the middle of Sanpete County where my mom's family is from. Eventually it goes down through, Piute, Garfield, and Kane Counties, literally right through the ancient red cliffs of Zion National Park.

I was already beginning to feel a little tired and I'd only been driving about 20 minutes. I knew this would be against our agreement but I decided it was too soon to wake up Marty so I turned the radio up and rolled down my window. I waved my left hand in the wind and sang along with the song "Thank God I'm a Country Boy" by John Denver. I made it through Spanish Fork and into Sanpete County with Marty out cold in the passenger seat. I started shaking my head every now and then, wiggling my toes and singing as loud as I could out the window. I didn't think anything could wake Marty up.

I started shifting my weight back and forth in the seat. I did everything I could think of. Eventually, I decided that I just couldn't keep driving and be safe anymore. I pulled over somewhere between Spanish Fork and a little town named Mount Pleasant. I rolled the car to a stop in the darkness somewhere on the shoulder of the road and I reached over and shook Marty's shoulder. To my surprise, he woke up right away and he turned to me looking disheveled and he said, "Thank you, Peter, for waking me up. I'd be happy to drive for the next hour or so." He stood up, got out of the car and stretched there on the highway next to his door. He ran in place for a second or two and then he did a couple of jumping jacks. I stumbled out of the driver's seat and around to the passenger's side of the car. I don't remember much else now except that I fell rock hard and resoundingly asleep.

This back and forth of drivers went on a few more times. The amount of time each person drove got shorter and shorter as it got later and later. We drove down through small towns with turkey farms all over the place. They were towns with names like Mount Pleasant, Ephraim and Manti. The time each of us spent driving on his "shift" went from an hour in the beginning to about a half hour. Eventually, about every 15 minutes or so, whoever was driving the car would pull over and politely wake up the passenger. The passenger would thank the driver and jump around half-heartedly for a minute. We would trade places and the guy who'd been asleep a moment ago would turn the key, try to get comfortable and awake enough to drive, and head back down the road.

Eventually, every ten minutes or so the car would crawl to a stop and we'd stumble around and switch drivers. By this time, all the pleasantries were over too. We were getting very efficient in our driver switching. We were still being nice to each other, but each time we stopped things were also getting to be a little ridiculous. We tried to maintain the protocol, mostly because we thought it was funny, and it was even funnier than normal at that time of night. Whoever drove would motor down for only a minute or two wiggling and turning and contorting his face and arms and hand muscles, flexing his butt cheeks in the driver's seat, singing with all of the lousy 70s music on the radio, doing everything he could in a vain attempt to just stay awake and drive.

Since orneriness and impatience were off the table based on our pre-approved protocol, our competitive and sleep-starved brains took over. We'd switch drivers mumbling our thank yous, and the passenger would fall into an almost coma-like sleep. The driver would wait a minute, pretending to listen to a song on the radio or get his seatbelt all fastened, and then he'd start the car and roll forward about 25 feet and stop again. There wasn't even time to pull back onto the road. The car would roll to a stop as if a half hour had gone by and the driver would poke and shake the other and we'd repeat the whole process.

Within two hours of starting our drive, excited with the adventure of it all and the idea of driving straight through the night all the way from Ogden, Utah to San Diego, we had been reduced to sleep deprived, babbling creatures, teased by the briefest hints of completely unsatisfying sleep. Our drive south, while it was a fun idea, had become like a scene from an Austin Powers movie. We were making absolutely no progress.

The two of us were just stubborn enough that, even though it clearly wasn't very funny anymore, we kept doing it. At least, I should say, neither one of us was laughing. In my mind, somewhere it was registering that it could be funny, or that it should be funny, but by now all of the humor cells in my brain were completely turned off. We started and stopped our way down the shoulder of Highway 89, making absolutely no progress, for some time. We even kept going as it started to rain. The thank yous were getting more and more uncontrollably sarcastic. Finally, Marty was creeping along the edge of the highway and I heard him say something about finding a place to park so we could sleep for an hour or so.

I had no idea how long I'd been asleep at this point. Although I think it is truly impossible to get any restful sleep in the passenger seat of an old Audi Fox, I had nodded off. I was in a deep fog. I had "AUDI" imprinted on my forehead where the plastic emblem on the door had dug its way into my flesh. I can't say I was really thinking clearly. Time passed but I don't remember it passing. In fact, I don't remember anything. Marty didn't nudge me. I didn't thank him. I just slept. I was really, really tired at this point. We'd both known that driving straight through wasn't a good idea anyway, and we both had figured we'd end up asleep somewhere. I was so tired now that the idea of sleeping somewhere in the darkness of remote Sanpete County didn't bother me one bit.

The next memory I have is of a hard rain and the sound of cows mooing. I was groggy and my back ached. There were big grunting and mooing cows around our car. I could see that we weren't out on the highway anymore, but parked somewhere in a field. It looked like the cows were trying to stay warm from the heat of our car. The rain was driving down and bouncing and steaming off the backs of the cattle. I had no idea what time it was now, but it was definitely still night. My body ached for sleep. The cows were grunting and stomping. The rain was pouring down. Now, finally when we had decided to get some sleep, between the cows and the rain and the horrible smell of wet cow poop being shuffled around and hoofed up and down by the herd of cattle, we both knew that falling back asleep was absolutely impossible.

I don't know how we ended up in a field surrounded by cattle, but I looked over at Marty, who at this point was getting frustrated. We had to move, he said. Marty sat up and put the car back in gear. He started to beep the horn and start and stop his way out of there. Luckily, the car didn't get stuck in the cow poop. The cattle moved out of the way and let us go.

When I woke up again it was almost morning. The car still smelled a little like manure. Marty had driven us down and stopped in the parking lot of the historic Manti Temple. I'd seen pictures of it before in church magazines. It's one of the most distinctive and beautiful buildings that the early Mormon pioneers ever built. We were still out in the middle of nowhere but at least now we were parked in a clean parking lot.

I remember how different I felt looking through the windshield and seeing this temple come into focus than I did with the cows and the rain. I still felt sleep-deprived but I also felt a little safer by the temple. I never thought we were going to get attacked by the cattle at our last stop or anything like that, but I felt alone out there and a little more vulnerable. I must have read something somewhere or heard a story about crazy ranchers and nonexistent gun laws in the Wild West. Maybe stories in the news of hitchhikers driving cars off cliffs and serial killers had snuck into my brain a little. Here, though, at the Manti Temple, I felt safe, like I could finally rest. Even the bad guys would choose someplace else to attack innocent people sleeping in their cars.

    I lay there sideways in my seat all knotted up and uncomfortable. The car was a mess. There were fast food cups and wrappers all over the floor and in between on the seats. We had both given up on the idea of driving through the night and it being a wonderful adventure. This idea had died back in the field with the cattle. I opened my door and fell out of the car onto the asphalt. Then I stood up by the clean, perfectly coiffed lawn of the temple. It was dawn, or just before dawn. The dark air was still cool. The very edge of the sky, where it touches the mountains in the east was just barely beginning to turn from dark black and glow a little. It was almost not noticeable. The night would soon be over. I think we needed the daylight; we still had about ten hours of driving ahead of us.

    Marty was still there behind the wheel. He wasn't moving either; it was almost like he was dead, he was so asleep. I waited a few minutes and I nudged him and shook and poked him until he woke up. I thought he might be mad at me for waking him up but he wasn't. He looked at me and he smiled and said, "Thanks for waking me up. I'd be happy to drive!" I laughed hard.

    We took a second to clean out the inside of my little car. Throughout the night, items like wrappers and cups and papers seemed to have appeared on the floor and between the seats. We picked them up and carried them to a nearby trashcan. I felt like we needed to pause for a second and clean up. Maybe it was the temple grounds and how they were so meticulously groomed. Maybe our drive through the night adventure, turned sleep trading slobber-fest, didn't fit well in my mind with the order and history of this particular parking lot. I'd slept in my car in the same clothes I'd worn the day before and woken up all twisted and sore and kinked up at the foot of this beautiful stone building. I felt like I needed to show some small amount of respect.

After I woke Marty up and we picked up our stuff, we drove away. I felt like we needed to get going. I didn't feel like I'd done anything wrong sleeping there in my car. I even felt like it was a good idea. I just felt a little irreverent, like I shouldn't laugh so loud and we should clean up more quietly out of respect.

The Mormon Temple in Manti is one of four or five temples built in the 1800s throughout Utah by early pioneers. Salt Lake City was the first place in Utah founded by early Mormon settlers. They had walked there, pushing handcarts, from the East Coast. They did this so they could live their religion without being harassed or killed by angry violent mobs like ones they'd dealt with in states like Missouri and Illinois. They went through horrific hardships on the trail from Nebraska to Utah, and many of them didn't survive. They froze or starved as they walked, with all of their possessions, to Salt Lake City.

Right after settling down in Salt Lake City, small groups of these early pioneers had been asked to spread out and start little towns and settlements about a day's horseback ride apart to the north and the south throughout what was then the territory of Utah, and beyond. The places they set up, the forts they built, grew over the years and eventually became towns and cities like Logan, Brigham City, Farmington, Bountiful, American Fork, Spanish Fork, Payson, Nephi, Scipio, Manti, Beaver, Fillmore, Cedar City, St George, Mesquite and even Las Vegas.

In a couple of these towns, they built temples where they could get married, remember their ancestors, and worship. The temples weren't just important churches. They were symbols to these people that they had done it. They had beaten the mobs and the trail and they had survived. They laid the foundation for a great civilization that would come to this area. I knew I was one of those who would come. I think this is why I felt reverent and cleaned up my car a little. There was just so much care put into that temple.

    The temple stuck out in Manti. Manti, Utah was, back then, a small town of little homes, farms, hay and sheep and cattle and old barns. And then there was this temple. It was important, and I didn't understand why back then, but I did stop for a minute with Marty in the darkness to try to stumble through a small show of respect. We didn't say anything. We just stood there by the trashcan in the parking lot for a minute and looked up at all the granite and all the history. Then Marty drove us down to get a fast food breakfast and we started to refill the inside of the Audi with more wrappers and cups. We then headed out on Highway 89 toward Southern Utah. A wispy cloud was hovering over the fields on each side of the highway as the sun came up. The windows of our tiny car hadn't even had a chance to defog yet.

    I fell asleep with my head against my shoulder and my arm jutting weirdly and uncomfortably straight up by the metal post of the door. It was a solid sleep. It was probably a continuation of the same sleep chemicals that had gotten started in the temple parking lot. In fact, whatever the scientific designation for deep, restful, rejuvenating, sleep-deprived sleep is, that is the kind I was finally experiencing. I was gone, profoundly, finally, restfully asleep. It was the kind of sleep they put you in at the hospital before they operate on you. My brain and my body had finally had enough.

    I don't know how long I lay there while Marty drove down the highway, but I absolutely remember what happened when I woke up. For some reason, we were stopped on the side of the highway. Something was wrong. Marty was fidgeting around, panicky. He was yanking my arm over by the driver's seat. He was pulling and pushing and jerking, and his foot hit the stick shift knob and he jumped or wiggled over me. It was completely freakish behavior and totally outside of what we had established earlier as acceptable. All I could do was try to move out of his way. He was squirming and pushing and shoving me over. I heard the word "Move!" and I tried to shift up and out of my seat over and around the emergency brake and the steering wheel, trying to avoid Marty and his desperate, spasmodic, forceful pushing and shoving. I landed hard somewhere near the driver's side. "This is a major breach of seat-changing protocol," I might have said. "What's going on?" There was no damage. We hadn't been in a wreck. I was dazed. This was absolutely out of context and…. "Go!" Marty shouted as he finally settled into the passenger seat where he closed his eyes and acted like he was fast asleep.

I sat there straddling the emergency brake, my left arm poking through the steering wheel and AUDI imprinted backwards on my forehead. I looked over at Marty as I sat the rest of the way down behind the wheel. My thoughts were coming in brief strobe-like episodes. It was too soon to actually form sentences. I sat there in the driver's seat, blinking and shaking my head. My hair was mashed up unevenly in a big awkward looking clump where my head had been pushed up against my arm by the window a few seconds before when I was asleep. Heavy duty sleep chemicals were still coursing freely through my veins. I was lucky I was even able to talk.

I had been awake for a maximum of 45 seconds when I heard someone pounding forcefully on the outside of my window. I couldn't figure out what was happening. The side and back windows were foggy so I couldn't see through them. There was clearly something out there, though, thumping on the glass—something that made Marty act very weird. I turned slowly and rolled the window down. There, leaning towards me, completely blocking out the morning sky, stood a hulking, emotionless Highway Patrol officer. I squinted a bit as I looked up at him. He seemed unnaturally huge. He had a gun, and a badge, and he wore big mirrored dark glasses and a Smokey the Bear-type hat. He was definitely not smiling. I rolled down the window and he looked into the car. He saw Marty "sleeping" and he asked me for my license and registration.

What could I do? I was, after all, sitting in the driver's seat. He had every reason to believe that I had been the one driving the car. I was sure he couldn't have seen us switch places. I couldn't very well point at Marty who looked like he was deeply asleep and say, "It was him!" At this point, the Utah State Trooper could have asked me for my name and I would have had a difficult time with the answer. I had to resist the urge to shake my head to wake myself up for fear that the officer might think I was on drugs or something. I wiped drool off of my cheek and I nudged Marty and told him I needed the registration from the glove compartment. Marty put on one heck of a show. He was yawning, and acting tired, and stretching like he'd been asleep for hours. "Your leg, I can't open the glove box," I said. Marty cleared his throat and rubbed his eyes and acted all disoriented. He said, "What?" and he looked up at me. When he did, he looked past me and said, very politely, "Oh, hello officer." Then he went into super polite and respectful Eddie Haskell mode. He straightened right up, sat up, opened the glove compartment, pulled out the car registration, and gave it to the officer. The policeman looked at Marty and said, "Thank you, Son."

His demeanor changed when he looked back at me. He glared with a deadpan highway patrolman stare and said impatiently, "Do you know how fast you were driving?" I just looked back and with total honesty said, "No sir, I really do not." He took the license and the car registration and he turned a crisp, disciplined turn and walked back down the shoulder of the road to his car.

What does one do in a situation such as this? I suppose I could have gone completely berserk and tried to beat the living daylights out of Marty, but I liked Marty, and I wasn't sure if I got in a fight with him right then that I could win. More importantly, the Utah State Trooper seemed to like Marty more than he liked me and it seemed unwise to start a fight while we waited for this officer with a gun and a Billy club on his belt to come back to the car. Plus, I was pretty sure he was considering, based on how I must have looked, whether he should check me for driving under the influence. Also, he liked how Marty was so respectful and obedient.

I could have refused to talk to Marty, which I did for a second, partly because I had no idea what to say and partly because I just couldn't believe what he'd done and how he had completely sold it and gotten away with it. I suppose I could have done a million things. What I did finally do, though, was laugh at how I was asleep, and then I was awake and behind the wheel, and then rolling down my window to the law. Marty beat me to the punch anyway. As soon as the policeman made his military style turn and walked back toward his patrol car, Marty begged for mercy. He just fell all over himself with apologies. He told me he had a terrible driving record in Utah. This, I thought, was a detail that might have been better to know at the beginning of our trip when we decided to drive through the night. He told me his license was a probationary one because he'd gotten too many tickets when he was in high school. He said that he was on the 362nd day of a 365-day driving probation in the state of Utah. If he got a ticket in the next three days, his license would be revoked and he wouldn't be able to drive on his mission. Most likely, because of that, he wouldn't hold any leadership positions on his mission, which I agreed was kind of a big deal.

I told him I'd take the ticket. I told him that he owed me big-time, though. He nodded like he knew he did. I told him he was paying for the ticket too. He agreed. I should have told him he was buying my lunch too but the Utah State Trooper was back staring at me and having me sign the ticket stating that I was acknowledging receipt and that I would show up when I was supposed to. He leaned in again toward us and tipped his hat to Marty. Then he looked at me. He handed me the ticket and said, "Slow down!" and he walked away.

Marty told me years later that he forgot to pay the ticket when it came due. He spent the better part of a day, about three days before he left home for his mission, calling the applicable law enforcement people in Sanpete, Piute, Garfield, Kane and Washington Counties. This was long before anyone had contemplated using the internet for something like this. Marty tells me that he'd call whatever number he got from the information operator in each one of the counties. Most of the time it was the home of the county judge or the justice of the peace. He had to hold each time because the judge was "out in the field" meaning he was out tending to his livestock or his wife would tell Marty she'd try to get him to come in 'cause he was out feeding the dogs or the chickens. Finally, after several calls, Marty found the right guy who found a copy of the ticket in his cardboard "ticket box" by the phone, and Marty sent him a check in the mail.

After we made it home to La Jolla, I stood up to the pulpit in my shiny, new Mr. Mac 3-piece suit, which was the fashion at the time. I didn't mention the Utah State Trooper, or the cows, or the Manti Temple parking lot. Instead I told the congregation about Waterfall Canyon and what Marty had said up there. I told them how I believed that all the struggles and sacrifices we make in life are worth it. I said that the efforts of all the people who went before us to find meaning in their lives weren't wasted. I said that I believed that God knew about it all and that he loves us. I told them that I'd be serving in Guatemala because I believed in the people down there and that their lives were as important and meaningful as my own. That's what I told them. That's why I'd decided to go on a mission. That is where I'd be for the next two years.

By the way, after I wrote this whole story, I drafted a letter for Marty to sign to confirm that everything happened the way I said it did. There is a copy of it following this page

Peter Nielsen
2615 Burrier Lane
Tustin, CA 92782

Dear Peter,

I read through your draft of our experience on Highway 89 back in 1977. You asked me to read it and send you my comments. First off, let me preface my remarks by letting you know how well it is written and what a funny, funny man you are. Secondly, allow me to say that you have captured things exactly as they happened. I wouldn't change a word.

Your friend,

Marty Newey

> Peter,
> I was driving. I pulled over and politely woke you up and asked you to take the ticket because I only had 3 days left on probation. I don't know where you came up with all the rest.
>
> — Marty

Figure: Marty's letter about traffic ticket

SIXTEEN

Guatemala Arrival

I had made arrangements to have my grandpa and Janice meet me at the airport before my plane left for Guatemala. I sat on one of the fiberglass seats in a very busy airport and listened to announcements over the public address system, hoping to see them once more before I left for the next two years. But after the last passenger went out the door onto the runway to get on the plane, I knew they were going to be late and I had missed them. There was a flight attendant standing at the gate. She nodded at me and frowned. I knew I had to get on so I handed her my ticket.

    I walked out onto the runway and then up the big set of rolling stairs they had pushed up against the door of the plane. I unenthusiastically smiled at the pilot who was there at the top of the stairs. He said something like, "Well, I'm sorry but we have a schedule to keep." I looked at him as I ducked into the plane and I told him it was okay. I didn't really mean it though. It wasn't really okay. I was sad and had said that in an attempt to be polite. He handed me a *Sports Illustrated* magazine and said maybe I could read it to take my mind off leaving home. I got choked up and almost cried and I said thank you.

I sat down in my seat, buckled in for the flight, and glanced back out the window. I sat back and closed my eyes and wondered what it would be like in Guatemala. I knew that I was going to find out in a few hours when our flight landed. I sat up and peeked out the little oval airplane window and noticed that something was going on outside the plane by the door that led from the waiting area onto the runway. The person at the gate was trying to remain calm but struggling with something or someone. Of course, this was before all the security lines and restrictions that resulted from 9/11. It looked like more than just an argument going on down there, but it seemed I was the only one who saw it because no one else appeared alarmed. I didn't see anyone getting ready to shut down the airport or call Security (which barely existed at airports back then).

I pressed my nose up to the plastic window and tried to look closer. The window was smudgy but I could see the gate attendant was wrestling with someone. In another second it was clear that it was my grandfather pushing his way out onto the tarmac, limping like he did back then, toward the airplane. He was swinging his cane around the best he could and demanding to go out on the runway. Janice was right there behind him. He was pointing and speaking forcefully. It was clear that in his small town, he usually got what he wanted. He looked annoyed and insistent, like nothing was going to stop him.

I unbuckled and jumped up from my seat and ran to the front of the plane. They were readying the heavy metal airplane door to be closed and I pointed through the opening at my grandfather and Janice. I pleaded with the flight attendant to let me go down and say goodbye. I could see both of them now, only a few steps away from the bottom of the stairs. The flight attendant stepped in front of me blocking my way and said, "No!" She held up her hands and frowned and told me that she couldn't hold up the plane for every passenger that wanted to say goodbye. I didn't know what else to do so I begged. I told her I was going away for a long time to a place I'd never been to before. I tried to tell her how they were my grandparents and how they were old. I said I might never get to see them again. I think I clutched my hands together like someone does when they are really desperate or when they are praying.

She would not have any of it, though. She ignored me and instead continued to prepare the area around the door so it could be closed. She acted like our conversation was over. I stood there for a second, not sure what I was waiting for. I could see Grandpa now all the way out on the airport runway, still arguing with the man from the gate who had followed him out. The flight attendant looked insistent and sure of herself. Grandpa Doctor and Janice didn't see me. They were too busy maneuvering and moving toward the plane. I didn't want to leave without being able to say goodbye, especially when they'd driven all the way up from Payson to see me off. I felt like shouting but there was too much noise and I was too far away, so they wouldn't have heard me.

Just as the flight attendant was about to grab the door of the plane and swing it around to close it, the pilot poked his head out from the cockpit and into where we were standing. He turned and looked out the door and saw the struggle with Grandpa and the gate agent. Then he looked and saw me standing there. He shrugged, like he hadn't thought of it before that moment, and then he said to the flight attendant, "Give him a break, he's going to be away from home for a long time. Let him go down there and say goodbye." The flight attendant glared back at the pilot for a second like she hated him and then she looked at me and said, insistently, "Then hurry! Go!"

I ran down the stairs and, like something from a movie, I ran over and hugged my grandfather and grandmother like I might never see them again. My grandfather seemed old to me that day. Maybe I hadn't hugged him like this in a long time. He felt frail. I hugged Janice too. She brought me some peaches in a glass mason jar. She said she thought maybe I could snack on them during my flight. My grandpa stood up as straight as he could and grabbed my shoulders and stared into my eyes like he was about to say something profound. He knew I had to hurry. I smiled at him, relieved that they had made it after all. He said, "Pierre, you be good. You know how. I know you do!" And then he turned me around and gave me a little nudge and told me to go get back on the plane.

I remember sitting down by that same little airplane window flying southeast towards Guatemala for hours. I thought that Guatemala was just south of Mexico and that Mexico was just south of San Diego. I didn't think it would take anywhere near as long as it did to get there. I learned from reading the world map in the magazine in the seat back pocket in front of me that Mexico is a huge country. Even though it seemed like it should be closer, Guatemala is way down there at Mexico's southern border. Because Mexico curves down and around, Guatemala is actually further east than Chicago and much further south than San Diego.

Pretty soon I fell asleep in my seat by the window. It wasn't until late afternoon when I woke up and looked out the window again. I could see blue skies with white chunky clouds and tall green mountains and volcanoes. They were steep and jagged and some of them actually had smoke coming out of them. I couldn't tell if we were over Guatemala yet but I did know that what I was looking at outside my airplane window was completely different than anything I'd ever seen before. It looked like I was somehow going back into the past. I thought it looked prehistoric. I didn't see any roads or cities, just tall majestic volcanoes and wide open verdant fields that led up to them. It was incredible.

I thought of my grandfather, The Doctor, and Janice and how, for the first time, they seemed old. I smiled as I pictured them fighting off the gate agent with Grandpa's cane to get out on the runway and say goodbye. Then I sat back and ate some of Janice's peaches with a plastic spoon I got from the mean flight attendant, and I read the *Sports Illustrated* the pilot gave me.

An hour or so later, after the plane landed in Guatemala City, I was lining up with the other passengers and then slowly stepping out onto the stairs that led down to the runway. I felt like the air down there was thicker somehow. It felt heavy on me and foreign. I wondered if I was ready for this. I told myself that I was, that this was going to be a big adventure. I felt like I had a real direction and purpose and that I was going to do everything I could to try and help anyone I could. I didn't know anything about this new country, but I told myself I would throw myself into any task I was given and I would do it with everything I had.

A few weeks later, after traveling for hours through windy mountain roads, I stepped off of an old rickety bus in the blazing humid heat of a very small village on the foothills of one of those volcanoes. It was March, which I would learn was the beginning of the hot season in Coastal Guatemala. By this time, I felt like I had stepped out of my former life in San Diego into the middle of a *National Geographic* magazine. I had arrived in a small jungle town on the Pacific Coast along the Pan American Highway. It was a Wednesday afternoon. To the southwest of the little town there were endless fields of sugarcane. There was a refinery that was rusted and old but still taking in tons of raw cane stalks every day and continually pushing out refined sugar. The whole area reeked like sweet rotting sugar, and the smell was in the air everywhere. I could smell it in the room where we lived. After a few days, it was in my clothes too, and in my hair. I could not have escaped it if I'd tried.

It was also hot all the time and the sun beat down relentlessly. I felt like it was so hot that the sun had to have been closer to Guatemala than it was to any place else on the earth. I knew it wasn't but it seemed that way. It was humid and stifling like you would expect a jungle to be. It felt like the East Coast of the United States on its worst, hottest, most humid summer day. At home on the East Coast, though, whenever it got hot and humid like this, they would call extreme weather alerts and warn older people not to go outside. On the news, they would have declared it a "Weather Emergency" and updated the nation on it every evening until the extreme conditions cooled off and people were safe again.

At first, I thought I might not be able to bear it. There was just no relief from it anywhere. None of the little *tiendas*, or soda shops, or public buildings, or cars, or even bars were air-conditioned. The only thing I could do during the hottest part of each day was to tough it out and wait until evening when the temperature would drop a little. I don't know what the meteorological explanation is, but after lunch every day, big dark clouds would creep up slowly on the town and they would drop giant globby drops of warm summer-like rain everywhere. I could hear the rain coming from across the whole village. It splatted down on the dirt roads and the tin and fiberglass roofs. It rumbled softly at first. Then, with every minute, it got louder and marched and thumped inexorably towards me. The roads, the roofs and the people were all helpless against it as, every day like clockwork, it rolled across the tops of the houses and down through the gutters until the town was soaking wet. Then it would keep moving down the coast to the next little village.

The warm rain never cooled anything down like I thought it should. It just made things more wet and humid than they had been in the first place. It was fun for a minute, while it was actually raining, to splash around and pretend I was cooling off, but when the sun came back out and the clouds went away, you could actually see steam start to ooze up from the cobbled streets like they'd been holding their breath and now had a moment to exhale.

Almost every morning before the village had a chance to warm up all the way, I used to sit out on a small step that led from the sidewalk to the front door of the little room we rented. I'd sit and watch the town wake up in the mornings. I watched the people drinking their coffee. The few who had cars or trucks were getting in them and starting them up. Every morning I said hello to one of the clergy from the Catholic church across the street from our room. He was young, like me, and he was nice. He told me once to stop and visit if I ever needed a rest. I told him thank you. I can't remember if I ever took him up on that. I would have done it, but I just don't think I would have ever let myself believe that

I was too tired and that I needed the rest (although there were times when I definitely should have).

Once a week, every Sunday morning, I sat on that step and watched as Mayan villagers who lived out in the mountains and fields all around would come into town for market day. They flooded in from all of the tiny villages where they worked on different plantations. There were hundreds of them, maybe even thousands. Some of them would walk for miles. They poured in until the town was almost overcome.

The Mayan people from each different village wore a distinct style of clothes. It was as if they all had a dress code except that nobody was making them do it — it was just the way they dressed. Men from one area wore white button down shirts, long shorts with wide colorful stripes, and leather sandals worn smooth on the bottom. Men from other villages wore different but equally bright outfits. Some of them had fedora style, or bowler, felt hats with bright bands around them. Their hats and outfits were all amazing and, I thought, worn with pride. They were at the same time grimy and stained from years of giving shade and being worked in under the hot sun. I could see old men with leathery skin standing, waiting for something, on the sides of the street. They looked worn but not tired and they stood there emotionless and unyielding.

The Mayan women dressed even more brilliantly and colorfully than the men. They wore hand-made wrap-around skirts with embroidered blouses they made themselves called *huipiles*. Sometimes they wore hats or scarf-like things wrapped around their heads made with ribbons of bright, colorful textiles. The women were the ones I remember negotiating, buying and selling at the market. While they did it, some of them carried their babies close to them in traditional and almost blindingly colorful wraps. I could see old Mayan women talking, negotiating and maneuvering, in and out of the crowds, and the tables of food and clothes and other things.

Every Sunday, as these people flooded into town, I watched the colors, textiles and people all weaving back and forth like they were synchronized. I heard them talking too, but I couldn't even begin to understand them. They spoke hundreds of amazing and completely foreign-sounding ancient dialects. The area hummed with strange and wonderful sounds. The smells of spice and dirt and people and the clicking and humming sounds of their talking were everywhere, just like the smell of sugar cane was.

They crowded into the streets and moved together like a sea of moving, swirling color. It was almost like a dance of some sort, fluid, connected, social. Looking at them from up the street over a period of months, I could see a real community on market day, almost like it was a living thing. It was a strong, beautiful, stubborn way of life.

A few weeks after I arrived, I met an old Mayan woman we called *Hermana* (sister) Poncio. She lived just outside of town in a small wooden home with a dirt floor and a low tin roof. She lived there with her common-law husband and two young sons. She was like a community midwife, except that she'd never been to school. She was respected by other villagers and they would call for her if they had a problem. She was the closest thing they had to a doctor. I went with her a couple of times when she visited people who were sick or hurt. One day I helped rub some weird gooey salve she'd made into a man's arm where he'd somehow been cut with a machete. When I wasn't rubbing it in hard enough, she corrected me and moved me out of the way. She ignored the man's complaints and started talking to the family louder than the man was complaining, and she worked that salve right into the tenderest part of his arm. Another day I went with her and watched as she set a little boy's broken arm. He sobbed and told her he'd hurt it spinning tops with his friend. I couldn't imagine how he could break his arm playing tops, but it was verifiably crooked where it shouldn't have been and it was most definitely broken. The boy cried when Hermana Poncio walked in, but she reset his crooked arm and wrapped it up in a splint she made from wood slats and some old rags.

I cried along with them all, and didn't think I would ever recover, when a little baby girl died of some unknown infection. I was sure that medicine I could have bought back home would have easily cured her, and I would have bought it for them if I'd known what it was and where I could get it. It wasn't even in their field of vision, though. I felt like I'd failed them somehow and I held the little girl's parents' hands and prayed with them for strength when things were at their most bleak. More about that later.

Months later, I went to dinner in this same family's little hut and I sat on a chair made from an old tree stump. They asked me to pray and bless the food. I prayed with the whole family and then we ate the family's only chicken. For a minute or two during that dinner, I sat back and watched everyone almost as if I wasn't there in the room with them. They were speaking Spanish that night and I could understand a bit. I watched as they passed their food around to each other, talking and smiling. I remember thinking about home and my family and how, really, their family was a lot like mine. I was comfortable there. It felt peaceful and calm and I liked that.

I lived in that town for four or five months beginning in March of 1977. I was still learning to speak Spanish back then. I used to force myself to read a story from the newspaper each morning to try to brush up on my skills. I would stand in the corner of my little room and read out loud so I could hear myself saying the words. I was just starting to be able to make out some of the headlines. When there were words I didn't know, I wrote them down in a little spiral notebook I kept in my front shirt pocket. Most of the time they were everyday words that had difficult conjugations or they were just new vocabulary I hadn't heard before. Later, when I had time, I would look them up. I couldn't remember the articles they were in or the context they were used in, and they were definitely not words a missionary would use every day. Sometimes they were about violent, bad things. I would think back and try to remember which article I'd read them in, but it was difficult to imagine what the stories could have been about. Over the next weeks and months, I tried to pay closer attention when I read to myself, and I slowly began to realize that the part of Guatemala where I was living could be dangerous. In fact, most of the time I was down there, I felt like I was close to this danger, like it was lurking around the next corner. I saw people who had been hurt and I tried to help them like Hermana Poncio. As my Spanish got better, I started to understand that most of Central America, including Guatemala, was getting to be a very dangerous place. I didn't want to be near any of this. I was there to help people, but sometimes the danger and violence was closer than I wanted or realized.

Early one morning, I was riding on a bus named "La Fortaleza" down the Pan-American Highway toward Guatemala City. I was sitting in the front row right across from the driver. I chose La Fortaleza because it was a luxury bus and it had air conditioning. I picked the seat next to the driver because I could feel the cool air on my face right when it came out of the vent. It was a huge, modern Greyhound-style bus and it was extremely comfortable. I sat and looked out of the big windshield with the driver and absolutely basked in the wisps of cool air on me. It was, I think, the only time I felt air-conditioned air for the whole two years I was in the country. This ride into the city was going to last about an hour and a half. I was looking forward to cooler weather in the capital and I was glad I'd paid the extra dollar or two to ride in comfort.

After about half an hour, we passed a small town named Esquintla. It was a hot and grimy town. People were just getting up, shuffling around, drinking their coffee, and getting ready for the day. The sun was up and just starting to exert itself. The town looked like it needed a transfusion or something, like it was starting to wilt. The cool air pumped out of the AC vent and I relaxed in my seat and watched out the window as we rolled smoothly past it down the highway toward Guatemala City.

I was beginning to feel a bit drowsy when the bus started slowing down. We were out on the highway, past Esquintla now. There was really no reason for the driver to stop. Nothing was around us but open sugar cane fields. I sat up a little and looked out my window to see if I could tell what was going on. It slowed down even more and then rolled to a stop by the side of the road.

We all sat up in our seats as the driver pushed a button by the steering wheel. The big bus door made a swooshing sound and opened wide. When the door opened, I could feel the heat outside push its way in. In a second, a soldier, wearing a dark green Guatemalan army uniform, stepped on board the bus. He seemed annoyed by us, like we were a waste of his time. He had a gun at his waist and a belt with rows of meticulously placed and ordered bullets draped over his shoulder and across his chest.

He stepped up and looked into where we were on the bus. Then he slowly took off a pair of *Top Gun*-style dark glasses. He pointed at the driver and squinted threateningly at him. The soldier never smiled. No one was smiling. The soldier spit out some orders and pointed through the windshield disgustedly to a small grassy area just ahead and to the side of the big bus. Then he turned and got back down out of the bus and stood there, in the sun, where I couldn't see him or hear him anymore.

The bus driver got up slowly and started walking down the aisle of the bus telling us that we had to get off. It was getting hot now and I didn't want to get up. But everyone filed out in line and moved forward slowly. One by one we stepped down out of the bus onto the side of the road. There were 5 or 6 dark green or gray army trucks out there now and all kinds of very serious soldiers standing with their weapons and their uniforms. They all seemed disturbed or angry. There were probably thirty of them standing there in the sun. They were deathly serious.

The one who stepped onto the bus and talked to the driver, the one with the dark glasses, was clearly in charge. He barked orders at the other soldiers in rapid fire, authoritative Spanish. There were big trucks covered with canvas tarps. The soldiers stood by with machine guns and pistols. The people on the bus were starting to push and shove each other to get all the way off the bus. Then we stood around and asked each other what was going on.

    The man in charge ordered all of us to line up on the grass by a little hill. Then he came over and one by one he stopped and looked at us. He held his hand out in the air in front of each one of us. He stood so close to me I could see myself in his sunglasses. He held his hand out insistently. One by one we handed him identification papers. He never spoke to me. It would have been beneath him. He knew that he was in complete and absolute control.

    I watched the hands of a man standing next to me shake as he handed over his wallet. I could feel sweat dripping down my back on the inside of my shirt. I reached for my ID in my front shirt pocket where I always kept it, next to a picture of Kathie. When the man was almost to me I pulled it out. He looked through his dark glasses at my identification and then he looked at me. I couldn't tell if he was feeling disgusted or if he was bored to death. After a minute and without a hint of care, without any acknowledgement, he gave me back my identification and he moved to the next person in line. The morning sun burned down on us as we stood there in line until we all felt like we were going to wilt. Other younger soldiers—and there were a lot of them—stood by leaning on their trucks, not talking, just looking at all of us. The whole thing was surreal.

    The general in charge, the man with the glasses, walked away from our lineup. He went over and started to argue with another man I couldn't see who was in the back seat of a black town car that had dark tinted windows. The sun was really pounding down now. Sweat was dripping on my face and my nose. Finally, the general stepped away from the town car and signaled to his men. He said something I couldn't understand, or didn't hear, and he made a dismissive kind of motion with his hand. The other soldiers eased and started to get back in their trucks. He whistled at us to get our attention and he pointed to our driver and then back at the door of the bus. He never said a word to any of us. He just pointed at the bus and grunted.

We all climbed back into the bus and sat down. I climbed into my seat near the front. When I sat down, I could feel that the man who had been next to me in the lineup was still shaking and almost crying. I put my hand on his shoulder and I smiled. The driver came in last and sat down too. He didn't speak. He just started the bus and drove away.

I remember looking around and wondering what was wrong. I looked over at the driver and then at the man next to me on the bus and I thought about the soldiers, and the general, and the general's argument with the man in the town car. I thought, right then, for the first time, that we might have been in danger. I thought it was awful that a place could be so incredibly beautiful and at the same so inhospitable. I could see why the Mayan men seemed so stern and stoic.

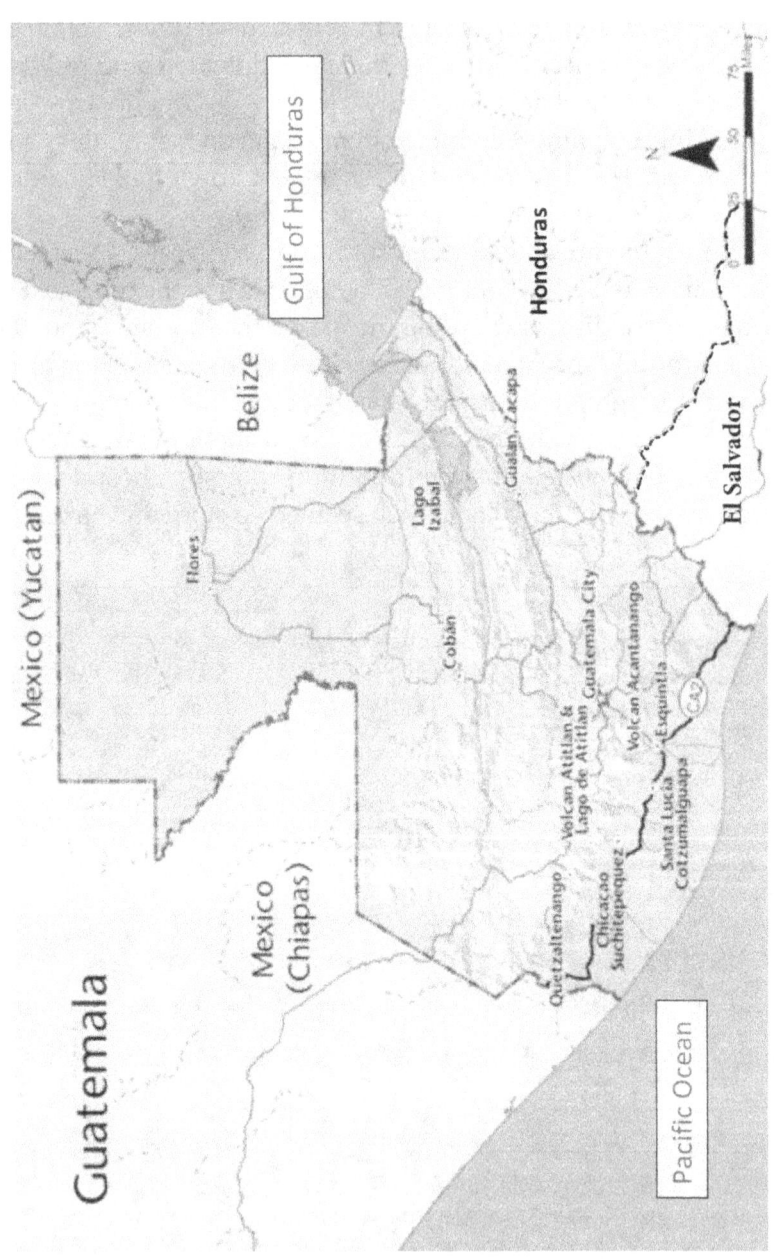

SEVENTEEN

Volver, Volver

Months later, I was in another little town in Eastern Guatemala named Gualán. It's in the *Departamento* of Zacapa just about half way between Guatemala City and the Caribbean Sea. Actually, Gualán is almost not big enough to be referred to as a town. The people who lived there described it as a *pueblito* which is like saying it's too small to be a real town.

I was there in 1978 during the Guatemalan hot season. The sun blazed down and made everything it touched hot. The locals told me it was like living in a *sarten* or frying pan. It was a Las Vegas-type intense, dry heat. I don't know all the meteorological reasons, but on the Caribbean side of Guatemala, the coastal towns were hot and dry during this time of year. On the other side, the Pacific Ocean side, it was also hot but always humid and sticky, too. Where I lived now, in Gualán, it was just bright and hot like they'd forgotten and left the sun turned on too high. At least Gualán, which was only a few miles from the southeastern border with Honduras, wasn't humid. I guess it had that going for it.

I was nineteen years old at the time. I had dreamed about going on a mission to a far-off foreign country almost as long as I could remember. I used to sit back in high school and daydream about learning to speak a new language and working until I was bone tired helping poor people and getting to know them in some far-off land. When I finally made it to Gualán, Zacapa, I was convinced that this part of Guatemala was as far-off and foreign as any place in the world could ever get.

One night I stood there on a muddy path in front of an old abandoned wooden building that had a rusty tin roof. The air was still warm and it was late afternoon, almost dark. I thought I could see fireflies beginning to blink in the fields. I stopped to rest when an old Mayan man with a beat up felt hat walked past me on the trail. He had a clump of firewood pressing down on his shoulders. He looked up and smiled and said something in an almost extinct Indian dialect that I could not understand. I held up my hand and waved to him and said, *"Buenas!"* He passed me on the trail. After he did I turned to watch him walk by me. Behind him there was an abandoned, decaying adobe building. It was darkened against the sky and creaky looking, like it could almost fall down if the wind blew hard. The thick adobe walls looked like they had been damaged by age and by the great earthquake that had beat the living daylights out of the country a year or two before I got there. The old building wasn't that much different from other buildings in town.

I noticed, though, in the evening sky, a creepy and ominous looking cloud oozing in and out of the top of it by where its failing corrugated tin roof was now desperately clinging on to its crumbling outside walls. I ducked when I saw this dark wind coming towards me out of the old structure. It was weird. It came at me, slowly at first and then, in a minute it got frantic and intense, like it was angry, like I imagined an evil spirit would.

I could tell in a few seconds that it was a swarm of bats. I'd never seen them fly together like this. They flew and swirled from the building and made the sky even darker than it had been. As a whole, the mass looked effortless, like the wake behind a boat only in the air. But the sound was frenetic like each individual bat was fighting and needing to grasp at the air to pull itself along with the group. After a second, I figured out that they wouldn't hurt me and I stood under them as they fought each other for open sky and moved as a group across the evening like a strange, graceful phantasm. The thought struck me then that I could not possibly be on a more foreign mission.

    I walked up the narrow trail into town and saw a man I knew standing outside the radio telegraph store. This store was my only access to the outside world. It was a very small room in a large concrete building that also served as the town's market on Sundays. Only one man worked the radio. He would tap out telegraph messages I could pay for by the letter and send them into Guatemala City. I don't recall ever sending a telegram but I always knew I could.

    One time I had to call into Guatemala City to talk to our Mission President. He lived in a beautiful two-story home that was built on the same lot as the very first church building in the country. He lived with his wife and his job was to look out for the welfare and safety of all of the hundred or so missionaries serving in the Guatemala City Mission.

    I walked into the telegraph room and asked if they had a telephone for emergencies. The man there said that they did not have a phone but they had a two-way radio they used for things like this. They could radio their office in a nearby, equally small town named Zacapa and somehow, in Zacapa, they could connect to a telephone landline and put my call through to Guatemala City. So, I sat at an old wooden counter with a small plastic speaker in my hand and I spoke to the Mission President. I could barely hear him through all the static of the two lines connecting and the last part of the message traveling through the air to me by radio waves. He could not hear me either and we both ended up yelling back and forth to each other and shouting, "What?" over and over again.

    I needed permission to travel by bus up to a very small town named Salama in the central mountains of Guatemala. I had a bunch of reasons and persuasive arguments ready in my mind when the static rolled and the line went live, but the noise and buzzing on the line were so loud and electric-sounding that after several "What's thats?" and "I can't hear yous" shouted back and forth, I finally just yelled into the little CB radio style handset, "Can we go up to Salama?" and I heard a "Yes!" fight its way back through the line. We didn't even say goodbye because the connection was so awful. I just gave the handset back to the man who ran the radio and got up and walked back out into the sun.

While I was there in Gualán, Argentina won the World Cup. I had never seen anything like it. No sporting event anywhere compared. In fact, no event of any kind got the kind of attention the World Cup did. Two Popes died while I was there, and most people didn't really notice, but the World Cup…they noticed that.

First of all, soccer is far and away the most popular sport in Guatemala. It's everyone's favorite sport in all of Latin America. In fact, in pretty much every country in the world besides the United States, soccer completely rules. After I got home from Guatemala, a defensive player on the Columbian World Cup team who accidentally kicked the ball into his own goal was murdered when he got home after the tournament. They've had wars related to the outcome of soccer matches.

I knew that soccer was popular. I'd learned about that back in high school. I had a friend named Javier who played on our high school team. I even went to a couple of games. But nothing could have prepared me to be there in that small town deep in Latin America when a fellow Latino country like Argentina was in the World Cup finals. They played Holland in the final game and when they did, the little dirt and cobbled streets of Gualán became completely deserted and silent. Usually, they would be filled with people talking, cars, buses belching out big black clouds of smelly exhaust, and vendors trying to sell food, or candies, or drinks.

This day, though, the day of the finals, the streets were all silent. It was like something out of a *Twilight Zone* episode, like a post-apocalyptic absence of anything at all going on.

The streets were, for the few hours the game was on, totally and completely neglected and ignored. There was only the game.

I kicked a small rock and listened to it bounce and echo around on those empty streets as I walked home during the final game. I could see in every window I passed (and I am not exaggerating) that every single one had a black and white TV with the game on. People were crowded around their TVs and they were all rooting for Argentina. It was very serious business. If I'd spoken Spanish better, I could have followed the game without missing a beat just by listening to people's TVs as I walked down the street from window to window.

When all the TVs showed a blurry image of one of the Argentines breaking free and scoring the winning goal in overtime, the whole town roared. It didn't sound like a group of people cheering, either. Right as the ball was kicked into the net and Argentina took the lead for good, I could hear every single person in that town and, I imagined, in all of South and Central America in that very same second, bellow and shout. It was the sound of vindication, like they were all finally getting even for what the Europeans had done generations ago to their ancestors. It was one full-throated cry of joy—that's what it sounded like.

After the game, people slowly reemerged from their front rooms and filled in their places in town and on the streets again. There was a song called "You're My Everything" that was everywhere on the radio back then. It must have been on all those TVs after the game because I could hear it everywhere as I walked the rest of the way home. I didn't know who sang it but people in this town tried to sing along with it even though they couldn't speak any English. They had no idea what the words meant but they sang anyway.

I went back to my small empty house and sat down on the edge of my bed out on a balcony that dangled over a small green hill. At night, you couldn't see anything there but gaping darkness. In the day, you could see the tops of trees and pieces of a narrow road that led out of town and eventually, somehow, home. I made a determined effort to not think about home too much. I'd only been in Guatemala for about a year when I was in Gualán and the two Popes died and Argentina won the World Cup. I had committed to be there for two years, I still had a long time to go, and thinking about home made me sad. The only way I could get up every day and have energy and be strong, was to try not to let my thoughts wander to my family and the cool weather back home in San Diego.

The problem was that when I got tired and would sit out on our little balcony and look out on the treetops or the darkness, my thoughts would always somehow end up at home. I would look at the sky at night and I'd wonder if they could see the same things I was looking up at. I would sit down sweaty and hot and a clear picture of me belly flopping into our backyard swimming pool would present itself in my head. I thought of my mom and dad and how they were probably busy living and paying the bills. My brother was at Stanford and my little sister was a cheerleader in high school. I had a grandfather living alone in Fullerton, California who I wasn't sure would still be around when I got home again. When I thought of them I got the most homesick.

One day, I had just finished eating my lunch of deep fried black bean cake with scrambled eggs and rice at the house next door to where we lived. We missionaries paid an old woman about $30 per month to cook our meals and wash our dirty clothes. She was diligent and very happy to have the work. I was happy too because, although I had never before eaten any of the things she cooked for us, I had been developing a taste for them and was starting to like them.

I was leaving the kitchen, walking across the concrete floor of their family room, when I saw that the old woman was watching her TV. She was pretty happy she told me because she loved Mexican Ranchero music and, she said, if I waited a few minutes Vicente Fernandez was going to sing. I'd never heard of Vicente Fernandez and I'd never listened to ranchero music either but she was nice so I stood there and I watched.

She had an old black and white TV like most of her neighbors. I watched as the camera panned across the stage till it found a small group of sombreroed men who immediately began playing their trumpets and guitars. They were wearing classic mariachi costumes and were completely decked out. I looked at the old woman and how in love she was with Vicente and I started to listen and try to understand the words to the song he sang which was "Volver, Volver." It means "return, return," and it's all about going back home. I knew it too. I felt it, but I also knew I had a long time until I could.

Vicente Fernandez belted it out. He sounded homesick like me. The music and the way they sang it dripped of sadness. The song was about a man who was wandering after leaving the woman he loved. I couldn't understand most of the words, but the hook or punch line of the chorus, where the song really makes its point said something like, "I know what it's like to lose something and … I am dying to return." I didn't move. I couldn't move.

I just stood there and listened and watched, thinking about the old man on the trail with the wood on his shoulders and how I had to use a radio to make an emergency phone call. I remembered walking in the street, knowing that every single person south of the Mexican border was watching the soccer game on their TVs. I thought of home and my mom and dad and how they might have been thinking of me, but I wasn't sure. I knew I would come home one day. But, to be honest, that day watching that TV with the old Guatemalan woman sitting next to me, it seemed like it would never happen.

EIGHTEEN

I Didn't Think He'd Get Up Again

The first time I came face to face with a dying man was at the end of a day that was so otherwise uneventful that I felt like I was invisible to everyone around me. I was walking in the hot and sweaty streets of a small town in coffee bean country, drinking Coca-Cola and wearing a John Deere trucker's cap. It was afternoon. I was working in a very small town in Northern Guatemala. I had just eaten lunch and was walking down a side street. I had started wearing a hat that had a green patch on the front that said "John Deere" to keep the sun off of my face and out of my eyes. The town I was working in was on the coastal, humid side of Guatemala. Although I couldn't see it, the humidity from the ocean must have been churned up each day into the air, rising slowly up the side of the volcano we lived near until it combined with the sun in some sort of radioactive brilliance that was so bright and so hot that I started getting headaches. So, I wore the hat.

I was walking on a small concrete sidewalk past stores that were closed until after the heat of the day passed by the town and the people woke up from their siestas. I can't remember where I was going but I remember that it was a grey cobblestone street and the town was pretty much empty as everyone was either taking their mid-day naps or awake and getting ready for people to come out of their hiding places and walk around and say hello.

I was daydreaming as I walked. I had something in my hands—a book of some kind—and as I walked, I tossed it back and forth from one hand to another. I stopped at a small *tienda*, which was really more like someone had opened their front door and had a refrigerator nearby with cold sodas and water that they would sell, along with a small assortment of treats like Hostess Twinkies or *Pan Dulce*, a sugary bread that people eat at breakfast time. I usually passed on the treat because out in these little towns there was no way of knowing how long it had been on the shelf in the heat. I started drinking Coke on my mission in this little town because I'd been told it was safer to drink than the water. I'd been sick several times and I was pretty sure it was from drinking the water, so I started drinking Coke or Diet Coke. Up until then I'd thought Diet Coke was something we Mormons avoided, but I had been assured that it was okay. I was learning a lot of stuff in Guatemala. Things weren't always how I had felt sure they should be.

I walked past a *carniceria* or butcher shop that had big hunks of beef hanging on hooks out in the air outside. There really was no way for a butcher to preserve things here. They didn't have commercial air conditioning systems, so they just hung the meat out in the sun and people came by, if they could afford it, on their way home from working and bought a piece of meat and took it home for dinner. The big slabs hung there all day with a dull, bruised, slightly off, rotting smell. I casually waved my hand in the air to scare away the flies that were buzzing around in the sunshine by all the meat. It seems a bit barbaric to think of them hanging and selling their meat that way, but by then, to me, it seemed normal, like it was just the way it was.

I passed a *cantina* next. It was closed up tight and the door was locked. Whatever party had raged in there the night before was now ended and probably forgotten. I was flipping my book back and forth in my hands trying to walk in whatever shade I could find. I came to a corner and stepped out past the last store on my side of the street and almost out onto the cobblestones. I was about to step down onto the street when, from some shadow or place I hadn't noticed, a man grabbed my arm and my book fell onto the street. I turned, but before I had time to see anything, he was on me.

There was struggling and he was pushing me. I stumbled but didn't quite fall. I caught myself and tried to stand up straight but he was pulling on me. He was so close to me that I couldn't see him or maybe it was that he was all I could see. It was mostly blurry and it all happened very fast. *"Ayudeme!"* (help me), he groaned. I braced myself and stood up so I could see him. He was messy and dirty and there was dark red blood on his hands and his face. The blood was everywhere. I wondered for a second if it was my blood, if I'd been hurt, but I didn't think so.

He staggered and cried and yanked on me to try to keep from falling down. He was dirty, bloodied, and beaten. He cried and kept on saying in Spanish, "Help me, please." I had no time even to process what was going on. I slipped around as he jerked on me and held on to my white shirt with his sticky, frantic, shaking hands. He must have been the victim of a robbery or a bar fight that went too far, I thought. He was a poor man, an Indian. His clothes were ragged and worn like someone who was used to being bent over in the sun cutting sugar cane all day. Maybe he owed someone money, or maybe it was payday and he'd been robbed for the pathetic wage he'd been paid. Maybe he'd been caught looking at the wrong Mayan woman. I guess I'll never know what really happened to him before I got there.

He was desperate. He had what looked like spit, sweat, dirt, and blood all mixed together and clinging to his hands and clothes. I reached out and I tried to steady him and have him stand up. I told him we would get him some help. He looked up at me very slowly like he was dying. I could smell his breath as he leaned on me. There was some kind of bright red awful looking fluid coming out of his head somewhere near his ear. He stumbled and pulled and pleaded for me to help him.

    I looked around for someone else as I struggled to stabilize the man. I heard myself shouting for someone to go get an ambulance. I was so close to him and he was up and in my face crying and moaning and stinking. I didn't dare let him sit down. I don't know why. I guess I didn't think he would ever be able to get up again. His blood, sweat, and desperation were all over me now. My hands were now bloodied too. I had splatters of blood on my face and in my eyes. It was in my hair and all over my clothes. I just kept telling him it would be all right. I tried to pull myself away but I couldn't, or wouldn't. I tried to tell him that we would get him some help. I was now out in the street with this man as he fought with me to remain alive. He slapped at me and grabbed on to me and wouldn't let go. I tried to stay calm, but I couldn't.

    Finally, slowly, more slowly than I thought I could stand it, a small minivan with a red cross painted on it inched down the road toward us. The man was sitting now and I was holding his head in my hands, thinking it would help him breathe. He took big gasps, and gurgled, and spit out blood toward the ground. I was shaking and trying to stay calm and think of what to do. Finally, the man in the van got out and came up to where we were. I leaned over the man I was holding and told him he was going to be okay. He looked up at me weakly and said something. I couldn't tell what he was saying. It sounded a little like *ayudeme* but it was weak. The man from the ambulance stayed at a safe distance and looked down at us. He was tall and clean and detached. He was not willing to get any closer to us. I couldn't tell if he was assessing the situation or if he was simply annoyed for some unfathomable reason. He had on grey, neatly pressed clothes. He looked at us for a second and then he stood straight with his hands on his hips and said in sterile, emotionless, perfect, educated Spanish, "I can't take that man in my ambulance. He'll get it dirty." For a second I saw what I thought was a look of disgust in his eyes. Then he went and climbed back in and sat down behind the wheel. Without looking at us again, he started up his van and drove away.

I had thought it was over, my part at least. I thought the ambulance would take him away and save him. But now, instead, I had to stand and grab the man and pull him up and tell him we had to walk. I wasn't sure if he could walk but I told him that he could and I made him start walking up the street. We struggled, and limped, and pulled each other up the street. It felt like it took hours.

I honestly think it would have been difficult to tell which one of us was hurt and bleeding by the time we made it to a little first aid room at the top of the street. I pushed and pleaded until the man was finally leaning on a flimsy wooden counter waiting for someone to come and admit him. After what seemed like forever, the man who had been driving the ambulance walked in from a back room and smiled as though the whole scene had never happened. He greeted me without any emotion, as though I hadn't just been staring at him in disbelief a few minutes ago down the street. He handed me a form to fill out for the injured man, but I didn't know anything about him. So I made up a name and wrote it on there and handed it back across the flimsy counter. He took the form from me and then he looked up at the beaten man as if this was all a big inconvenience. It was a look of pity, not for the pain, but for something else I could not understand. Then he ordered the beaten man to go over to a cot that was against the wall and sit down.

I left and went and sat down on the little step outside my room where it led out to the street. I sat there in the hot sun with this man's life all over me. My white shirt was dark red now and I remember thinking how odd it was that I really felt nothing. I couldn't move off the step, though. I was sure that something was probably wrong with me because, except for being at the very limits of what a person should have to bear, I felt almost bored.

The man I had helped died that night, right there on the cot in that first aid stand with the unhelpful ambulance driver there to clean up.

NINETEEN

Baby Blessing

Late one evening I was sitting on the front step of my room somewhere deep in Central America. The night was balmy, still hot, even though the daytime had slipped away and a heavy darkness had taken its place. I was sitting there with the creaky wooden door open behind me so the light from inside could shine through onto the pages of a small book I was flipping through. I had been stationed in this very small town for two months. It was my task to try to talk to people and, if they were interested, share a message of hope. I thought it would be accepted pretty well in the highlands of Guatemala where everything was so difficult for people. But we had knocked on every door in town in the first week, trying to get people to come to our little church. I had spoken to the *alcalde* or mayor of the town; I'd invited the priest of the local Catholic church; I'd gone to one of the local schools and invited the *directora* or principal of the school. We had talked to everyone and nothing was working.

One day I had the idea to eat breakfast at the small family-owned cafeteria and then walk out along one of the muddy, steamy trails that led out of town to the *fincas* or large coffee plantations. I would walk with another missionary for hours on these trails talking about home, or our favorite songs, or anything really to pass the time. We passed a lot of people each day who were walking the other direction into town. They were Mayan people mostly, balancing water, or wood, or food, in big baskets or buckets on their heads.

I had learned how to greet them in their own ancient dialects from the local midwife in town, Hermana Poncio. She taught me to say, if it was a woman, "*Sacaric nan!*" which meant something like "Good morning, ma'am." If it was a man I was to say "*Sacaric tat!*" Every time I would say this to an Indian woman on the trail, they would look up wide-eyed like I had surprised them. I'm sure I looked out of place to them with my blond hair now almost white from being exposed to the burning sun each day and my short-sleeved white shirt glowing almost as brightly in the hot sun as my hair. We also wore ties, which I don't think most people had ever seen on anyone else in their whole lives.

One morning, I was walking up a trail on a hill. Near the top there was a short, extremely old Mayan woman. She was standing at the top of a hill resting for a minute. She could not have been over five feet tall. She was dressed in typical Mayan clothing with a brightly embroidered *huipil* (blouse). I guessed she had to be at least eighty years old by the way she walked. She was a little bow-legged and limped like my grandpa did when he was out in the pasture feeding the sheep. She stood there catching her breath with a big plastic jug balanced on top of her head. It was full of what I guessed must have been water that she was taking back to her village.

I walked up, also a bit short of breath from climbing up the hill on the opposite side. When I reached the top I stood there for a moment and I nodded to her. She just looked back at me. I said, "*Sacaric nan.*" She nodded back and said, "*Sacaric tat.*" She didn't move. She just looked at me. I couldn't tell if she was angry or just cautious, the way she stood and looked at me, blank, without emotion, still catching her breath. I smiled, and as I did I remembered another short phrase someone had taught me to say in her language. I can't remember it now, all these years later, but I nodded and said it to her.

She continued staring, emotionless for just a moment. Then slowly she began to smile. She looked at me a little perplexed but she could not keep the smile away as she looked at me half confused and half amused. Then, with the big container of water still up on her head, she began to laugh. She didn't say anything; she just started to quietly smile and laugh. I was not only unsure what I had said to this Guatemalan grandmother, but I also had no idea how to respond. She couldn't stop laughing and my surprised or confused look seemed to make her laugh even harder.

Soon she leaned her head forward a bit between roaring, cackling, gasping laughter, and she grabbed hold of the big plastic bucket on her head and hefted it off and put it on the ground next to her. Once it was safely on the ground, she held her stomach and she leaned back and really began to belt out loud, sustained laughter like she couldn't have stopped if she had wanted to. I smiled a weak smile and then turned and walked down the hill in front of me. I could hear her still laughing as I walked away. In fact, after several more ups and downs on the trail, I stopped and I looked way back. I could see her still laughing, pointing me out to some others on the trail from all the way across the countryside. They all looked like they were laughing too. I wondered what I could have said. On my way back home in the afternoon, I half expected them all to still be there with the old lady leaning on her plastic pot of water telling everyone who passed by about the skinny, blond missionary and whatever it was I had said.

That night, I was having dinner with the Poncio family. Hermana Poncio was more than just a midwife. She helped people when they were sick or injured. As far as I could tell, she was the heart of this community. She kept in touch, knew everyone, and when she could she helped them. People loved Hermana Poncio. She sat across from me at an old wooden table her husband had made from scraps at his job cutting lumber. I sat on a woven hammock they stretched across the other side of the table whenever visitors came. I told her about the old woman on the trail and how she'd laughed so hard and so long at what I had said. Hermana Poncio smiled and then she laughed too. She asked me to repeat the phrase. When I did she looked over quickly at her husband and they both smiled and then started laughing too. When she caught her breath she said something like, "No...you did not say that?" I told her I had said those exact words and she leaned over the old table and told me that I'd said that the old Mayan grandma I'd met on the trail was a "very desirable woman." I turned a little red and then finally I laughed too.

A week or so later, late in the afternoon, I had sat down to eat dinner at a family-owned cafe on the other side of the same small town. I was a few blocks away from the Poncio family's little homestead out in the jungle. I remember I sat down at a picnic style table. They had a red and white-checkered vinyl tablecloth that stuck to my sweaty arms when I rested them on it. A young boy who I assumed was one the sons of the cafe's owners brought me a plateful of black beans and rice. There was a small piece of cooked beef or pork and some tortillas I was sure they had formed by hand back in the kitchen. It smelled good.

I picked up my fork and I leaned over the plate and breathed it in for a second. I'd been working hard and I was hungry. Just as I was about to scoop up a big mouthful of beans, a very large spider whose legs reached out to about the size of a silver dollar lowered itself down on an invisible line from the ceiling and landed right on top of the meat in the center of my plate. It landed, and then stood there like it was on watch against an unseen insect enemy. It was erect and unmoving. It had successfully taken the highest ground on my plate. I sat up in my chair and then I looked around to see if anyone else noticed. If they did notice, then they didn't think it was a big deal. They all just kept on eating and talking. I didn't think I should have to deal with a great big spider standing right on top of my food. I was sure, when I pointed it out, the people who owned the place would be horrified and they would fix me a new plate. It seemed reasonable.

I stood up and waved at the young boy who had been waiting on me. He smiled and came over and stood by me wondering what I needed. He was looking at me, though, and did not notice the spider standing guard on top of my food. The spider was ugly and strange, with a grey balloon-like abdomen and eight spindly legs. It stood there on my dinner, looking dangerous. I pointed down at the creature on my plate. As soon as the young boy saw the spider there, he shrugged and reached down with his fingers and grabbed it, rolled it up into a death ball, and flicked it out the front door of the café, and then he walked away.

The spider was gone. The food was still warm. The boy was satisfied. It was breathtaking, how efficiently he had handled the whole thing, and he was probably very happy with the fine spider removal service he'd done for me. I wasn't sure what to do next. I looked down at my plate and wondered if there could be some residual spider goo that ended up on my meal. I couldn't see any and, although it was one of the biggest spiders I'd seen in a long time, it didn't seem big enough to damage the food. I was, after all, very hungry. I thought about it for a second and figured that, if the boy could pick it up with his bare hands and roll it up in a ball with his fingers and flick it calmly away from my table, then the spider probably presented no real threat. So I picked up my fork and started eating.

After dinner, I sat down on the little concrete step facing out to the cobblestones of the main road through town, my back to our front door. I was flipping through the pages of a book I was reading hoping the light from inside the room, if I sat just right and bent the book a certain way, would illuminate what I was trying to read. It was a delicate effort, as the light over my shoulder from the house battled with the darkness out on the street. I was tired. Even though it was dark by then, it was still uncomfortably hot. The air was still and black outside my room. Once in a while I would hear a dog barking or moaning from some closed in place off in the distance. I read and wiped sweat from my forehead. I tried to just sit and rest and un-clutter my mind. It was hard to do. I worried about our efforts in that town. I wondered if I was doing my best. I felt like I should do more but I could not figure out how. It seemed like nobody was interested in what we had to say.

I had tried everything I could think of—I even showed movies outside in the dark on the side of the Catholic church across the street from where I lived. I ran an extension cord from somewhere in the church and borrowed a movie projector once when I went into Guatemala City. I sat out in the courtyard with the priest and a small crowd and watched church movies in the night. But nobody wanted to know anything more after the movie was over. They just stood up and left. That's when I asked the priest if he would like to come over to our place for church on Sunday. He smiled and then told me he couldn't. He was always too busy on Sundays.

I sat on the step in the night and tried to read my book, but either the weak light from our little room was dimming or the darkness outside was getting stronger, and it was getting harder to see the pages. Right then, between the light and the dark, I heard two young boys running toward me. They were hurried and frantic. When they came close I could see that they both looked pained, like something urgent and dangerous was going on. They were Mayan boys. One of them I recognized as the boy who had broken his arm playing tops. They pleaded with me to follow and asked if I could come and pray with a family. Someone was very sick in their village, they said.

I pushed myself up and threw my book into the room and followed these two boys into the darkness. I'd never gone the way they were taking us that night. I ran hard and followed them behind the big Catholic church and then down a slippery muddy path through the jungle. We scrambled through overgrown areas with big leaves that were heavy from rain that slapped at us as we ran. I could barely keep up. After a few minutes we stopped at Hermana Poncio's little wooden hut in the jungle. It seemed like we'd cheated time somehow. I guess the boys had taken us a faster way that only kids their age knew.

There was a big group of Mayan men and women there. They were agitated and talking like I'd never heard. They were anxious and there was anguish and pressure in the air like something serious was happening. The boys slipped into the little house through the wooden opening to the family's main room and I stepped in behind them. The ceiling was made of branches pieced and nailed together to hold up the roofing outside. It was a low ceiling and I had to duck my head when I entered. When I did, Hermana Poncio hurried across the room to me. The room was a mess and people— Indian people—were crying and holding onto each other. Everyone was in some kind of pain.

It was then, when I stepped into the room and they all looked up at me, that I realized they were looking to me for something. Hermana Poncio looked up at me like I was her last option. I stood there quietly trying to figure out what was going on, when Hermana Poncio introduced me to a young couple. They were weary and the woman was almost unable to stand. Her husband stood beside her and looked like he hoped I could do something to help. Hermana Poncio slipped away for a second and came back with a baby girl in her arms. The baby wasn't moving. She held out her arms to give me the baby and asked me to pray for her. She told the couple that a miracle could happen—that *I* could make a miracle happen. I closed my eyes and took the lifeless body of this little infant in my arms and held her close to me. I was alone amongst people who could barely understand me, holding the body of this infant in my arms. Everyone in the room was waiting and hoping for what I would do next.

The truth was I had no idea what to do next. I was nineteen years old. I'd never even seen a baby that had died. I was pretty sure that in the Bible there were stories about how Jesus had once brought people back from the dead. Of course, He was the Son of God. I was a missionary. I was a pretty good one, too, but I was completely unprepared for this. But I had to do something—I couldn't just stand there.

The mother and father looked at me like they believed I could actually bring their child back to life.

I didn't know what happened to the baby or why it had died. Perhaps, if I'd known about it beforehand, I could have bought medicine that they could not afford and given it to them, and the little girl might have survived. Everyone was staring at me hunched over holding the child in this dimly lit room wishing, hoping that I could perform some kind of a miracle. I felt the dead little baby's lifeless weight in my arms. I looked down at her. She looked like she was asleep but I knew she was not.

It was difficult to speak, but I bowed my head and I prayed. I didn't pray for a miracle like everyone wanted and was waiting for, though. I prayed instead for comfort. I meant it with all my heart when I asked God to bless these people and help them to find a way to survive this night. I hoped that they would be able to be happy again one day. I hoped that I would too. I prayed with all the intensity and fervor that was in me. I wanted to pray for a miracle. I wished I could have, but I didn't. I finished and I said Amen and everyone in the room started crying and holding each other. I moved over closer to the baby's parents and I held their little baby out to them. They took her and held her and it felt like everyone everywhere was crying. I turned to the little girl's mother and I looked into her eyes and I felt like I had failed.

It was hard to go on as usual and have the same interest in my days after that night. Maybe I didn't have what it took to be an exceptional missionary. Maybe, when it came right down to it, there was some kind of a hole in my faith. Maybe life was just flat out hard and unexplainable sometimes. The experience was hard to even think about; it hurt me in my soul. There were years in my life when I thought about it every day. That night, though, I went back and sat down in the sliver of light on my front step and cried.

TWENTY

Bottle Caps

On a cloudy day months later, I ducked into an old bus on a dirt road in a part of Guatemala City that was decidedly past its prime. The road we were on was rutted and dirty. There were bottle caps that had been dropped on the ground over the years by drunks as they left a nearby cantina. The caps had been mashed into the dirt by hundreds of thousands of buses and taxis as days and months and years came and went.

I was twenty years old and I used to, on occasion, try to pry an imbedded bottle cap up out of the pounded road and dig the dirt and gunk out of the inside of it and flip it into the air with a motion like I was snapping my fingers. I got pretty good at bottle cap flipping, that is when I could find a clean enough one. They would spin like tiny Frisbees with a flick of my fingers and arc up and away from me into the air only to bounce down on the dirt road to get stomped on and beat back down into the dirt somewhere else.

The road was lined with block-wall houses painted bright colors that had long since started to crumble and fade. There was a man standing on the concrete sidewalk. Every day he had a new clump of plantains. They were green and claw-like and they hung upside-down in the air from a small metal rack. I never bought one from him. I never even spoke to him. People, mostly women, would approach, give him a couple of small coins and he'd pull a long gun-metal grey machete from his belt and he'd chop a bunch of plantains away from the clump and make the exchange. There were people selling, among other things, black beans by the bag, meat, or produce. They set up folding card tables right there on the sidewalk and sold their goods.

This was a residential area, several blocks away from the bustling retail and business part of Guatemala City where every store window had a mannequin with tight blue jeans and stiletto heels like Olivia Newton John wore in the movie *Grease*. Bee Gees music pumped out of giant black speakers from, it seemed, every single store. The area where I sat that day, in the back of an old bus, was a quieter but more desperate part of Guatemala City. Sometimes I felt like this area was crying or something, like it had been beaten down into the ground just like the bottle caps around the cantina.

It was in this area that a skinny, hollow man we were teaching had shown me multiple scars on his arms that he said were from him cutting himself. He said he wasn't trying to kill himself or anything. He was just trying to see how it felt. I bought him a plate of steaming beans and scrambled eggs and then stood a little bit away and watched him try to find someone he could sell them to so he could buy glue to sniff out of an ugly plastic bag.

One day as dusk was falling I sat with another man who had sores on his arms and bare feet. The only light in the room was from a long, white candle he'd lit and stuck by its own wax on a tin plate. He looked around like someone might be listening and then he leaned in close to me. His eyes were glassy and unfocused as he asked if I believed in the ghost of *Siguanaba*. He said that there was a legend down there about a woman named Siguanaba who would wander around at night crying and washing clothes in the river. He said that she was so miserable and ugly that if I saw her and looked into her face, I would freeze from fright and turn to stone. I was pretty sure I didn't believe in Siguanaba, but the thought of her, and him with his sores, and the candlelight—it was all very creepy. The image of this hideous, frightening ghost haunting these poor people in Guatemala clung to me, though, as if she might appear to me at any moment around the next darkened, bottle cap-strewn street.

I never saw Siguanaba and I was pretty sure I never would. I believed that she was more of a place for people to hang their fear than she was a real being. Maybe, though, it was Siguanaba who was responsible for the *desaparacidos*. Maybe it was she who grabbed these poor young people from their families without a word and snuck them away into the darkness, never to be seen again. Maybe it wasn't the government of Guatemala, desperately trying to control things. Maybe it was a cruel, miserable, frightening ghost who caused all of the misfortune in this town—misfortune that was everywhere. Maybe it *was* Siguanaba at the heart of it all. I'd seen people shot and others hit by cars. I'd bumped into candlelight vigils for young people cut down by government guns without ever knowing why, almost like it was sport to their assassins. Then again, maybe it *wasn't* Siguanaba. Maybe it was just anger, or competition, or greed, or selfishness all piled into the hearts of people who had guns. Maybe it was just ruthless, unfeeling, cold-hearted men who would just as soon kill a person as leave him alone. Maybe it was the fact that some people, a very few, had everything they needed and many others, millions in fact, didn't even have enough to feed themselves or their families.

In truth, I knew it wasn't Siguanaba causing all the misfortune I saw around me. It was just that there was too little for too many people, and it made the ones who had everything do whatever it took to keep it. Sometimes if they didn't have help, the little people, the ones with no say so, would get caught up in things and get overpowered by wheels that had been put in motion a long time before. They'd end up diseased, bent, hurt beyond repair—or even dead. I was frightened, too. Not for my own safety, but for the general sense of abrupt, matter-of-fact, unflinching evil that was out there, like Siguanaba, lurking behind the next corner or down the next alley.

That cloudy day I climbed onto the bus and sat in the back row with my knees pressed up on the metal back of the bench seat in front of me. I leaned on the little window and looked out at the people selling their goods. I saw people sitting, some of them, in their doorways, just waiting for the days to pass. As the bus I was on moved slowly forward down the bumpy, rutted road, I saw a man carrying a large package awkwardly under his arm as he balanced on an old bicycle, up ahead on our right. The package was a big one, and though it didn't look heavy; it was awkward and the old man struggled to ride and balance and carry his load. The package was important—I could see that. I couldn't tell if what he was carrying had any real value, but he was being very careful not to drop it. He teetered quietly along the road on his rusty bicycle until he came to a corner where he stopped and waited so he could cross the busy street. I don't know why I focused on him but I sat in the back of the bus and kept looking as he waited at the corner to move on. Our bus rolled up next to him, belching and spitting out black smelly exhaust as the driver coaxed it forward.

Now, we were at the corner and I was looking down out of the window at the man on the bike. The bus started to turn right onto the next street. As it did, the gap between the bus and the raised concrete sidewalk narrowed. As the bus continued to turn, the gap between it and the sidewalk narrowed even more. At first, the man on the bicycle with the big package under his arm didn't notice that he was right there in that narrowing gap. I noticed, though, and started banging on my window. The man was just below me now as I tried to get his attention. The bus never once even hesitated. It lumbered slowly, mercilessly ahead and to the right.

Exhaust from the bus choked the air as the driver downshifted to take the corner. There was a sick, cold grinding sound as the gears struggled to lock in. More smoke billowed from the exhaust. The old man on the bike looked up almost too late to see that the bus was going to overtake him. I was looking down on the top of his head out of my window when, at the very last second, he jumped off the bike with the package still balanced under his right arm. He grabbed hold of the stub of an old post with his free hand and somehow yanked himself up onto the sidewalk to safety. As he did this, his bicycle lost its direction and fell under the back wheel of the bus and got twisted and mashed into the road just like one of the bottle caps, another victim of Siguanaba's wrath.

The bus was so big and heavy and the bicycle was so small that I couldn't feel any bump at all when we rolled over it. I don't think the driver, or anyone else for that matter, had any idea what had happened. As the bus turned the corner and pushed down another street, I twisted around to look out the back window and I could see the owner of the bicycle trying to lift the mangled bicycle up from the mud. He was shaking his fist in the air at our bus. No one on the bus cared or even knew that we'd just nearly ruined or possibly killed this man, but I did. I saw it. I was a small part of it, too, because I was on the bus that did it and I didn't do anything about it. I just sat there and let the bus take me wherever it was going.

My time as a missionary in Guatemala was an adventure all right. It was beautiful and completely one hundred percent foreign. It was ancient, and stubborn, and hot, and smelly and full of things I had to fight to understand. It was at the same time warm and comfortable. I was starting to see that it could also be dangerous and cold-hearted. All of it is now part of me. I've tried hard to forget some of the things I saw there, but I can't. I've learned over the years that I don't want to. A part of me still feels a little like Guatemala is home.

TWENTY-ONE

Mission Ends

In the fall of 1979 my mission ended. My two years were up. My mother and father flew to Guatemala City to pick me up and have me show them some of the places I'd worked and some of the people I'd met. The day they flew in, I went to the airport and waited for them next to a window where I could look in and see arriving passengers as they stepped into the airport and then waited in a long line to clear customs. I remember standing there and watching through the window when Mom and Dad came into the room.

I felt something intensely comfortable and familiar inside me when I first saw them enter the building and join the customs line. It was something I hadn't felt in a long time. They couldn't see me where I was standing on the other side of the room, but I couldn't look away. It seemed to take forever as they moved up to the front of the line.

I was a little surprised because they looked the same to me. I don't know what I was expecting, but for me, two monumental years had passed since I'd seen them last, and I guess I expected them to look older or somehow changed. I felt as though I was in one of those time travel movies where you go back into the past for months or years, and then you squeeze back through a wormhole and find when you get back to the present that no time has passed at all, or that just a minute or two have gone by. Mom and Dad looked like no time had passed for them, and the way they walked and greeted people just felt right—it felt like home. I could feel myself breathing easier just seeing them. I knew that I had changed forever during the two years since they'd seen me last, and I wondered if they would notice.

I could feel myself becoming a little less guarded, more like I was back home, than I had at any time since I stepped off the plane in Guatemala two years before. These two years seemed like forever in some ways, and I found it difficult to know how to think about my experience, how to feel about it, or how to remember it. Parts of it had been beautiful, touching, and truly incredible. But other parts had been hard, very hard. It's funny how the good parts and the difficult parts were both tender and scary to me. I couldn't even start to sort them out that day at the airport. Sorting them out would take years.

When Dad and Mom finally made it through customs and walked over, they stopped in front of me for a second and they both smiled at me. Then Mom grabbed me and hugged me. I smiled too, and a wave of relief that I'd been holding back for a long time swept over me. I got all choked up. She put her hands on my shoulders and held me there with her arms out straight. She looked me over. Then she frowned a little and said, "You are so skinny!" Dad put his arm around me and we walked out to the curb. Honestly, I hadn't noticed that I had lost any weight. I don't think I'd ever weighed myself the whole time I was in Guatemala.

I walked up to a taxi in front of the airport and asked the driver how much he would charge to take us to the Hotel El Camino Real where we were staying while Mom and Dad were in town. He looked up at me from his seat and answered like he didn't care. I told him he was much too expensive and I started walking toward another cab. As soon as I started walking away, the cabbie jumped out of his car, hurried up behind me and immediately dropped his price. I stopped and turned and we discussed the price in Spanish for a minute or two. He started to pick up Mom's suitcase but I told him to put it down. I knew that if he picked up the suitcase and put it in the trunk of his car, we would have to go with him. He just looked at me with the suitcase in his hand as I—almost shouting now—told him we had to agree on a price first. He didn't want to let go of Mom's suitcase but I told him firmly to put it down. He set it down next to Mom and then we agreed on how much the cab fare to the hotel would be. I nodded and then he grabbed Mom and Dad's luggage and put it in the trunk, and we all got into the taxi.

    I remember Dad staring at me looking confused for a few seconds while I climbed into the front passenger seat and the driver pulled out onto Avenida Reforma, a traffic-choked avenue in the heart of the city. The cabbie took us around a busy traffic circle. It felt normal to me but Mom and Dad's eyes widened as he honked, shifted and maneuvered in and out of traffic and over to our hotel. Dad said something about how he'd noticed that I'd been able to negotiate with the cab driver. He said he was really impressed. It was nice that he had noticed, but I knew it was just the tip of the iceberg in terms of things I could do and ways I had changed. Negotiating with a cab driver was merely child's play compared to all the ways I had grown, ways I could not then even begin to comprehend.

    A day or so later, I was showing them around Guatemala City near the Parque Central where the giant, pale green National Palace and the huge Catholic cathedral are. I was showing them how to get a shoeshine from one of the young boys that hung out with their wooden shoe shine boxes full of inks, dyes, and pastes. We were standing at a corner near the entrance to the cathedral and I was explaining that there was scaffolding all around the cathedral because it was still being repaired from the horrible earthquake that had shaken the whole country years before. For a second, as I was talking, I felt lightheaded, like the whole day was just getting to be too much for me. I had been on my guard for a long, long time and my body, whether or not I wanted it to, was starting to ease up and relax. But it was much more than that. I felt tired and weak or even a bit ill. I looked around for a place to sit down but I couldn't see one. I put my hand up on a brick wall in front of a store because I felt like my knees might buckle. I leaned on the wall for a minute and blinked my eyes and shook my head. Then I looked up at Mom and Dad, who were worried, and I asked them if it would be all right if we went back to our hotel so I could lie down and rest.

I tried to tell them I was okay but, honestly, I was scared. We walked back to our rental car and I sat down in the back seat and closed my eyes. It was as if my body had suddenly realized that my mission was over, and it had begun to shut itself off or relax somewhere deep down inside, like I had a sudden drop of blood pressure. It was real, too. Although it was only midafternoon, I felt exhausted, and I knew that my day was over.

I fell asleep in the back seat on the way back. I have no idea how my dad figured out how to make it through all the honking and traffic back to our hotel. After we arrived I stumbled down the hall to our room and laid down on one of the beds.

About 9 a.m. the next morning I woke up; I'd been sleeping for many hours. My dad heard me rustling around and he came over next to me, sat down, and asked me if I felt well enough to get a bite to eat and talk about things. I felt awkward and self-conscious, but hungry too. I hadn't talked directly to my father about anything important for at least two years. I knew he was proud of me and my time in Guatemala, and I knew he loved me. I could also see his concern. He had never been a member of my church, and I didn't want him to get a bad impression of it. I worried that if I told him everything that I'd gone through, he might.

We ordered breakfast; I think he'd already eaten. He ordered a cup of black coffee and I ordered some scrambled eggs and black beans. We sat there for a minute and then he said, "So Peter—what's going on?" I could see concern on his face and I could tell that he was asking a serious question.

A part of me wanted to completely lay it all out and tell him everything that had happened. I wanted to tell him about *Siguanaba* and about the horrible moments I'd had with the Poncio family up in Chicacao. I wanted to tell him about the poverty. I was mad, too, at stupid, flaky missionaries I'd known whose families had made them come on missions, and how they spent their time goofing off and breaking the rules. My mission had been hard, and it bothered me that other missionaries seemed to be just playing around. As my mind raced though images of the last two years, I knew also that part of me loved my mission. I had grown up and gotten stronger and learned to speak Spanish, living among the tough, stubborn, noble, beaten down people in towns like Santa Lucia and Chicacao and Gualán. I wanted to tell him how proud I was of my efforts. But another rogue part of me felt secretly, almost over-poweringly, ashamed, like I had in some way failed. This was all tangled up inside of me and I didn't know where to begin. If I shared my bruised, insider view of this amazing, difficult, threatening, dangerous experience, how would he react? Would he ever think well of the church? Would he think well of me? I was still a missionary, at least until I got home, and it was important for me that he like the church.

He just sat and watched me shoveling down my breakfast like I was starving. Maybe if I ate fast enough I wouldn't have to talk about things. He waited, I am sure, wondering what was making me tired and worn out. I didn't say anything at first. I just sat there. Then I remember deciding that he was my father and that he wanted to know about my experiences out of concern and love, so I decided to tell him everything that was on my mind. I told him how some missionaries were great but some were lazy, and some tried to wiggle their way into leadership positions by manipulating or lying. I told him how I almost got in a fight with one of them one day. I had said some bad things that I really didn't mean and I let my own anger get the best of me. I told him about how hard it was and how much I'd tried to be a good missionary, and how I'd seen people die after they'd been right next to me. I told him how unbearably hot it was on the coast and about the poverty. I talked until my voice got all choked up and my heart was pounding and I didn't feel like I could talk any longer.

He reached across the table and put his hand on mine and he told me it was going to be okay. Then my dad, who has no religion that he adheres to and who describes himself as "agnostic," said, "Peter, here's my advice." I looked at him hoping he could somehow tell me something to restore my faith in the world, and in the church, and in myself.

"First off, these things about some missionaries working harder than others, or lying, or cheating, or promoting themselves to get ahead—well, you are just going to have to figure that one out. It happens everywhere. It's definitely not unique to your mission. It will happen at school. It happens in business. You'll see that one for the rest of your life, and you're just going to have to figure out a way to deal with it."

He paused and thought for a minute and then said, "Second, and this is important: all of these things, everything you've told me about your time here, it doesn't have anything to do with what you believe. They were hard things you went through, but you'll be okay and, if you believe this Peter, you go for it!"

He told me not to tie all of the confusion, pain and trauma I'd experienced to my faith in God. The many challenges of my mission in Guatemala had been difficult to think about because I had twisted them all up with what I believed as a missionary and as a young man. The things I had experienced were threatening and scary for me in many ways, but in that one thoughtful comment, my dad enabled me to think about all of it without the sting and without the pain.

That day, at that table in the little restaurant in the lobby of the Hotel El Camino Real, I decided that I would move ahead anyway. It's okay to believe, I decided, even when it's hard. In fact, that's when it's the most important. To me, that's what faith really is.

TWENTY-TWO

Pheasant Hunting

This story begins with a friend of mine named Hod. One day he told me that he loved to hunt, but more specifically, he said he loved *pheasant hunting*. It was an off-hand comment. I could have ignored it. I was sure that Hod would not have believed me if I told him about how my uncle owned a pheasant hunting ranch in Utah and that I thought I could get him to open it for us one day so we could do some hunting. I am sure that in Hod's mind the words *hunt*, or *pheasant*, or any kind of gun were not in any way associated with anything he knew about me.

Hod has been a friend for many years. He owns a concrete construction company that builds the dividers that go in between the lanes of traffic on freeways throughout Southern California. I guess things are going well because he drives a nice car and lives in a good area with lots of people who are between young and old, like Hod and me, and live in attractive houses with green lawns and big backyards. Hod mentioned the pheasant-hunting thing almost as an afterthought. We were at a church social and our wives were talking and he said something about how he was a bit tired because he had just driven a long way back from a day of hunting. It was an innocent sort of ice-breaking conversational moment. I could have taken it a million ways. I could have talked about driving long distances. I could have asked where he had driven from. I could have asked what he was hunting. But, as I popped some candy covered popcorn into my mouth that the church activities committee had laid out on the table, I said, "Oh, hey Hod, I have an uncle who owns a pheasant hunting ranch. If you ever want to go to Utah and do some pheasant hunting, let me know." With that, I bit down into the popcorn. Hod looked at me with reverence, like I had performed some kind of a miracle, and he said something like, "Definitely! Sign me up!"

I hadn't spoken to my uncle for about ten or maybe even fifteen years. I was going to explain this to Hod but he had locked in like a hunting dog does when it sees a bird out in the field. I could tell by looking at him that I was going to have to try to set something up. The very next day on my way into work I scanned through the contacts in my phone looking for my uncle Jay Russell's phone number. It wasn't there but there was a number for his sister, Kay Marie. Now, it had been even longer since I had spoken to Kay Marie, but I couldn't shake this picture in my head of how excited Hod had gotten since I bragged about my cowboy uncle Jay Russell. So, I dialed up Kay Marie's number. It was early in the morning but there is an hour time difference between California and Utah, so I thought she might be available and I gave it a try.

When Kay Marie answered and I recognized her voice, I felt like I was ten years old again. She has the same twang or accent that my mom did whenever we were in Payson for longer than a day or two when I was a boy in the 1960s. "Hello!" she demanded. In the true language of Payson, one says hello as if you are a little annoyed with the emphasis on the first syllable. It's like a statement, not a question. Kay speaks Payson, Utah with the fluency of a real insider who has never lived anywhere else. "Kay?" I responded, "This is Peter Nielsen." I was about to explain that my mom was her step sister but I couldn't get a fragment of another word in.

"Who?!" she yelled through the phone. "It's Peter...Marilyn Oldroyd's son." There was silence on the other end of the phone for a few minutes as she was putting this all together. Then her tone softened and she said (also in perfect Payson-speak), "Peter, well...bless your heart!" I told her I was trying to get in touch with her brother Jay but I had lost his phone number. "Well, shore" (which translates to *well, sure*), "I've got it here somewhere." She rummaged around a little and then came up with the number. "You heard Jay's house burned down didn't you?" "No," I said with a concerned tone. She just said, "It did." Then she gave the number. I think she said "bless your heart" a few more times and then we hung up.

I remembered Kay Marie's voice and it sounded familiar the second she started talking, but thinking about Jay Russell was a completely different level of remembrance. I'd spent every summer of my youth following him around and riding shotgun in his pickup truck, but it had been a long time since I'd talked to him. I'd grown up and I had a family now, with children and grandchildren, even. I wondered, as I looked down at the phone, if he would remember things the same way I did. He had to be at least 65 years old by now. I knew that after my grandfather died, Jay Russell had ended up with the pasture land down by West Mountain. I'd been out to see him a while back and it was fun. But I got busy, and he did too. Too much time had passed since I'd contacted him.

I had heard somewhere that he'd been living with his wife, Jane, and their three children down at the pasture in a house he built. It was no surprise to me that he could build his own house. Someone told me that one of Jay's sons had gone to Utah State University and studied to be a large animal veterinarian. That was no surprise either. I don't know who told me, but I'd also heard that he'd studied up and applied for a demolition license. The story I heard was that he passed all the tests and got the license, and a few months after that 9/11 happened and the State of Utah made it much harder to get an explosives license. Somehow Jay Russell had one, though. I hoped his new-found abilities with explosives had nothing to do with his house burning down.

I was on my way to work that day. I had arrived at Union Station in Los Angeles and I was walking to the little shuttle that taxis a group of us from the train station to our office every morning. I remember I sat down in a courtyard there and dialed the number Kay Marie had given me. It rang a few times and then, with the same annoyed-sounding twang as his sister's, he half shouted, "Hello!" "Jay?" I said, "It's Peter Nielsen." I don't know why but I waited for a second before I said anything else. Before I could add anything, Jay Russell laughed out loud and said, "Peter? Well you just made my day! What are you doing? Are you up here in Payson?"

I smiled. It was Jay Russell all right. It's amazing how, even though I hadn't spoken to him for ten or fifteen years, the minute we started talking it felt like zero time had passed since I was riding around with him in his truck. It was the same voice I remembered, laughing and talking at me through my cell phone. He said he was "jus' goin' up to the pasture to check on some things" and he wondered why I was calling him. I told him about Hod and how excited he was when I told him I had an uncle who had a pheasant hunting ranch. Jay said they didn't operate the ranch anymore, unless I wanted to come up. He told me to wait until the season in November and call him back then and they'd open it back up. He said they would definitely put something together for us.

Months passed, and to be honest, I probably would have forgotten to set something up except that I would see Hod at church every Sunday. I knew he was one hundred percent on board with the idea. I stopped him once in the hallway and told him about my conversation with Jay Russell. He said he and his sons and his hunting dogs were ready whenever I called him, once the season was open. November did finally roll around and Hod was still as excited as ever. My son Jeff, and my son-in-law Alden were both on board too. When I called my other son-in-law, Thomas, who lives with Sara in St. George, Utah, I asked him if he would like to go pheasant hunting with us. Tom just said, "Freak yeah!"

So, it was set. After a few discussions, we settled on Jeff, Alden, Tom and me staying together up in Provo and driving down and meeting Hod and his son, Mitchell, and Mitchell's wife Alexis at a McDonald's near the Payson exit on Interstate 15. Hod had been up in Idaho hunting with a mutual friend named Matt. Matt came with Hod and brought his daughter, who was in her first semester at BYU.

So that was the cast of characters on our end. I was a little uneasy. I'd never been to a real pheasant hunting ranch and I wasn't sure if this one would meet with Hod's elevated expectations. Jay met us in his truck at a parking lot next door to the McDonalds and we followed him on the same route I took as a boy, out of town, down the dirt roads, to the pasture, with gravel spitting out behind our rental car. I hadn't been on this old road for an extremely long time, but somehow it seemed like I was there just yesterday. I couldn't tell where my grandpa's old piece of land was situated, mostly because I had never paid attention when I was riding in the back of his truck. I was sure, though, that when I saw it I would know it.

We followed Jay down the road. It had seemed so far away and such a long trip when I was a boy, but we'd only been following for a minute or two when Jay turned off of the skinny road onto a double rutted dirt path. I recognized it immediately as the spot where Grandpa used to whistle or yell at me from the cab of his truck and I would jump down and unlatch the gate. I drove our Nissan Versa compact rental car onto the pasture land and I said something like, "Okay guys, welcome to my childhood!" I was only partly right, though. This was the exact same spot where I'd helped corral the cattle and feed the sheep, but it was clear that a lot had gone on in the intervening years. There was a giant new barn standing out in the field. It was painted red and it had clearly been built with all the latest construction technology. It stood roughly where the old gray wood barn that my grandfather must have built in the early 1900s had been. I walked over and stood right where the old barn had been. Jay told me it had finally "wore out" and blew away one day in a big storm.

Jay and I walked around where the old barn had been and I thought about my grandpa and how he could whistle so loud at the animals and how the sheep sometimes ran toward his truck when he did. I thought about how many years he got up every morning and came down to this spot whether it was cold, or snowing, or raining, or anything. It was clearly the same piece of land. I could look over and see the dry, brown slopes of West Mountain or look the other way and see the tall rugged edges of Loafer Mountain and Payson Canyon. I remembered a day when I stood right there and asked my grandpa, already an old man, if he knew the names of all of the mountains and he pointed at each one and rattled them off like he didn't even need to think about it. He saw them every single day.

Everyone had gathered near the gate waiting for Jay to let us know how to get things started. I walked over by them and listened as Jay Russell started asking questions like how many people brought shotguns and how many pheasants did we think we'd need out in the field that day. Then somebody drove off to wherever you buy pheasants for hunting in Payson, Utah. Jay started telling them all about hunting and the pasture and living out there. I interrupted him and asked him if his house had burned down. He said, "It shore did, yup!" Then he said, "It wasn't because of the explosives, though!" He did tell us how he'd been asked by the state to seal up a mine over in West Mountain. He said that a young man had gotten stuck in the mine and died and they'd finally found his body and notified the family, and now they needed Jay to close it all up. I got claustrophobic just hearing about it. Next, Jay said to us, "You was probably wonderin' why there are gun safes all dented and scattered out in the field." I hadn't noticed, but there were about five or six gun safes, each one the size of a small closet, strewn about the field. He told us he'd been hired by one of the safe manufacturers to do a commercial where they blew them all up. He said that only one still worked. It was the right one, too—the safe made by the people who'd hired him to do the commercial.

The car came back and one of the people in it said they'd placed the pheasants out in the field and everything was ready. Jay immediately stopped talking and handed me a shotgun. Hod let his dogs out of the back of his truck and we started to hunt. We followed Hod's dogs all over the field. They would scamper around with their tails wagging, like I remember Jay Russell's dog Jethro doing. Jethro was a sheep dog, though, and he was best doing what he loved and what he'd been trained to do. Hod's dogs were hunting dogs; they would run around sniffing and looking at the world from their view about two feet high. Hod would bark out things like, "Get a bird!" and they would put their heads back down and get more intense. I'd be talking to Jeff or Jay Russell when one of the dogs would stop and lock his eyes on something in the brush, something we couldn't see. The dog would freeze and stare down the poor bird while the bird did everything it could to lie there, completely motionless.

In fact, pheasant hunting is pretty unfair. There are two dogs, and while one is frozen "on point" staring down a bird in the brush, the other one stops in its tracks and "honors" the other dog's find. Then (and this is the unfair part), on the day we went hunting, there were about eight people wandering around the field with shotguns, waiting for the dogs to find a bird. We would all line up next to each other and start to slowly walk toward where the dog was pointing. As we approached, the bird became more and more nervous until it would make a move and try to wiggle out of its trap by flying up into the air. Right then, all eight shotguns would rise to our eight shoulders and the guns would explode everywhere! Pellets would fly all over the place. The bird would almost always be hit and it would fall out of the sky back onto the field. Then, we would all reload and get ready for the next, while Hod "released" the dogs to go pick up the dead bird and bring it back to him. The birds never had a chance. In an effort to be totally honest, I do have to say that one pheasant was able to fly away unscathed. It was when we had just started hunting and everyone was still figuring out their guns and things like the safety that won't let you shoot unless it's switched the right way.

Mostly I enjoyed being out there with everyone. I think my gun was on safety about half the time. I'm not sure if I actually shot one bird. I was alone in my thoughts walking around in my childhood remembering calling the sheep and unlatching the gate and riding around that field on an old, gentle and very fat horse named Freckles. I kept asking Jay Russell where the old barn was or if we came in through the same gate as we used to. Jay nodded and waved me over closer to him. I was done with the hunting. It had been fun but not as fun as just walking around on this particular piece of land.

I walked over to him. He was brushing something off of his shirt and leaning on an old fence post. "Wanna blow something up?" he asked. I looked around like we were about to do something forbidden. Then, I told him I did. I really didn't want to, but I thought everyone else would like to see it. Jay said he'd put together a bomb made of "ANFO" which he told me was the same thing terrorists had used to blow up the Oklahoma City Federal Building. ANFO stood for *Ammonium Nitrate Fuel Oil*. He told me to go out in the field and he'd tape together a box of the stuff and put it down in the cow pond and we'd see how big a mess we could make.

I was now sure that I had somehow gone back in time and he was seventeen and I was ten and he was showing me how to brand a cow or shoot at a tin can or catch a fish in the irrigation ditch. We were both a lot older now but nothing had really changed. He was setting it all up so I could do it. He told me I would push the button on the switch after he yelled, "Fire in the hole!" a bunch of times. I was laughing and he was too. He got me up in a huge backhoe and he had me drive it over to where the cow pond was. When we got there, he stretched the mechanical arm out over the pond and had his son-in-law get in the little bucket above the muddy water. He said that the first time he tried to put the bomb he made in the pond, it didn't sink and "we couldn't rightly blow up a pond with the explosive resting on top of it, now could we?" I just shrugged my shoulders. We were way outside my area of expertise.

Jay had his son-in-law reach down and pick up the floating bomb and then he duct taped some muddy rocks to the outside of it. Then he put the bomb back down onto the pond where it immediately sank. I was about 50 yards away hiding under the upside down larger metal bucket of the backhoe. It was just about dusk when I heard Jay talking to the police department about how they should not worry if they heard or felt a big explosion or if they got any calls about it. He said he was just blowing up the cow pond for his nephew. Then he ran out near the pond and shouted, "Fire in the hole; fire in the hole; fire in the hole; fire in the hole!" He shouted for me to push the button.

I did, and for a second nothing happened. Then, well, I don't think I can adequately describe what happened next, but I'll try. Mud, rocks and water boomed upward more than 100 feet into the darkening sky. A second later, great blobs and splats of mud and manure and water from the pond were landing with great thuds all over the field.

I heard a monumental cry of joy and happiness from the rest of the people there that day. I stepped out from under the bucket of the backhoe and, when I did, everyone cheered again. I could not have been more popular had I been the MVP of the Super Bowl. They all came running to me like I had done something monumental, something worthy of adulation. I half expected them to lift me up on their shoulders and carry me to a nonexistent locker room somewhere. It was a glorious five or ten minutes.

I am not kidding when I tell you that, for some reason I do not understand, the people who were there that day have treated me differently since I pushed that button and blew the living daylights out of Jay's small cow pond. Jay said he needed to expand the pond but I think he just wanted us all to have some fun. Using ANFO to make a little cow pond bigger is a lot like using a crossbow to shoot a fish in an irrigation ditch. It's a sure thing if you have someone around to shout "Fire in the hole," or show you how to stand and watch for some fish movement.

TWENTY-THREE

We Shall Overcome

I started this book with a banking story so it seems fitting that I end with one. In the United States, we are in the middle of a political season that is very difficult to understand. Everywhere you look, there is a complete blindness to any other way of thinking or any other point of view beyond one's own. It seems like the era of contentious debate is ending or perhaps has ended. Many people see things so differently that they cannot even *have* a debate. Here's an example of what I am talking about.

A few weeks ago, I was at dinner at a restaurant in Newport Beach with my dad. We were eating and talking about all kinds of things when he asked if in all my travels I had ever been to Florida. I set down my fork and I thought for a second and then I remembered my one short visit there. It was back when I worked for the FDIC, and the trip had started in Florida but ended up in Alabama.

When I was hired on at the FDIC, they told me that I would be working in a job that had *heavy travel requirements*. One day, after I'd been working there a while, I got an email from someone official telling me I'd been "deployed" again to a bank in the South that had lost all of its money and was failing. The message said I'd be leaving the next day. So, I packed up a small suitcase with enough business clothes to last me for the weekend and I hopped on a plane going to somewhere on the Gulf of Mexico side of Florida.

I made my travel arrangements with the government-approved travel agent because there were complicated rules about how and when we traveled, and fortunately the travel agent knew all of them. Also, I'd heard that the government travel agency had the ability to find hotel reservations when there didn't seem to be any available, and I was a late addition to this particular bank closing. I wanted to make sure I could stay in a decent hotel. I'd tried to get a reservation all afternoon by myself, to no avail. In only a minute or two after I called them, they found a Hilton somewhere in Tampa Bay and made a reservation for me. It was pretty impressive. I think I may have even been turned down minutes before by that very same hotel.

My flight to Florida took all day. It always takes all day when you are going to the East Coast because you fly toward the night and you lose time. When I arrived, I was tired and I'd stress eaten a lot of cookies and other unhealthy things on the plane. For the last hour of the flight I sat, feeling bloated, and watched reruns of *I Love Lucy* on one of the TVs that hung down from the top of the fuselage. When the plane finally landed, I was ready to get my suitcase and go find my hotel and collapse.

I got off the plane and wandered over to baggage claim and waited as every single other person who had flown with me came and picked up their suitcase and lugged it away. Even people who had to go to the special counter to pick up the oversized things, like those giant golf cases made of bullet-proof looking, Kevlar-type space age materials, had already come and left. I stood there until the black conveyer belt stopped running and everyone else was gone. My little weekend bag was not there. I wandered over to the baggage claim customer service counter and spoke to a completely uninterested attendant. She handed me a "lost bag" form and said something in a thick southern accent that I couldn't understand. I don't know if it was her accent, or if she was just talking really fast and impatiently, but she barely looked up and waved me on. I had traveled as light as possible. I'd only carried on a couple of magazines and a copy of *USA Today* that I picked up for free at the gate when I boarded. I hadn't put any clothes in my carry on and I wondered what I would do if I had to show up at the bank the next morning wearing the same old Levi's and T-shirt I had worn on the plane.

The air in Florida was heavy and humid as I walked out into it and flagged down a cab. He drove me to the Hilton Hotel, somewhere in Tampa Bay or St. Petersburg. I knew it would be embarrassing the next morning if the airline didn't find my bag, and there wasn't time to stop, find a store, and buy something more appropriate to wear. Plus, I was in a taxi—what would the driver do while I went shopping? Maybe, I thought, there would be something at a hotel store off the lobby where I could buy something to wear the next morning.

I sat in the backseat and looked out at the city lights reflecting off of the surface of the water. It was late and dark now but it was beautiful and completely different than anywhere I'd ever been. Everything looked like it was right at sea level. The roads, it seemed, were only a foot or two above the waterline. It was a clear August night and the water was calm and glassy and the lights from the buildings shimmered off of the water almost like I was in a dream of some kind.

When I met the desk clerk at the hotel, he mentioned something about how I should really have called first if I was going to be a "late check-in." He looked over my identification and asked me when I made my reservation. I told him I knew I was late checking in but the airline had lost my suitcase and it took a long time to fill out all the forms. I said that they told me they would deliver it to the hotel once they found it. He could not have been more than about twenty years old and he looked me over suspiciously like I might have been a con man or something. I told him I was sure I had a reservation and I was tired and I would like to go up to my room and rest.

He looked into his computer screen like he had a decision to make, and then he told me I was lucky and that they only had one room left. He smiled insincerely and said they would call me if my bag came. I reminded him that I'd only be there for the weekend and that I had an important meeting in the morning and I asked them to call me if the bag came, no matter what time of the night it was. And, for the record, I didn't feel lucky. I felt tired and I was pretty sure that my suitcase was in some place like Alaska. I was also convinced that there was more than one empty room left in that hotel. I got on the elevator and I started trying to think of ways to explain why I would dare to show up at the bank group meeting the next morning dressed in a T-shirt and Levis.

Even though it was late at night in Florida, my body and my mind were still on California time. I watched some Thursday-night movie and then *David Letterman* and then I lay down and tried to go to sleep. I knew I had to be awake first thing the next morning and get myself down to Sarasota to get instructions on the bank that was closing. I wondered about my suitcase and my clothes. Worrying about all of it only made getting to sleep more difficult. I lay there with my eyes closed in the dark trying to will myself to sleep. Finally, long after the show following *David Letterman* ended, I drifted off and fell asleep.

What seemed like only seconds after I fell asleep, the phone by my bed rang loudly. It was the front desk. They said a van from Delta Airlines had just brought my luggage and dropped it off in the lobby. So, I pulled myself up out of bed and put my clothes back on and I stumbled down and got my suitcase and brought it back up to my room. I rolled it inside the door and lay back down and thankfully fell back asleep until morning.

Early the next morning, I arrived at the bank in Sarasota groggy but ready to go and dressed in my navy blue suit. I was walking into another FDIC meeting, through another hotel lobby, about to show my ID at the conference room door when my Blackberry buzzed in my suit pocket. I pulled it out and saw an urgent message from my employer. It said that they needed me in Alabama as soon as I could get there. I stopped right where I was and read it because the message was very insistent. It directed me to leave Sarasota that very moment and make a plane reservation for the next flight to Alabama. It was confusing. After all the trouble I'd had finding my clothes and getting up and getting down to Sarasota that morning dressed like a banker, I almost didn't do it. I read the message over a few times and then I called our regional office in Dallas and confirmed that I really should drop what I was doing and leave. They told me that I should. They said it would all be explained when I got there.

This was unusual. The FDIC operated very methodically and its moves were usually well planned out. They analyzed and scrutinized every bank they closed far in advance, and they had the timing and the scheduling down to a science. I'd read detailed reports written about banks that weren't going to close for months. I knew some kind of weird financial crisis had to be happening in Alabama for them to yank us off the Florida assignment so suddenly. I called the government travel agency and made a quick reservation for the next flight to Birmingham, Alabama, and then I got in a cab and went to the airport. When I got there, after I'd cleared security and knew I'd made it early enough to catch my flight, I sat down and I wondered what was going on that could have caused them to re-assign me like this.

Long before I found myself in Florida that morning, I'd worked on the IndyMac Bank closure and I knew how difficult things could get if people didn't understand what was going on. When IndyMac failed there was a run on the bank and people lined up in the sun and waited to talk to people from the FDIC. The media was there covering the whole event and the people were upset. IndyMac was most likely the FDIC's worst-case scenario for a bank closing, I thought, and maybe history was about to repeat itself. Maybe they were having another old-fashioned bank run. Maybe the depositors were panicking and lining up and trying to withdraw their money.

The problem with a bank run is that banks don't keep depositors' money in a safe somewhere. They make loans with it and they only keep a small part of it on hand. If depositors panic and demand their money on a first-come, first-served basis, the slow ones, or the people who got in line last, will be out of luck. The bank will always run out of cash before the last guy in line gets up to the window. When this happens, things tend to get very ugly and the FDIC has to step in and shut the bank down. Then, everybody gets up to the amount that their deposits are insured for. I was thinking about all of this and how I was pretty sure that most of the people at the FDIC hated the way the IndyMac closing got so ugly.

I'd never been to Alabama before but I'd read about it in school and I knew it was where a lot of the action during the civil rights movement had happened. There was a Neil Young song called "Alabama," and the only lyrics I could remember from that song was a line that said, "The devil fools with the best laid plans." I tried to go over that song in my head. I could remember the tune but I couldn't remember any more words. My mind, as if it was making its own decisions now without my permission, kept humming those words over and over.

I bought a sandwich at a little sandwich stand and then I stood there alone with Neil Young singing in my head and waited for my flight. For a few minutes, I just stood there and read the sports section of *USA Today*. I read an article about Barry Bonds. When I saw his picture, I was sure he had taken steroids. His rookie baseball card made him look like a kid out of high school but his picture in *USA Today* made him look more like an orc from *Lord of the Rings*. I read some more and then I looked up and began to wonder—if there was a big emergency in Alabama somewhere, why was I the only FDIC person in the waiting area for the flight to Birmingham? It seemed unusual that they would send out an emergency notice and I would be the only one going. I started looking around and saw, down the hallway, a group of about 15 people I knew from my office in Irvine. They were waiting in line to get on the next plane to Montgomery.

One of them waved me over and told me to look again at my Blackberry. She said I was in the wrong line, and it turned out she was right. I read the message again and it clearly said "go to Montgomery" and not Birmingham. This was a problem because I was already through security, my ticket clearly said Birmingham, and the flight to Montgomery was beginning to board. The only ticket I had would take me hundreds of miles away from where I needed to be tomorrow morning. My friends on the Montgomery flight where chuckling at me and showing their boarding passes to the gate agent and getting on the plane.

I called the superpower government travel agent and told her all about Birmingham and Montgomery and how I had a seat on the wrong plane and I needed to get to the right place that night at the latest. I was rattled and I must have sounded like it because she told me to calm down. She said she thought she could help and she put me on hold. This trip, I thought, was a disaster. I nearly had to go to the bank group meeting in St. Petersburg looking like a high school kid in Levis and a T-shirt, and now I might miss my whole reason to go to Alabama because I had booked a flight to the wrong city.

It was getting dark outside now and the boarding gate for the Montgomery flight was closing. Everyone was on board and two very serious looking gate agents were closing the security door and getting things ready to leave. I started wondering how much it would cost to take a cab from Birmingham to Montgomery in the middle of the night. I was sure it would be too much. I would ask the travel agent when she came back on the line about maybe renting a car and driving it down there. It sounded like a miserable night but I knew I had to come up with something. It was too far to drive there from Tampa Bay. The door to the jetway was closed now and I was still thinking I would have to go back through security and get a new boarding pass. It was embarrassing.

When the travel agent came back on the line I told her I absolutely had to get on the flight. Again, she asked me to calm down. I interrupted her and said that I was serious, anything she had to do was okay, but it was critical that I get on that plane. She called me "honey" and told me to calm down again and listen. I told her I didn't want to calm down. She actually shushed me and then she said she'd had to use some special authorization, but *I was on that flight*. I started to tell her that no, I wasn't on the flight! I started to tell her that they'd already closed the door to the jetway but then I saw a man in a dark blue blazer walk over and unlock it and open it back up. A few seconds later, another man, a disgruntled looking man who I guess didn't need to be on the plane as badly as I did, walked back through the door into the terminal looking like he needed to find another way to get to Montgomery.

The travel agent told me to get on the plane. She said that a seat had become available. I asked her where to get a boarding pass and she told me that wouldn't be necessary. I would just have to show them my ID and they'd print me one right there at the gate and I could get on board. What a relief I thought, as I got on the plane and sat down near the front of the plane in the only empty seat. Then the plane taxied down the runway and took off into the darkness between Florida and Alabama.

The next morning, I woke up somewhere in Montgomery, like the whole plane drama had never happened. We all met, according to our instructions, in the conference room of a small hotel on the outskirts of town. A friend I'd met in California before the trip started was there too. I walked around the room shaking hands and introducing myself. Most of the people there had to have been from another department in the FDIC because I'd never met them. The Receiver-in-Charge was from our Dallas office and she brought with her about ten or so people who also worked in Dallas.

I liked the Receiver-in-Charge. She definitely knew what she was doing. It was clear that she had been through this many times before. She walked up to the front of the room and smiled confidently. Then she greeted us all as we sat down. She said that they had received word that a very big bank based just outside of Montgomery was in trouble. She told us all that there had been a story in the paper that evidence of fraud had been uncovered in the bank's mortgage division. The FDIC needed us all in Montgomery, not because the bank had failed, but because it was highly likely that it would fail. More distressing, she said, was that before it failed there could be a run on the bank. She told us that we wouldn't know until it happened and if it did happen, she said, we would need to be ready, at a moment's notice, to close the bank.

She went on to say that there really wasn't much for us to do unless there was a bank run. The FDIC's charge was to investigate banks before they fail, and then go in and help if they do fail. She told us we were going to remain strictly hands-off unless people started lining up outside the bank. We weren't even supposed to tell anyone where we were. She said that if the press caught on that there was an FDIC presence in Montgomery and if even a hint of it made it into the news somehow, just by being there we could actually cause people to panic and get in line. She also said that there were some large national charities—she wouldn't tell us who they were—that had deposits in the order of millions of dollars in the bank. She told us, "I sure hope they wake up and withdraw their money before the bank fails." The Receiver-in-Charge explained that if the bank failed, there would be nothing we could do to help them. She said we would have to follow the law. It didn't seem like a good law that would allow an organization that took care of veterans or raised money for sick children or something like that, to just lose its money. It made me feel sick to my stomach and angry at the banks for taking the risks they did and putting all that money in jeopardy. But we absolutely could not notify the charities that a failure was imminent. Tipping off these charities would not only be unfair to everyone else who had money in the bank, but it would be illegal. So, with millions of dollars from some big-name charitable groups hanging in the balance, and, I imagined, hundreds of people getting ready to line up and try to withdraw their funds from the bank, all we could do was sit in this hotel conference room and wait.

During the next few days I rarely left the conference room of that hotel. I googled the bank and I read all the newspaper accounts and I worked on some reports. It was supremely boring and minutes absolutely crawled by like they were hours. If there had been a run on the bank we would have been able to jump into action, but short of that, time just stood still.

There must be some unwritten rule somewhere that says if you're part of a group in a hotel conference room, you are required to continue sitting, every day, wherever you sat the first time you walked through the door. That first morning I walked in and sat down next to Wilma McMillan, an African-American woman about my same age. She was self-assured and always dressed smartly like she was going to church. She was tall, or at least taller than I am. She was nice to me but I could tell that she was not one to be trifled with. I would learn that she was always willing to speak her mind.

One morning I did decide to go out for a walk to try to clear my head. I only made it out onto the sidewalk in front of the hotel for a second or two before the oppressive, sweaty Alabama heat rudely forced me back inside. It had been a long time since I felt heat and humidity pushing down on me like that. There was no relief anywhere. Shade from the trees in front of the hotel didn't help at all. I mentioned the heat outside to a woman I'd met while we were waiting. She shrugged and told me it was "the same way back home." Then, for some reason she used the phrase "by the grace of God" to explain that "by the grace of God she was from Texas." I couldn't figure anything at all that being from Texas or the Alabama summer heat and humidity had in common with the grace of God, but she was nice so we kept talking. I was reaching for something we had in common to talk about. Somehow, in our rambling conversation, I asked about the

Civil War and if it ever made it down here to Alabama or to Texas. She looked at me a little confused. I couldn't tell if she was teasing me or if she really hadn't heard of the Civil War. She waited a second and then, like she was remembering something trivial or hidden deep in her memory, she said, "Oh...you mean the War of Northern Aggression!"

I also sat down that first day next to several people who had worked for the FDIC for a long time. I could tell they were from Texas by the way they spoke. They talked about things like Longhorn Football and one of them said he drove down from his house in Dallas. He had family in Montgomery and he was going to stop by and see them at night. I don't think I'd ever really known a true "by the grace of God" Texan before that week, but come to think of it, I don't think I'd ever known an African-American woman like Wilma either.

Wilma told me about her family and how she was happy to be working for the FDIC. She also used the phrase "grace of God" when she told me that she had grown up in Mississippi in a poor family, but she was able, by the grace of God, to get a good education and a good job and she and her family had never wanted like that again. I asked her if she visited her family in Mississippi often and she said no. She said they all moved to California to get out of the heat. We talked for a long time about all kinds of things. She started to go on about the food they ate back home. I mentioned that I'd never eaten Southern food. Wilma just stared at me incredulously like I'd just admitted I was guilty of a capital offense. Then she composed herself and she reached across the table and put her hand on mine and looked me in the eye and said, "Peter, you must accompany me today, at lunchtime, to The Piccadilly Cafeteria." Then she turned and said to the group, "Who would like to go to the Piccadilly for lunch with Peter and me?" Several people said yes.

I'd never heard of The Piccadilly before. I didn't know what the word Piccadilly even meant. It reminded me of one time when I was traveling in Oklahoma and I stopped at a convenience store called the Piggly Wiggly. But whatever initial reaction I had about the name, it was immediately erased when I tasted their food. Wilma walked me though the lineup of foods on display and told me about each one. I had the Chicken Fried Steak and Crawfish Etouffee. Wilma told me they were time-honored classics. They came with turnip greens and fried okra. I had never eaten anything like it, and I ate it all including a slice of sweet potato pie. Wilma was delighted. She sat next to me and told me, "There was nothing like having a good home-cooked meal at the Piccadilly."

On Wednesday, the Receiver-in-Charge stood up and announced that if we kept our Blackberry's turned on and ready to get messages, we could go wherever we wanted the next day. I was pretty relaxed by then and I shouted out, "I know where I am going!" People shouted back their guesses "To a bar?" "To the Indian Casino?" "To a strip club?" People were relieved to be able to get out of that hotel room. They were laughing and talking. They weren't really waiting for me to answer. Still, even though I thought no one was listening, I sat up and said, "I'm going to the Rosa Parks Museum." I'd seen an ad for it in a tourist brochure in the lobby of my hotel. As others were making their plans to go to a casino somewhere, Wilma shouted, "I'm going with Peter!" A small group of Texans sitting next to me said they'd like to go too.

There is something understated and normal and, at the same time, almost sacred about the sidewalk where Rosa Parks got on the bus back in the 1950s. There's just a little plaque there imbedded in the concrete. Of course, there is a giant library and museum that now covers the entire block, and a modern university that seems like it must own the whole downtown area around it. It was captivating and moving going through the museum with all of my new friends. There is a mockup of the bus where Mrs. Parks sat down and refused to get back up and they showed how it was laid out and where she sat and how the bus driver, who sounds like a complete jerk, got up and told all the black people in her row to get up and move back because there were white people up in the front standing up. The museum had her actual booking arrest sheet with her fingerprints on it from when she was taken in and charged with a crime.

There was a room dedicated to the Montgomery Bus Boycott where all the black people in Montgomery walked or carpooled or took taxis for about a year after Mrs. Parks' arrest. I had known all this but standing there looking at her booking sheet and knowing that she'd been arrested basically for being black in Alabama in 1955 felt like it was kind of evil. Now I'm not sure if this is true, but I also heard that when the bus boycott gained momentum, the white people in charge passed a new law that made it illegal to carpool. So, the black people of Montgomery walked sometimes, I read, over 20 miles just to get to work each day.

I knew this was all in the past but I felt insulted. I felt like somehow I'd been hurt by this mess that had gone down decades before. I felt like the people involved were heroic and noble. I loved the story about Rosa Parks even more when I learned that she never wanted to be out front like that, in the limelight. Everyone I knew anywhere knew who she was and what she did, but, as I read the plaques all over the walls, I was amazed to learn that she never believed it was about her. The message I got was that it was about injustice and basic human dignity—that's what she demanded. Eventually, I thought, she saw the world change under the weight of her quiet determination. It was inspiring.

At the end of our tour, we circled back into the room we had started in and saw the replica of the bus. Music was playing from some speakers near the door. It was Pete Seeger singing "We Shall Overcome." It kind of caught me off guard. I knew that that song was like an anthem during the civil rights movement, but when I heard Pete Seeger singing, it sounded so familiar like I'd listened to it as a child. I knew the words, too. They're simple words. Everyone in the room was quiet and we stood there next to the bus and listened.

That's when I saw Wilma McMillan, who was standing next to me, crying. She lifted her arms into the air and started singing very loudly, "We shall overcome, we shall overcome, we shall overcome some day!" I looked around the room and no one else was singing, just Wilma. She didn't care. She started softly but soon she was belting it out, "Oo-oh deep in my heart, I do believe. We shall overcome some day!" In between one of the lines she looked at me and shouted, "I remember this! I *lived this* as a girl in Mississippi. Sing with me!" So, even though it was a bit against my nature, I decided I didn't care if I stuck out or sang off tune, and I threw my hands up in the air and I started singing with Wilma, "We are not afraid, we are not afraid, we are not afraid today." I got very emotional and I sang out loud with gusto. When the song was over, I put my hands down back at my side and Wilma hugged me.

    The group of Texans we were with stood there stiffly. I didn't think they objected to anything in the museum; I don't know how anybody could. They just stood there while Wilma and I were waving our arms around and singing and hugging. When the music stopped, our little group moved out of the main room of the museum and into the gift shop. I looked through the cards and puzzles with pictures and quotes from the civil rights movement and I found a small button for my wife that said, "Well behaved women seldom make history." I bought it because I thought she would like it, although I never once got the idea that Rosa Parks was anything but well behaved. I thought, in fact, that was why she ended up being so perfect for this moment in history. It wasn't about her as much as it was about ending an unspeakable, arbitrary, incredible injustice.

    As we walked out of the museum, Wilma stopped on the sidewalk by the little plaque and told us all that this was a good day. She said she'd felt some things inside of her she thought she had long laid to rest. I just smiled and walked to the car.

    When we climbed back in the rental car, one of the Texans asked if we could make one more stop. He very politely said the afternoon was still young and if we had time he'd like to go and walk through the home of Jefferson Davis. He called it "the first white house of the Confederacy." I was sure he was joking. It was completely unbelievable to me that he could even think of someone like Jefferson Davis after leaving the Rosa Parks museum and seeing the pictures of the bus boycott and the booking sheet of Mrs. Parks with her actual fingerprints on it, and hearing Pete Seeger singing "We Shall Overcome," and seeing Wilma so emotional and proud. Could he have been on the same tour? Had he not noticed that the theme of our afternoon did not include things like a visit to the home of the vanquished President of the "War of Northern Aggression?"

I must have not answered right away because Wilma said to me, "Peter, it's all right. Let's go see that house." We went there with the group and walked through the house. It was big, stately, creaky, and just what you would think of as an old Southern mansion. For a second, it didn't seem like things had changed that much after all. I was disappointed that we could all go on the Rosa Parks' Museum tour together, but my friends from Texas obviously didn't see things the same way Wilma and I did. I felt like some of them were just deciding to look the other way and ignore the significant and personal history we'd just experienced. Their minds were made up, no point in discussing, much like the current political times. A sadness overcame me and I felt again like I had when I was staring out the window from my hotel in Utah, after I'd just told all the bank employees their bank was closing and they were all losing their jobs.

I tried but I just felt it too intensely to leave that mansion and drive straight back to our hotel. As we left, I had an idea, and I didn't ask this time. I said we were going to stop at the Dexter Avenue Baptist Church. It was closed when we got there but that was okay. I just didn't want our day to end at the home of Jefferson Davis. I didn't want our day to be trumped by other, less meaningful history than what we had seen and felt in the Rosa Parks Museum. I parked in front of the church and got out of the car and walked up the walkway. I imagined I was there back when Martin Luther King Jr. was preaching and things were dangerous and unfair and electric and change was about to come.

TWENTY-FOUR

Final Thoughts

My dad's mom, who we called "Far Mor," which is Danish for grandmother, I think, passed away when I was a boy. I remember visiting her in the hospital in Fullerton with my dad when I was in the first or second grade. We drove down to the hospital from our home in a little town named Piru in Ventura County, California. She was very sick and couldn't really talk too much. I remember waving at her through a large glass window. We didn't stay long that day. Everyone seemed sad and serious.

A few weeks later, I was playing tether ball out in front of my best friend Eddie Smith's house. He lived on the other side of an orange grove near my home, about two blocks from Piru Elementary School. It was hot and dusty. Eddie had a big dog named "Blacky" that jumped up and down every time we hit the ball around the metal pole like he was a part of the game.

I remember stopping when I saw my mom drive up to the end of the gravel road by Eddie's house. She looked serious. She got out of her station wagon and came over to me. When she pulled up I stopped swinging at the ball on the rope and stood and watched her as if I knew something had happened. Blacky stopped jumping and Eddie grabbed the ball to keep it from swinging around the old pipe stuck in the concrete on the ground.

    Mom came over and got down on her knees in her dress and held my hands and told me that Far Mor had died. She said she had no way of calling my dad because he was playing golf that day. She looked into my eyes and smiled and asked me if I was okay. I remember that her question surprised me. I crinkled up my brow and thought. "Am I okay?" I knew I should feel bad, but right then, right when she asked me if I was okay, I didn't. I didn't feel anything. I felt the same as I had before she came when Eddie and Blacky and I were playing tether ball.

    Mom told me she had to drive off to Valencia to find dad and tell him. She asked if I wanted to come with her. I told her I was all right. She squeezed my hands and then stood back up and brushed the dust off of her dress and told me she'd be back as soon as she could. Then she backed the car down the alleyway and drove away.

    Eddie hit me the ball. I don't think he heard what mom told me about Far Mor. I swung at it. Then I wondered if I should have felt something. Why hadn't I? Was I bad somehow? My grandmother had just died and I was playing tetherball. I stopped hitting the ball and it fell to the side of the pole. Eddie and his dog looked at me. As they did I felt a deep, horrible, sick feeling overcome me. I felt intense sadness all of a sudden. It came to me without any thought on my part and it seemed to control my whole system. What I felt was like what I imagine complete and utter loneliness feels. It was everywhere in me. It was as though the sadness came at me on a cellular level and overpowered me in one moment.

    I blurted out, "I have to go!" and I bolted into the orange grove between our two houses. I ran and I cried and it didn't seem to help. I was running up through the trees all alone and crying with loud uncontrollable gasps. I ran as fast as I could to go home and to get away from my friend Eddie. I didn't want to cry in front of him. I held my stomach and I felt like, even though there was only a little ways to go to get to my house, I might get lost. Finally, just before I made it to the other end of the trees I fell on the ground in the dirt and sobbed with my head on my arm. I don't know how long I laid there.

Later, when I saw mom again, she was in her room and she told me that it was very sad. She said that if I felt like it I should cry. She told me to cry until I didn't need to any more. I don't remember much else about that day except I remember lying on my bed with my face in my pillow sobbing because I would never see Far Mor again. It felt so final, and horrible, and abrupt.

I once read a book about Harry S. Truman. It said that when his mother died he told people that he knew what it felt like to be an orphan. He was in his sixties then and he was the President of the United States. Even then, with all of his resources and as grown up as a person could possibility be, he felt the same terrible loneliness that comes when someone close to you dies.

I was only nine. This was my grandmother. My parents were both living then but it felt almost like I wouldn't survive.

I used to think that I didn't have a lot of experience with someone close to me dying. But, as I get older, it keeps on happening. My grandpa up in Utah, The Doctor, lay on his little bed in their old house in Payson long enough that death finally came and took him too. I was older then, and so was he. By then, he was in his 90s and he was no longer a force to be reckoned with in that small town. Life had worn him down. All of the complicated parts of his life no longer seemed important to me.

Mom called me early one morning and told me that The Doctor had died peacefully in his sleep. Knowing the way he pushed and insisted his way through life, I had half expected him to struggle or negotiate at the end too.

Kathie and I took our three children and we all flew up to Utah to support Janice and help with the funeral. There was a viewing the night before the ceremony and I took my son Jeff through the long line of people that had gathered there at the town mortuary to pay their last respects. Jeff and I stood there between The Doctor's old friends and some of our distant relatives. Jeff was less than 10 years old. I held his hand. He could sense that this was a serious moment. When we came to the coffin and the body of my grandfather. I stopped and thought about all of the summer days I worked with him out in his pasture. I remembered him trying to chase Janice around the house with a dead bat. I smiled for a second.

Jeff stared at him, trying to take it all in and figure out what was going on. Then he reached up and looked around and pointed at him and looked at me. I smiled trying to reassure him. He moved in closer and got right up by The Doctor's face and touched it with his finger as if to see if it was real, like he needed to confirm what he was seeing. Then he squeezed my hand and we moved on over to where the family was gathered in another part of the room. An old friend of The Doctor's from some town with a name like Goshen or Genola was there amongst the family. He said something about how the town wouldn't be same now that Doc Oldroyd had moved on.

Some movie star once said, "I'm not afraid of dying, I just don't want to be there when it happens." The hard part about death to me isn't that it will someday happen to me. It is the mystery of it all. It's the big final question mark. Does it all just end, and there is blackness, and it's all over? When my grandpa finally closed his eyes, what happened? Did a long lost relative in some other form come and take his hand and lead him somewhere beautiful, or did the curtain just close the way it looks like it does to those of us who are left behind?

One morning many years later, Kathie and I spent a difficult Saturday with my sister Kirsten, helping my dad move. It was early December and he'd sold his house days before. It was a nice house with an ocean view in Newport Beach. From his patio you could see the mid-rise office buildings and the primped and preened retail center known as Fashion Island. It's a beautiful center where nothing but the finest of things are sold. He'd asked us to help because he anticipated giving some of his things away. It turned out to be much, much more than that.

For you to understand why this day was so hard, you have to know first about my mom. She was a small town girl from a little town that Mormon pioneers settled in central Utah. She'd grown up there and graduated from Brigham Young University just as the airline industry was taking wing around the world. She took a job as a "stewardess" (they call them flight attendants now) for United Airlines. She did this to go out and see the world and also to get away from the confines of small town central Utah. She met my dad on a blind date in the Seattle area and they were married in her living room in Payson, Utah a few years later.

    My mom was fun. If she ever felt self-conscious, I never knew it. After they got married, Dad graduated from the Stanford Business School and took a job in San Francisco. Mom set up our home and we ended up moving around from house to house in areas that have transformed over the years from quiet little suburban neighborhoods into the heart of the high tech industry in America. We lived in little houses in places like Palo Alto, Sunnyvale, and Menlo Park.

    My dad is a serious, hard-working man who always seemed to have a genuine sense that he understood the world and his place in it. My mom was the other half. She was spontaneity and laughter and had an easy way. She was always accepting of others no matter what anyone else thought. My grandfather, her dad, once told me that, "Marilyn is the only person he'd ever known who is just as comfortable in a room meeting the President of the United States (which she did once while we lived in Washington D.C.) as she would be sitting down to a bowl of stew and sourdough bread with Dale Allred up at the sheep camp." I believed him because I'd seen it. She was real and she made dad's life have a fun texture to it that I'm sure he would have never known had it not been for her.

    The day Kathie and I went over to help my dad move ended up being more about my mom than anything else. She'd been sick by then for several years. She had a condition that robbed her of her ability to communicate with and really get to know other people. It's a savage, uncaring disease that ate away at her senses, a little at a time. It's almost not noticeable, then one day you look up and realize, by that point, the day we moved my dad, the mom we all knew was gone.

That day was less about my dad moving, and more about my sister Kirsten, Kathie, my dad and I going through her stuff and trying to somehow find a way to honor her and a life time of things she had accumulated. Some of these things were valuable—a diamond ring, some pieces of Hallmark silver—and some were just hard to figure out. All of these things, boxes and drawers full, were meaningless unless I could remember her with them. They were out of context. It was my mom that gave all these things meaning. Without her, the costume jewelry, the cookbooks, and the boxes full of balls of yarn and needles, and even the expensive jewels, or coats, meant nothing. It was a sad day. I'm still not all the way over it. I don't think I ever will be.

We had done our best, though, at the awkward task of trying to find the "mom" in all of her things. The only thing I could do on a day like that was put my head down and pray and hope for a miracle. But it was not long after that when we all sat around her bed and held her hands and told her we loved her and then she quietly slipped away.

I know we all do actually have to be there some day, but what is the deal? Why do we struggle and fight every day if the end is just a cancellation of our ride? How is it we come here pre-wired with feelings, and care, and hope, and love, if it's all just a game of survival of the fittest? I guess it could be a game like that. It would be a cruel trick that there is this illusion that things matter, that people matter, that what we do has some significance, if we just return to dust one day.

This came to me pretty clearly once when I worked at the National Bank of Canada, in the early 1990s. I had a breakfast meeting one morning in downtown Fullerton. Coincidentally, it was the same town where my dad lived as a little boy. The meeting was in the old part of town in a cafe near Harbor Boulevard which, back in the day, they called Spadra. I knew that the cafe I was eating at had to be somewhere nearby where my grandfather, my dad's father, had owned and run "Nielsen's Menswear" in the old downtown area.

After my meeting was over, I walked down the old street and tried to find where his store had been. It was and old area and no longer vibrant. I imagined that once it was alive with people from all over town doing their shopping. Now, there were a lot of closed down shops. There was a run-down looking tax preparation storefront, an armed services recruiting center, and an old taxidermy place. I didn't go in any of them.

It isn't a very big couple of blocks in the old part of town and I walked up and down trying to guess which old store had been his. It made me feel bad that he had spent the better part of his adult life working right where I was but I could not find anything that indicated that he'd even been there.

Before I go on, I need to say that I loved this man. He was funny and caring and after my grandmother died in the late 1960s he moved in with us for a while. He used to have me help him when he fixed things around the house. Before Far Mor died and they visited us, he brought me things that he had fixed, like an old canvas carpenter's apron. One time he brought a little broken transistor radio and we took it apart and I helped him fix it. Then he smiled at me and we crossed our fingers and he turned it on and heard Nancy Sinatra singing "These Boots are made for Walkin'." He wiggled his head around like he liked the music and it made me laugh.

When he was very young, he lied about his age and went off to fight in France in World War I. I tried to get him to tell me about the war once, but he wouldn't. He wasn't kidding either. He was funny usually, but when I asked him to tell me about fighting in the war, he got very serious and told me he wouldn't. He was happy to tell me all about after the war when he married my grandmother and they settled in Fullerton where they raised my dad and his older brother. When he was older, long after Far Mor's death, he lived all alone in their house. This was when I was a teenager and we lived way down in San Diego. We came up and visited as much as we could and my dad convinced him to stay with us sometimes in San Diego. We called him "Far Far", or "Farf" for short.

That day, the day of my business meeting in the old part of downtown Fullerton, I walked around until I started to feel sad because no one there had any idea about my grandfather or about Nielsen's Menswear. I got in my car and started it up. I decided that nobody at work knew how long my meeting was supposed to take and I was already extremely late anyway, so I decided to drive over to the cemetery on the other side of town where both of them are buried to see if I could try to find their graves.

I wasn't sure if I could find them because it had been so long since I'd been up there. But I drove my car up and parked it by a part of the cemetery that looked like where I thought they might be. I got out and walked around for a second and read the names on a good part of the headstones searching for something that would show that they had really been there once.

When he died, it was the early 1980's. Kathie and I had moved to Irvine and we used to take Emily up to see him on weekends. Farf had had a stroke a few weeks before and he didn't seem to be recovering like I wanted him to. We visited him a lot but it was getting harder for me because he was no longer recognizing me and he talked like there was someone else in the room with us.

It was like he was arguing with his brother, Art, who passed away years before. I don't know if Art was actually there in the room in some kind of spirit form or if my grandpa was just delirious. It was confusing to me and sad, but he didn't seem to be suffering, so I guess that was good. He would come and go and we would wait for those moments when he was clear and he seemed like his old self and he would smile and make funny faces at Emily, and then a minute later he'd fade back away somewhere else.

I found their graves and I stood there looking down at the grave stones. I felt emotional. I wasn't crying. I was feeling solemn, heavy like I was at church or something. I felt respectful and a little lonely. I was glad I'd found their graves and confirmed that they were a part of that town.

I remembered a morning. I think it was a Saturday morning, years before. Kathie and I lived in a little house in Irvine. The phone in our kitchen rang and I picked it up. It was my dad. He said, "Peter, I got the call late last night. Your grandfather passed away in the night." I was sad. For days and weeks, I almost could not believe it. I felt sure I'd be doing something and he would just walk around the corner and smile at me and tell me he was happy with the way my life was going. At least I hoped he would.

Dad asked if I could say a prayer at Farf's graveside service. I told him I would and I spent a long time thinking about what I could say to sum up his life and honor it like it should be honored. I remembered when the time came, we were all standing around the grave in the very same spot where I was standing that day years later. My dad and mom, and my brother and sister were there. Kathie was holding Emily and my aunt and uncle and cousins stood next to the grave.

I stepped up when the minister motioned to me and I bowed my head. I prayed that this spot would be a place of peace where people could come and rest and feel good. I prayed that we could all remember those who were there and live our lives to best honor their memory. I opened my eyes after the prayer and looked around. I hoped I had done right by my grandmother and grandfather. I hoped I would somehow see them again.

Death is such a sudden thing though, even when it creeps up slowly and gives good warning like it did with Far Far. It was final and over like he'd just been brushed aside. One minute before death takes someone they could be one hundred percent with you and then when they leave, you are left with the puzzle of what happened and where they went. What was it all about—my relationship or friendship with them, I mean? How to go on remembering without knowing? It is a test for me. It is something I hope for…that I'll see them again.

I had stood there by my grandfather's grave for a while trying to remember how much time had passed since I'd prayed there at the funeral. I was the only one there in the whole cemetery except for a groundsman I'd seen driving around in his utility cart quietly fixing faucets and trimming the grass and doing other things that cemetery grounds people regularly do.

I could only talk so long to the gravestone without running out of things to say, so I stood there for a moment and took a deep breath and looked at the carvings in the stone. It said "Harold Nielsen 1899 - 1985" but just above his name it says one more thing. It says "Far Far." We had all called him Far Far. It means "Father's Father" or something close to that in Danish.

I almost stumbled when I read it and I thought about the words Far Far and something clicked in my mind and my heart and I realized that I am the evidence that I'd been looking for. Me, my brother, my sister, and our cousins are what he did that really mattered. I stood up a little and I got all choked up and I looked around to see if anyone else was around. I felt a new resolve to go out and do something with my life. I knew part of him was in me. I felt like I had to go make it the good part of me.

After my son Jeff graduated from college and moved back to Orange County near us, we were cooking some hamburgers on the barbecue in our back yard and he told me that once, when he was in High School, I took him aside when he'd done something I thought needed parental attention. He said that I looked at him and said, "Jeff, you are my greatest life's work. Don't mess it up!" I felt like that there in the cemetery. I felt like my grandfather's gravestone was telling me that I was a big part of his life's work, like I had better be getting things together.

One last thought, early in my career I was working at a Canadian-owned bank and I was feeling a lot of pressure to come up the learning curve and be a smarter, better banker. The economy was in trouble, as this was the very early 1990's. It seemed like all of the client's I had at the bank were in some kind of financial crisis. I knew that I worked for the bank and that they signed my paycheck and that I represented them in everything. My clients were all frustrated and angry and work was kind of like a battlefield every day.

My commute to Downtown Los Angeles was hideous and when I arrived each day I realized that the City of Los Angeles was going through the worst five or six years in its history. This was when an all-white jury found some police officers who had beaten a black motorist nearly to death, not guilty, and the city erupted into several days of total anarchy and riots. In those years, while I was commuting to Los Angeles, they had big fires that burned down parts of Laguna Beach and Malibu. There was a huge earthquake one morning that knocked down several freeway overpasses and caused traffic to be rerouted and made everyone's commute even worse. To top it all off there was the world's obsession with, and the 24-hour news coverage of, the O.J. Simpson murder trial.

It was hard to stay focused. I had this feeling that I was in a fight somehow. It was hard on me and I started to not be able to sleep very well. That made me feel tired and uninterested in work. I knew my family was depending on me, so I had to keep moving ahead.

One night in the middle of all of this, I hadn't slept well for weeks. I lay on my bed looking up at the ceiling trying to still my mind and find some rest. I did eventually fall asleep and I had a dream that was as clear as if it had been real, like if I wasn't really sleeping at all.

When it began, it was fuzzy and thick like I was disoriented. Then I was standing in a big room, like a hotel conference room. It was full of people and they were all dressed up like it was some kind of a formal event. People were talking and laughing and I walked around through them all looking for someone I knew. I remember that the dream was in black and white for some reason and I was wearing a grey suit. I walked over by a big black piano and stood there, hoping someone would recognize me. I felt like I should know these people but I didn't. I could hear glasses tinkling and the sound of people talking but I couldn't tell what they were saying. I leaned on the piano and I tried to get myself focused so I could understand. That's when I saw standing next to me, Wesley and Lillie Lloyd, my wife's grandparents, who'd died many years before.

At first, I couldn't believe my luck to have run into them and I shook Wes' hand and he looked me over and smiled. He leaned over and whispered something in my ear. I couldn't hear him over the voices in the room and I leaned in close and asked him to say it again. He was still shaking my hand when he cleared his throat. Everyone in the room got quiet. Lillie was standing next to him, looking at me, like they had agreed ahead of time what he should say.

I think it's great, by the way, how in dreams you can sometimes tell what other people are thinking. Lillie was clearly agreeing, although I still didn't know what he'd said. He shook my hand and leaned in. He had a smile on his face and he said, "Thank you for taking care of Kathie." I nodded and told him that he had it wrong. I said, "Kathie takes care of me." Wes and Lillie Lloyd then saw someone else they knew and started to walk over across the room to see them.

When they did, I saw Far Far.

He was there alone, looking calm and at ease. I couldn't believe he was there. I knew, in the dream that he had died and I thought I would never be able to see him again. He held out his hands and I put my hands in them. When I did he squeezed them so tight and he looked into my eyes like I was a little boy again. It was a look of absolute pride. I knew that he believed in me. I knew I could do it too, whatever "it" was. I knew if he believed in me that I should too. It was pure love.

I woke up and grabbed Kathie's arm and woke her up and I told her about the whole thing. It was vivid and clear and the message was undeniable. I don't know if dreams have meanings or if they are just random firings of tired sleepy brain cells. But I am telling you that this one felt real. It was meaningful. It made me feel more hopeful, like I was more ready and capable to deal with the world and all of its complications. I was sure that the struggles in life are worth it, that this big mystery of life and death has some important meaning to it.

ACKNOWLEDGEMENTS

Special thanks go to my big brother, John, who read the drafts of a million stories. He encouraged me, and he always offered great advice. To Axel Forrester and her husband, Stephen, for reading and providing feedback, to Marty Newey, who's always been a great friend, and to Debbie Moncrief and David Hansen, for agreeing to let me use their real names.

Also, I'm grateful to Nancy Smith for book design, to Tessa Roper for editing and to Mark Neal for preparing the Guatemala map. Photo credits are to the Peter Nielsen family.

About the font: Palatino Linotype was designed by Hermann Zapf and initially released in 1949 by the Stempel AG typefoundry in Germany. It is named after Giambattista Palatino, a master calligrapher and contemporary of Leonardo da Vinci, and utilizes classic Italian Renaissance forms.

ABOUT THE AUTHOR

Peter Nielsen was born in California in the late 1950s. He has strong ties to pioneer Mormon family members living in Utah, where he spent many happy summers as a child. In the late 1960's the family moved to Washington D.C. at a time of exciting and dangerous developments in the world. At age nineteen he lived in Guatemala as a Mormon missionary. His view of the world was forever changed as he learned to understand and appreciate the plight of the people there. After two years he came home, graduated from college, and began a career working for various multinational banking organizations. He had a front row seat when the "Great Recession" of the late 2000's came crashing down on the banking world. He was an important piece of a team of professionals who were employed by the Federal Deposit Insurance Corporation and were tasked with helping to resolve the terrible financial crisis that ensued. He now lives with his wife, Kathie, in Tustin California. They have three children and six grandchildren.

THANK YOU FOR READING

If you enjoyed *All That I've Seen*, we invite you to share your thoughts and reactions online and with family and friends.

www.ingramcontent.com/pod-product-compliance
Lightning Source LLC
Chambersburg PA
CBHW071412070526
44578CB00003B/554